The Human Body and the Limits of
Medical Intervention

Emerging Issues in Biomedical Policy Series

Vol. I: *Setting Allocation Priorities and Genetic and Reproductive Technologies*

Vol. II: *Debates over Medical Authority and New Challenges in Biomedical Experimentation*

Medicine Unbound

The Human Body and the Limits
of Medical Intervention

Edited by

Robert H. Blank
Andrea L. Bonnicksen

Columbia University Press New York

Columbia University Press
New York   Chichester, West Sussex
Copyright © 1994 Columbia University Press
All rights reserved

Library of Congress Cataloging-in-Publication Data
Medicine unbound: the human body and the limits of medical intervention/
edited by Robert H. Blank, Andrea L. Bonnicksen
p. cm.—(Emerging issues in biomedical policy)
Includes bibliographical references.
ISBN: 0–231–08148–0
ISBN 0–231–08149–9 (pbk.)
1. Medical policy—United States—Moral and ethical aspects.
2. Medical ethics—United States. 3. Health policy—United States.
4. Medical technology. I. Blank, Robert H. II. Bonnicksen, Andrea L. III. Series
R855.5.U6E44   1994
362.1'0973—dc20   94—41829
CIP

Casebound editions of Columbia University Press books are
printed on permanent and durable acid-free paper.

Printed in the United States of America

c 10 9 8 7 6 5 4 3 2 1

Contents

General Introduction

❖

Health care has moved to the center of the domestic policy agenda in the 1990s. Incumbents and challengers in the 1992 campaigns at both the state and federal levels recognized the growing public concern over the state of the U.S. health care system. Prior to assuming the présidency, candidate Bill Clinton stated that health care was the critical problem facing the U.S. and that it would be a major priority of his administration. He promised to propose comprehensive legislation to slow the seemingly uncontrollable escalation cf health care costs and to guarantee health insurance for all Americans.

The ascendance of health care from a largely private undertaking to a highly visible policy issue over the past several years has been accelerated by rapid advances in biomedical technology. As the capacity to intervene in the quality and prolongation of human life has increased, the costs of health care have continued to expand well beyond general inflation levels. Moreover, as biomedical innovations have proliferated, public expectations have risen accordingly, thus producing heightened pressures to develop even more impressive—and expensive—interventions. Concurrently, medical decision making has become considerably more complex, in part because of questions as to when to use these often life-and-death capacities, who should make such a decision, who should have access to health care, and who should pay?

This series, *Emerging Issues in Biomedical Policy*, was initiated to address the policy issues raised by changing biomedical technologies. Recognizing the need for an authoritative, interdisciplinary debate of these issues, with this series we endeavored to create for biomedical policy a forum where scholars, practitioners, and policymakers could address overarching and timely themes that structure the issues as they unfold. Each volume is designed to provide coverage to substantive topics that represent important policy areas. Volume I focused on two sets of emerging issues: setting public priorities for allocating scarce medical resources and framing policy responses to rapid changes in genetic and reproductive technologies. Volume II directed attention to debates over authority in medical decision making and to new challenges in biomedical experimentation.

In Part I of this volume, "Inviolability of the Human Body," biologists, ethicists, theologians, and political scientists examine the issue of whether there ought to be limits to medical intervention. Although medicine has always stretched the boundaries of intervention in the human body, new technologies of organ transplantation and genetics and the emergence of revolutionary drugs raise concerns over how far we should go in moving from mere therapeutics to actual enhancement of the human body. Is there some point at which we change the person by changing the organism? Questions of inviolability also arise in situations where treatment of the fetus requires intrusion into the bodily integrity of the pregnant woman. The contributors debate what is meant by inviolability: where, if ever, it should be used to preclude certain types of intervention; and to what extent, if any, this should be a matter of public policy.

Part II, "End-of-Life Decision Making: Issues of Power and Policy," brings together authors from bioethics, medicine, psychology, journalism, and politics to examine the intensifying debate over empowerment of patients in making their own decisions regarding the end of life. The heightened public debate over physician-assisted dying is but one aspect of a broad range of policy issues that follow our newfound technological capacity to control the circumstances and timing of death. As such, they bring to the forefront the issues of who ought to make these decisions and what role, if any, the government should play. Legislative attempts to enhance patients' power through advance directives and other legal mechanisms are analyzed, raising the possibility that this may be an area where legislation is in fact undesirable. These chapters demonstrate the difficulties of framing a public policy that legalizes aid in dying, and they return us to the more general question of what is the most fair and effective relationship between private medical authority and public legislative action.

Both topics covered in this volume, inviolability of the human body and empowerment at the end of life, exemplify the problems facing policymakers and medical decision makers in the 1990s. At a more basic level, they also illustrate the extent to which advances in biomedicine challenge traditional notions of decision making by introducing more contingencies and players to the process. Importantly, both sets of issues again demonstrate how difficult it is to frame public policy in a morally pluralistic society where there is little consensus over appropriate public action. The authors reiterate the ongoing need to expand the dialogue among persons of many disciplinary, ideological, and political persuasions if we are to move toward resolution of these emerging issues in biomedicine.

Medicine Unbound

*The Human Body and the Limits of
Medical Intervention*

I

Inviolability of the Human Body

Introduction

Robert H. Blank

We have entered a dynamic and volatile era of advances in medical technologies that promises to significantly transform the human condition. At least three million people worldwide live with artificial implants such as cardiac pacemakers, arterial grafts, hip-joint prostheses, middle-ear implants, and intraocular lenses. Another 300,000 patients are kept alive by kidney dialysis machines (Galletti 1988:35). Vast improvements in surgical procedures, tissue matching, and immunosuppressant drugs such as cyclosporine are making repair and replacement of organs increasingly routine. Whereas in the recent past we were dependent on cadaver organs and low patient survival rates, now transplants from brain-dead individuals, other species such as baboons and pigs, and artificial organs are revolutionizing organ substitution (Mathieu 1988).

Likewise, human genetic technology offers an expanding array of diagnostic and therapeutic applications that are giving us considerably more control over determining the health and the characteristics of future generations. Similarly, biotechnology now offers among many other products unlimited supplies of pure human insulin, interferon, and human growth hormone, as well as monoclonal antibodies that promise widespread benefits to society. Furthermore, advances in cosmetic surgery, computerized prosthetics, and the development of artificial skin (Fisher 1990) extend our capabilities to improve upon nature or restore individuals to a full life. Finally, the development of more effective chemicals to enhance physical and mental capacity suggests that there will be few limits to manipulation of the human body in the future.

As remarkable as these advances in science and technology are, however, they should force us to pause and reflect on the implications of where they might be leading. Historically, in our attempts to overcome disease and illness, we have always stretched the boundaries of intervention into the human body. In many ways, this continual expansion of our ability to intervene has, in fact, defined progress and therefore seldom has been questioned. However, the rapid developments outlined above are perhaps directed at giving us greater control over what it means to be human and have taken on a new urgency, thus giving us little time to adequately assess where these are leading us. Our unrealistic dependence on technology alone to cure human problems, many of which have complex social causes, has translated into a potent desire to find nothing more than quick technological fixes to our perceived shortcomings. Moreover, the search for cures for diseases readily gives way to demands for improvements on nature or for control over the aging process through a techological fountain of youth. We strive for perfect bodies through chemicals and cosmetic surgery, for enchanced mental powers through "smart" drugs, and for replacement of worn out body parts. In all these cases, technology becomes the perceived liberator from human limitations.

As Reiser (1984:171) cautions, however, technology can be addictive because it takes on a life of its own. Because they have powerful symbolic meaning as purveyors of human life, medical devices such as the artificial heart are difficult to limit once they are introduced. Reiser (1984:173) contends that an overreliance on a technological fix is generally inadequate in accounting for the complex consequences of technology on the way we think. Furthermore, our heavy faith in technological solutions often has the added danger of diverting attention and resources from more appropriate nontechnological actions.

The time is ripe to stand back from our infatuation with our expanding newfound technological capacities to intervene in the human being and examine their long-term implications. There are two critical dimensions, the moral and the practical. The moral issue centers on the question of whether there is an inviolability of the human body beyond which we should not intervene? Or, conversely, are there no moral limits to intervention and modification of the human species itself? Secondary moral questions follow a positive response to the core question. If limits are warranted, where should the boundaries of intervention be set and, importantly, who should set them: the medical profession? Individuals? The government?

The practical dimension assumes that at some point scarce resources will preclude doing everything technologically possible for every person who needs or desires it. Although there is considerable debate over the need for rationing the use of medical technologies (Blank 1992; Califano 1992; Lamm 1992), we can no longer assume unconstrained choices in this area. The question then is whether there is a point at which intervention in the human body is not *practical* given finite resources and the inevitability of death in any event. In light of the burgeoning proliferation of intervention capabilities, and its potentially unlimited expansion of already stretched health care budgets, it can be argued that limits must be set on economic grounds alone if not on moral grounds. The real questions then might better be where such limits are set, who should set them, and on what specific criteria?

Medicalization of Preferences

One critical distinction that underlies all potential interventions in the human body is the motivation behind a particular application. On the one hand, these techniques can be directed at ameliorating or overcoming disease or deficiencies in the body. Transplantation of organs, gene therapy, and use of human growth hormone to correct a natural deficiency are examples of such applications. On the other hand, an intervention can be performed to enhance normal body structure and function in the *absence* of disease or illness. These interventions are based on individual preferences, which often reflect the social value placed on specific characteristics, such as physical appearance. Frequently, these applications are chosen due to simple vanity. Moreover, the line between these two categories of intervention may be obscure. For instance, cosmetic surgery can be used to correct physical deformities or to give a normal person the features he or she desires. Likewise, although orthodontics can be used to ameliorate dental problems, frequently its use is motivated by the desire to improve physical appearance according to cultural expectations. A broad array of interventions are now routinely undertaken without any medical indications in the narrowest sense.

American society especially is obsessed with the search for the "perfect" body. Our athletes and movie stars are rewarded for their physical prowess and looks. Although the purported extensive physical remaking of Michael Jackson may be an extreme manifestation of this obsession, reconstruction of the human body is a multibillion dollar industry, representing a rapidly growing sector of "health care." Countless young women starve themselves to achieve the model body as espoused by the popular media. Crash weight loss diets are marketed less for health reasons than for appearance—advertisements idealize the thin look, often with little or no mention of health benefits, or risks. Moreover, quick technological fixes, not long-term behavioral changes are marketed to mass consumers, many times under the rubric of "medical" solutions.

It is a small leap from this mode of thinking to the realm of cosmetic surgery as routine. Although most of the applications of cosmetic surgery are clearly not meant to address health problems, by packaging it as "health care," we in effect have medicalized physical appearance. In the process, we have also trivialized the human body and the uniqueness of individual identity. Biological diversity and variation in appearance gives way to socially defined or perceived correctness. The selection of model noses, breasts, pectorals, and buttocks is made through the use of computer imagery that allows potential customers a view of what they will look like with their new "enhanced" features. Likewise, widespread use of anabolic steroids and other body-building substances promises a technological shortcut to remolding the body. "Smart" drugs designed to enhance our ability to remember promise to do the same for the brain in the near future. We desire immediate results and in many cases they are delivered by an expanding arsenal of innovative procedures and substances.

Growing evidence of long-term problems with these technological fixes—for instance, silicone breast implants and steroid use—appears simply to shift the demand to alternative interventions that promise the same immediate benefits without adequate long-term testing for adverse effects. Rather than questioning the very premise that there might be something inherently risky in such intrusions into and manipulations of the human body, the tendency is merely to replace one *type* of intervention with another. That segment of the medical establishment with a significant financial stake in the continued use of such interventions reinforces this approach in the popular mind.

It might be argued that the diffusion of new methods of enhancing the body will have an "egalitarian" impact on society by enabling those persons less endowed naturally to become more competitive. In reality, however, the vast inequalities of resources in American society make it more likely that those who are already advantaged will have access to interventions, and at the expense of the least well off. With pectoral implants averaging $7,000, calf implants $5,000, and buttock implants $7,500, they will be available only for those individuals with substantial resources. So far as a society actually rewards individuals with these characteristics, those who will benefit will be those who have sufficient wealth to begin with. Although pressures may be exerted on society to share the financial burden of these techniques, the diversion of resources from genuine health procedures may make the costs unacceptable to the vast majority.

There is also a clear danger of oversimplifying complex human behavior in the use of "enhancement" interventions designed to "perfect" the species (see Wheeler 1992). The assumption that we can, through these interventions, find biomedical solutions to social problems tends to reduce all human frailties and deficiencies to medical problems open to technological fixes. Such thinking is already inherent in many of the applications summarized thus far. In the words of sociologist Howard Kaye, the result "will be a transformation of how we understand ourselves: from moral beings, whose character and conduct is largely shaped by culture, social environment, and individual choice, to essentially biological beings" (cited in Wheeler 1992:A8). Increasingly, we are extending this mentality in efforts to use similar methods to enhance human characteristics that until now have been defined within the normal range. Under such conditions, humans no longer are fully natural creatures—in effect we are merging with technology. According to Kass:

> We, on the other hand, with our dissection of cadavers, organ transplantation, cosmetic surgery, body shops, laboratory fertilization, surrogate wombs, gender-change surgery, "wanted" children, "rights over our bodies," sexual liberation, and other practices and beliefs that insist on our independence and autonomy, live more and more wholly for the here and now, subjugating everything we can to the exercise of our wills, with little respect for the nature and meaning of bodily life. We expend enormous energy and vast sums of money to preserve and prolong bodily life, but, ironically, in the process, bodily life is stripped of its gravity and much of its dignity. (1985:298)

Furthermore, some observers see these developments as leading to eugenics (see Kevles 1985). "But like the endless number of movie sequels that have overrun our movie theaters, eugenics is back with a new cast of characters and a slightly different script, but the same tired and dangerous plot" (Allen 1989:9). Allen argues that once again the proponents of eugenics are using highly dubious research on biological diversity as the basis for a social agenda to turn attention away from such causes of social problems as wage and benefit cuts, unemployment, and stress in the workplace (1989:11). For such critics, the new, implicit forms eugenics is taking are more insidious than the old forms because policies are being justified on grounds of maximizing socially acceptable goals, such as improving individual health, reducing social or family burdens, individual rights to a sound mind and body, and the best interests of the patient.

Mortality and Morbidity

There are many questions as to the efficacy of intensive intrusions into the body. A recent study by Olshansky, Carnes, and Cassel (1990), for instance, casts doubt that stretching the boundaries of intervention into the human body will give us the reductions in mortality (and morbidity) we have come to expect. Barring major advances in the development of life-extending technologies or the alteration of the effects of human aging at the molecular level, the period of rapid increases in life expectancy has in fact come to an end in developed nations. Although the size of the older population will continue to grow even if death rates remain at current levels as a result of the large baby-boom cohort, it will take increasingly larger reductions in mortality to produce equivalent increases in life expectancy (Olshansky, Carnes, and Cassel 1990:438). The data indicate that average life expectancy will not exceed 85 years at birth or 35 years at age 50, implying that the upper limit to longevity has already been approached. Further significant declines in mortality are unlikely because the "dramatic age shifts in mortality required for increases in life expectancy beyond 85 years appear unlikely" (Olshansky, Carnes, and Cassel 1990:638).

It *is* more likely that advances in medical treatment are allowing those elderly who are frail and who suffer from fatal degenerative diseases to survive longer after the onset of the disease than in the past. The result is that age-specific morbidity and disability rates and their duration will substantially increase. Unfortunately, "even if rates of morbidity and disability remain constant, the number of people surviving with conditions of frailty will definitely increase because of the rapid growth in the size of the elderly population resulting from population aging and declining old-age mortality" (Olshansky, Carnes, and Cassel 1990:639). Even while improved lifestyles and medical technologies are successful in reducing the major causes of premature death, we are—and will be—left with a rapidly growing elderly population whose additional years of life may be dominated by nonfatal but highly debilitating conditions such as arthritis, osteoporosis, and Alzheimer's disease. The result could be longer life, but worsening health, thus an actual decline in active life expectancy. Olshansky and colleagues (1990:639) suggest a major shift in research efforts from prolonging life to a strategy aimed at postponing morbidity and lessening the adverse effects of nonfatal but highly debilitating conditions to reduce the duration of frailty for that part of the population that has already approached its biological limits.

Redefining Humanhood?

A discussion of biomedical interventions takes us straight back to the most fundamental questions that have dominated Western thought since classical times. Basic questions regarding human existence and the meaning of human life, the role of society vis-à-vis the individual, and the just ends of government are central to these new interventions. At their base, all biomedical technologies focus on the question of the extent to which we ought to intervene directly in the human condition. They differ only in the level of intervention and in the means of accomplishing the intervention. The debate continues between the extremes of those who argue that it is irreverent and ethically dangerous to violate or bypass fundamental human biology, and those who contend that the benefits of such biomedical research and applications greatly outweigh the dangers. Although seldom explicitly stated, this debate centers on the concept of inviolability, which, depending on its definition, sets limits on the manipulation of human life. In essence, a discussion of inviolability forces consideration of differing conceptions of human nature itself.

Throughout the history of Western political thought, assumptions about the basic characteristics of human nature have been critical to the development of theories of politics. From Plato to the present, many philosophers have posited how humans ought to live their lives assuming a largely immutable human nature. Although human nature is often viewed as malleable to the extent that it is open to formation through habituation, human nature has been seen as fixed insofar as human beings have certain capacities or tendencies from birth (Arnhart 1988). Despite profound disagreements over what this basic human nature is like, the essential issue has been to determine what the good or moral life is for the sort of creature humans happen to be.

Although changes in technology have always demanded a redefinition of basic concepts, new biomedical discoveries and applications raise critical challenges to our fundamental notions of humanhood. The central moral issue, therefore, becomes much more complicated with the added capability of deciding to what extent we ought to effectuate changes in the nature of the human species itself. We must soon move beyond the traditional question of what is the best life for humans "given their nature" to questions as to what human nature ought to be in light of a new self-definition offered by these technologies. According to Stich, "sometime in the next century and perhaps much sooner, the age-old presumption of a more or less fixed human nature may begin to dissolve" (1983:11).

The current revolution in biomedicine and genetics is moving us rapidly into a world in which human features and faculties can be altered almost at will. Although in part still speculative due to the uncertainty of what will be technically possible, we can ill afford to ignore the implications of these developments on the definitions of human nature. At the least, a clarification of the term *humanhood* is critical at this juncture. If there is a genetic base to human nature, and through genetic engineering we are able to break the code, there is nothing to stop us from controlling or changing the nature of what it means to be human. If altruism or aggression, for instance, have a biological base, our burgeoning knowledge of the human genome and resultant methods for intervention at the gene level are likely to allow alteration.

Ironically, social norms themselves might encourage biomedical intervention to ensure that one's offspring can compete in a changing society. "The desire to help one's children excel is a powerful and widespread motivational force" (Stich 1983:9). With the availability of techniques for genetically engineering traits that convey a competitive advantage (from height and physical agility to increased intelligence, memory, and longevity, as well as advantageous personality traits), parental demand to maximize their progeny's chances will be substantial. Furthermore, those parents who lack the resources or are unwilling to use these technologies might find their offspring condemned to a second-class citizenry where what had been within the range of the "normal" gradually slips into the domain of the "subnormal." Given our litigious society, it would not be unexpected to have children sue their parents for failing to use available enhancing technologies and thus put them at a competitive disadvantage. Torts for "wrongful life" might be extended to recover damage for this competitive disadvantage caused by inaction on the part of the parents (Blank 1990:93–101).

This desire for "perfect" children has significant long-term implications on our very perceptions of children. As people limit their families to one or two children, their demand for the technologies that they believe can guarantee a "perfect" child has increased. According to many observers, young couples are now going to considerable lengths (including sex preselection) to ensure the birth of a "near-perfect" child (Bishop and Waldholz 1990:313). As more precise and effective gene therapy techniques emerge, pressure for access will intensify. Recent evidence of parents demanding human growth hormone "therapy" for their otherwise healthy children simply because there is speculation that their child would not be as tall as they desired attests to the strength of this quest for the perfect child (Grumbach 1988).

Although attention to date has focused most clearly on questions of inviolability of the human genome (see Zohar 1991), and issues raised by genetic technologies used to enhance the "perfectibility" of the child, similar questions are inherent in interventions directed at the brain (Office of Technology Assessment 1990). Should we be hesitant to alter that organ traditionally viewed as the center of personal identity, autonomy, and determination? If there is any inviolability of the human body, it is likely to be conceptualized either in the genes or the brain. As techniques for brain intervention advance rapidly in the 1990s, we must ask how far we can go in modifying the brain without inextricably altering the person him or herself. These heightened capabilities—chemical, diagnostic, electrical, and surgical—should raise genuine concerns over the inability to draw clear lines between acceptable treatment and potential abuses of these remarkable techniques.

Emerging Issues and Inviolability of the Human Body

The authors of the essays in this section are highly respected scholars in a range of fields including bioethics, biology, law, political science, and theology. Although the essays vary widely in style and approach, they all deal at some level with the concept of inviolability and present critical and often provocative views on where biomedical technology is taking us and how these developments affect our views toward humanhood. The diversity of the perspectives offered here illustrates the controversy surrounding inviolability and the difficulty of applying it to specific biomedical interventions. Although there is little agreement on inviolability, because all medicine focuses on the individual human body, it is essential that we come to a better understanding of how our notions of it affect or ought to affect modern biomedical interventions.

The first four essays directly analyze the applicability of inviolability to emerging biomedical technologies and offer various views on its foundations and importance. Carson Strong, an associate professor in the Department of Human Values and Ethics at the University of Tennessee College of Medicine, rejects the strict "inviolability-of-persons view" which holds that the physical integrity of the body must in all cases be preserved. Although Strong suggests this view can make a contribution to debates over emerging issues in biomedicine, he finds it unacceptable as a moral framework. Strong, however, is clear to make the distinction between therapeutic and enhancement technologies, the latter being more amenable to limitations on the bases of inviolability.

Lynton Caldwell, Arthur Bentley Professor Emeritus of Political Science and Professor of Public and Environmental Affairs at Indiana University, shifts attention to how cultural and religious values shape attitudes toward the human body. In fact, controversy over treatment of the human body reveals deep schisms in modern society. Instead of insisting upon an absolute inviolate condition of the human body, there is a wide range of competing interpretations. Caldwell argues that Western religion, generically defined, is the best point of departure to understanding these competing notions of inviolability.

Albert S. Moraczewski, adjunct professor in the Department of Psychiatry and Behavioral Sciences at Baylor College of Medicine, gives a useful summary of one of the most articulated conceptions of inviolability. After reviewing some of the critical biomedical applications, Moraczewski explicates the basic principles that guide the Roman Catholic Church's "reflections on the limits to human intervention on the human." Although the determination of those limits is very difficult, especially in light of the benefits of biomedical technologies, the bodily and mental integrity of humans must be safeguarded.

H. Tristram Engelhardt and Kevin Wm. Wildes, both of the Center for Ethics, Medicine, and Public Issues at the Baylor College of Medicine, argue that in a secular, morally pluralistic context, the only justified limits on alterations to the human body are those set by the individual him or herself. This is because in the absence of a single moral community for substantive moral discourse, a secular state has no moral justification for the use of state authority to impose a particular moral point of view.

Grobstein and Daniels introduce another dimension of the inviolability debate: to what extent can the bodily integrity of a pregnant women be violated in the interests of the fetus? Clifford Grobstein, Professor of Biological Science and Public Policy Emeritus at the University of California, San Diego, provides a brief theoretical framework for dealing with these increasingly frequent "tortuous dilemmas." Cynthia Daniels, a political scientist who teaches in the Women and Politics Ph.D. program at Rutgers, analyzes an array of sensitive policy issues raised by cultural, technological, political, and legal developments that have converged in the last decade to "push the fetus into public consciousness as an independent and autonomous being." Together these chapters illustrate how the varying conceptions of inviolability drive controversies surrounding the changing maternal-fetal relationship.

The next two essays, by Annas and Sinsheimer, focus on what Caldwell sees as potentially the "most subversive of the sciences" as relating to inviolability. George J. Annas, Edward Utley Professor of Health Law and Director of the Law, Medicine, and Ethics Program at the Boston University Schools of Medicine and Public Health, raises critical questions about the limits of genetic intervention in his *fictional* account of the workings of a top-secret federal interagency group called Perfect People 2020. The goals of this group are human immortality and creation of the genetically perfect human. Throughout this original piece, Annas weaves discussions of existing and potential technologies into a fictional, although feasible, account of the deliberations of this group.

Robert L. Sinsheimer, previously Chancellor of the University of California, Santa Cruz, and currently Professor Emeritus at the University of

California, Santa Barabara, looks at a future time well after the human genome project is completed. Sinsheimer examines the implications of a world where design and redesign of all living matter (including humans) to human purpose is commonplace. What impacts might genetic engineering have on humans as "we move from the natural world that bore us into the synthetic world created by our own intellect"?

In the concluding essay, Daniel Callahan, co-founder and director of the Hastings Center, asserts that we "are likely to be wrong in thinking we can find some self-evidently inviolable line we ought not to cross in manipulating life." He examines the conflict between what he terms the conventions of traditionalism and modernism and finds them unsatisfactory. Instead, Callahan offers four principles designed primarily to avoid circumstances that "would most likely push us toward lines we would be sorry to have crossed once we had done so." In the end, however, there is unlikely to be an effective means of setting boundaries for intervention unless medicine itself is part of a way of life that understands the need for restraints, accordingly to Callahan. The insights advanced by the contributors to the first part of this volume will become even more consequential as the capacities to alter the human condition expand into previously uncharted directions. As emphasized by many of the contributors, it may not be feasible in a pluralistic culture such as the United States to reach a consensus as to where to set boundaries on medical intervention. Yet, as we stand at the threshold of the introduction of new technologies, there is an urgent need to readdress basic questions as to medicine's ultimate goals. In other words, what do we envisage as the end result of these largely incremental alterations of the human body? Although a serious consideration of the basic concept of inviolability offers no simple answers, it does force a reframing of the debate toward these core issues underlying remarkable technological achievements.

References

Allen, Garland E. 1989. "A Dangerous Form of Eugenics is Creeping Back into Science." *The Scientist* (February 9):9–11.

Arnhart, Larry. 1988. "Aristotle's Biopolitics: A Defense of Biological Technology Against Biological Nihilism." *Politics and the Life Sciences* 6(2):173–191.

Bishop, Jerry E., and Michael Waldholz. 1990. *Genome*. New York: Simon and Schuster.

Blank, Robert H. 1990. *Regulating Reproduction*. New York: Columbia University Press.

———. 1992. "Regulatory Rationing: A Solution to Health Care Resource Allocation." *University of Pennsylvania Law Review* 140(5):1573–1596.

Califano, Joseph A., Jr. 1992. "Rationing Health Care: The Unnecessary Solution." *University of Pennsylvania Law Review* 140(5):1511–1523.

Fisher, Lawrence M. 1990. "Three Companies Speed Artificial Skin." *New York Times* (September 12):C1, C6.

Galletti, Pierce M. 1988. "Artificial Organs: Learning to Live with Risk." *Technology Review* (November-December):35–40.

Grumbach, Melvin N. 1988. "Growth Hormone Therapy and the Short End of the Stick." *New England Journal of Medicine* 319(4):238–240.

Kass, Leon R. 1985. *Toward a More Natural Science in Biology and Human Affairs*. New York: Free Press.

Kevles, Daniel J. 1985. *In the Name of Eugenics: Genetics and the Use of Human Heredity*. Berkeley: University of California Press.

Lamm, Richard D. 1992. "Rationing Health Care: Inevitable and Desirable." *University of Pennsylvania Law Review* 140(5):1511–1523.

Mathieu, Deborah, 1988. *Organ Substitution Technology: Ethical, Legal and Public Policy Issues*. Boulder, Colo.: Westview Press.

Office of Technology Assessment. 1990. *Neural Grafting: Repairing the Brain and Spinal Cord*. Washington, D.C.: U.S. Government Printing Office.

Olshansky, S. Jay, Bruce A. Carnes, and Christine Cassel. 1990. "In Search of Methuselah: Estimating the Upper Limits to Human Longevity." *Science* 250:634–640.

Reiser, Stanley J. 1984. "The Machine as Means and Ends: The Clinical Introduction of the Artificial Heart." In Margery W. Shaw, ed., *After Barney Clark: Reflections on the Utah Artificial Heart Program*. Austin: University of Texas Press.

Stich, Stephen P. 1983. "The Genetic Adventure." *Report from the Center for Philosophy and Public Policy* 3(2):9–12.

Wheeler, David L. 1992. "An Escalating Debate over Research that Links Biology and Human Behavior." *Chronicle of Higher Education* (June 24):A7–A8.

Zohar, Noam J. 1991. "Prospects for 'Genetic Therapy'—Can a Person Benefit from Being Altered." *Bioethics* 5(4):275–288.

1

What is the "Inviolability of Persons"?

Carson Strong

Medical advances in emerging fields such as neural-tissue transplantation and gene therapy are raising a host of ethical issues. What guidance for these issues is provided by the concept of the "inviolability of persons"? My first response to this question is that the meaning of the *inviolability* of the human body and of persons has not been clearly set forth. We are led immediately to other questions: What sorts of "violations" does the concept include, and what is its relation to other ethical concepts? Thus, we must begin by seeking clarification. To do this, I believe that it will be helpful to consider several types of situations in medical ethics in which commonly expressed views seem to presuppose a concept of inviolability. These are situations, for instance, involving surrogate decision making where there is absence of guidance in the form of the patient's autonomously expressed wishes. Patients for whom such decisions are made might include previously competent adults, as well as children and mentally retarded persons who lack the ability to choose for themselves.

Two Views on What is Best for Patients

In such surrogate decision making an important issue arises because patients often suffer from pain, handicaps, or other effects of disease that diminish the quality of their lives. For example, previously competent adults sometimes become severely debilitated and have a reduced ability to interact with others. Similarly, handicapped newborns sometimes have a diminished potential for cognitive development, while mentally retarded persons, depending on the degree of their retardation, might have a significantly limited capacity for rational decision making. In choosing what is best for these patients, two main views can be distinguished. According to one, regarding these impairments as morally relevant in deciding what is best for patients denies them the full status of personhood. In deciding what would best promote the patient's interests one should consider what would be appropriate for any person, regardless of degree of disability. In the second view, handicaps and suffering *can* sometimes be pertinent to judgments about what is best for the patient.

The contrast between these two views can best be illustrated by considering their implications for specific cases. The following is an example of situations involving previously competent adults (Ackerman and Strong 1989:89–91).

J. A. was an eighty-year-old man with senile dementia who was being cared for at his daughter's home. He stayed in bed all the time, hardly moving, and was fed by nasogastric tube. His immobility had caused bed sores and contractures [a deformity of a joint that results from its immobility] of both legs. His legs were bent at the knees in a fixed position with the heels near the buttocks. J. A. was brought to the hospital because of difficulty breathing and was diagnosed as having pneumonia. Although he was conscious, his interaction with others was minimal. When staff members talked to him or asked questions, he would not respond in any way. When awake, he would simply lie in bed and stare at the wall. Another daughter said that recently he had spoken briefly on one occasion, but she could not understand what he said. The physician found that the patient would react only to stimuli that ordinarily would be deeply painful. In senile dementia there is decline in mental functioning caused by atrophy of brain cells. The condition involves progressive degeneration and eventually death. The average survival time after onset is about five years. It was very unlikely that there would be a significant recovery of the patient's cognitive functions. The physician asked whether the patient had ever expressed wishes about life-preserving treatment if he were to become seriously debilitated, but family members could not recall such a discussion. The physician wondered whether antibiotic treatment of the pneumonia would truly be in the patient's interests. The question also arose concerning whether a respirator should be used if the patient's breathing worsened.

According to the first view, J. A.'s cognitive impairments and lack of interaction with others are not relevant to the questions about life-preserving treatment. The pneumonia should be treated because the patient's life has inherent value. In the context of such life-or-death decisions, this view is usually referred to as the "sanctity-of-life" approach. As Daniel Callahan points out, "the *meaning* of the 'sanctity of life' is that of signifying the ultimate respect we are willing to accord human life. It expresses a willingness to treat human life with consideration, to give it dignity, to commit ourselves to its furtherance" (1969:200). Endorsements of this view abound, especially among physicians, whose training emphasizes saving lives (Epstein 1979:919–920; Pertschuk and Heyman 1965:618).

The second view, on the other hand, holds that the cognitive impairments are relevant because they affect J. A.'s quality of life. Life has value to persons insofar as it enables them to pursue desired activities. Treatment decisions should consider whether patients will be sufficiently able to carry out valued activities to make continued life in their interests. One who holds a quality-of-life view might reason that J. A.'s prospects are so dim that continued life for life's sake is not in his interests. If so, comfort care should be provided, but not life-prolonging treatment.

A similar conflict of views arises over treatment of handicapped newborns. According to the first view, an infant's reduced potential for cognitive development is not relevant to treatment decisions. This view is illustrated by the U.S. Department of Health and Human Services (DHHS) "Baby Doe" regulations, which stipulate that withholding life-sustaining treatment from impaired newborns constitutes discrimination against the disabled. According to DHHS, "it is only when non-medical considerations, such as subjective judgments that an unrelated handicap makes a person's life not worth living, are interjected in the decision-making process" that discrimination occurs (DHHS 1983:30847). Similarly, Paul Ramsey states that "the standard for letting die must be the same for the normal child as for the defective child. If an operation to remove a bowel obstruction is indicated to save the life of a normal infant, it is also the indicated treatment of a mongoloid infant" (1978:192). The second view, however, regards the quality of life to be important in choosing what is best for impaired newborns. It might conclude in some cases that an infant's expected quality of life is so low that life will not be beneficial to the child and that there is no obligation to provide life-prolonging measures.

Another contrast between the two views concerns medical hydration and nutrition. J. A. was being fed by nasogastric tube, and according to the view that patients' infirmities are irrelevant to treatment decisions, his nutrition and hydration should not be stopped. Because providing food and water is a symbolic expression of care, withholding it would fail to respect the patient's status as a person. With regard to handicapped infants, this view is illustrated by DHHS regulations stating that "the basic provision of nourishment, fluids, and routine nursing care is a fundamental matter of human dignity, not an option for medical judgment. Even if a handicapped infant faces imminent and unavoidable death, no health care provider should take it upon itself to cause death by starvation or dehydration" (DHHS 1983:30852). On the other hand, the view that a patient's impairments are relevant might conclude in some cases that withholding fluids and nourishment is permissible, provided doing so does not increase patient suffering. Examples would include patients in the persistent vegetative state.

Decisions for mentally retarded persons are illustrated by the case *In re Guardianship of Gloria Sue Lambert* (1976): Gloria Sue Lambert was an eighteen-year-old profoundly retarded woman, with an intelligence quotient in the range of zero to twenty. She lived with her mother and required assistance in daily living, being unable to feed herself adequately, brush her teeth, or wash her hands. She suffered from a gynecological problem consisting of heavy menstrual bleeding and bleeding between periods, and was unable to manage her menstrual hygiene. She had received medical care for the bleeding problems, but efforts to control the bleeding with drugs had not produced satisfactory results. Her mother filed a petition with the probate court, seeking appointment as her guardian with authority to consent to hysterectomy. This surgical treatment was sought to remedy the bleeding problem and remove the possibility of pregnancy (Norris 1977:879).

The first view would maintain that the patient's mental retardation is not relevant to the decision. This view is illustrated by the judge in this case, who inquired whether the procedure would be medically indicated for a woman of normal intelligence with similar problems. The woman's physician testified that if she were mentally normal he would not recommend a hysterectomy. Based on this testimony, the judge ruled that it could not be concluded that a hysterectomy would promote the patient's interests, and the authorization was denied (*In re Lambert* 1976:1–5). Thus, the first view emphasizes that the patient has the same rights as persons with normal mental ability, including a right to noninterference with the capacity to reproduce. According to the second view, this case should be decided by weighing the various factors pertaining to the patient's interests, including her personal comfort and moral interest in procreating. The profound mental retardation would be relevant because if the patient never would be capable of raising children, then she would be unable to experience the rewards of childrearing. This presumably would diminish her moral interest in procreating. Also, a hysterectomy would eliminate the possibility of patient anxiety if she became pregnant and did not understand what was happening to her body. It would also eliminate the possibility of some common gynecological problems, such as uterine bleeding or pain, infections or cancer of the uterus, and benign uterine tumors. In addition, the patient would be free from menstrual problems. Taking these considerations into account, it might be concluded that a hysterectomy would promote her interests.

The Inviolability-of-Persons View

In contrasting these two views, we can see that they emphasize different ethical considerations. The first view emphasizes the patient's status as a person. It seeks to promote the equality of rights and interests of all persons, regardless of degree of handicap. The second view emphasizes the well-being of patients, while also considering their rights and status as persons. In the context of life-or-death decisions, these views are commonly referred to as the "sanctity-of-life" and "quality-of-life" approaches, but there is no standard terminology to delineate these views as they apply to a wider range of situations. When considering the first view's application to a range of situations, including those involving medical nutrition and sterilization of the mentally retarded, we find a common thread. According to the first view, respect for persons requires that the lives and bodies of persons be inviolable. Decisions should be firmly guided by concerns such as respect for life, preservation of the physical integrity of the body, and respect for the reproductive capacities of people. Thus, it is central to this view that respect for persons be secured by adherence to certain *rules* designed to protect the inviolateness of persons. These rules include the following: the lives of persons should be preserved; adequate food and water should not be withheld; the mentally incompetent should not be sterilized; and the physical integrity of the body should be preserved. This view appropriately can be referred to as the "inviolability-of-persons" view. Different versions of the inviolability-of-persons view formulate the rules in different ways. Some include certain exceptions to the rules. For example, one might stipulate that life should be preserved except when imminent death is unavoidable. Authors who advocate versions of the inviolability-of-persons view include Callahan (1969:202–211), Kelly (1979:5–11, 149–167), Marshall (1960:65–76, 97–110), and O'Donnell (1976:41–134), among others. By contrast, the second approach might be called a "beneficence-centered" view. It follows the important ethical principle that when patients' wishes are unknown, surrogate decision making should be guided by the patient's well-being. In the beneficence-centered view, decisions should be individualized to the specific patient's needs, rather than based on firm rules.

In further describing the inviolability-of-persons view, two additional points should be made. First, although the foregoing discussion focuses on incompetent patients, the inviolability-of-persons view also is applicable to mentally competent persons. For example, involuntary sterilization, as in the "eugenic" sterilization of criminals, would be a violation. Moreover, some versions of the inviolability-of-persons view forbid voluntary sterilization (McCormick 1981:260–268) as well as suicide (Kelly 1979:266). Second, there is a standard exception to the rule protecting the physical integrity of the body: surgery with "mutilating" effects is permitted if it is necessary to protect the integrity of the whole organism (Kelly 1979:262). Thus, a life-saving amputation or removal of a cancerous uterus would be allowed.

Critique of the Inviolability-of-Persons View

A main argument in support of the inviolability-of-persons view is that the human capacities or conditions protected by the rules in question have inherent value, rather than a value dependent on the person's ability to pursue desired activities. The specifics of the argument would depend on which rule one is considering. Perhaps greatest attention has been given to the rule that the lives of persons should be preserved at all costs. Arguments that human life has inherent value often have been based on religious doctrine. Human life is viewed as a gift from God of which we are the stewards. As Norman St. John-Stevas states, "Man is not absolutely master of his own life and body. He has no *dominion* over it, but holds it in trust for God's purposes" (1964:12). In this view, our stewardship therefore requires the preservation of life.

A major problem with this argument is that it presupposes a particular religious doctrine. Nonbelievers, or believers in other faiths, will consider the argument indefensible because it rests on that doctrine. As Daniel Callahan states, because "a considerable portion of humanity is not Christian and does not accept this foundation for the sanctity of human life . . . it does not readily provide a consensual norm to which all men have recourse" (1969:190).

Another serious difficulty with the inviolability-of-persons view is that it leads to conclusions that in some cases are at odds with our moral intuitions. For example, in the case of J. A., the question arose whether a respirator should be used if his breathing worsened. The sanctity-of-life approach would require such measures. However, our moral intuitions suggest that withholding respirator support with the approval of the family would be morally permissible in such a situation. Similarly, in the case of Gloria Sue Lambert the inviolability-of-persons view would prohibit a hysterectomy. However, a hysterectomy would seem to be reasonable for the purpose of promoting the patient's interests in this case. The inviolability-of-persons view leads to such implausible conclusions, I suggest, precisely because it focuses exclusively on the sanctity of the human body and life, overlooking other important considerations such as those emphasized by the beneficence-centered view. As in these cases, issues in medical ethics generally involve a plurality of values. Following strict rules sometimes leads to unsatisfactory results. Unfortunately, the strictness of its rules is integral to the inviolability-of-persons view; after all, to say that something is *inviolable* is to say that it *never* should be violated.

Application to Emerging Issues

Let us now turn to inviolability's application to emerging issues in biomedical intervention. I believe that the difficulties discussed earlier will continue to be problems in applying the concept to new issues. Of course, it is a feature of emerging issues that there are few actual cases with which one can test ethical principles, thus making it difficult to argue from moral intuitions about specific cases. Nevertheless, in general terms the problems with the inviolability-of-persons view will be its adherence to firm rules and its failure to consider the plurality of values involved. I believe these problems make it unacceptable as a moral framework for emerging issues, just as it provides an unacceptable framework for the types of cases discussed above.

Even so, the inviolability-of-persons view can make a contribution to the debates over emerging issues. The rules that are involved point to ethical concerns that should be considered, such as respect for life, the physical integrity of the body, and reproductive capacities. These are among the plurality of values relevant to emerging issues, but should be regarded as *prima facie* considerations rather than as protected by absolute rules.

To illustrate one way in which these considerations might usefully contribute to ethical debate, let us consider, for example, the physical integrity of the body in clarifying the ethical differences between procedures performed for therapeutic purposes and those aimed at enhancement of personal qualities. By "enhancement" I refer to interventions designed to produce "superior" characteristics in individuals.

An intervention that is life-saving, rehabilitative, or otherwise therapeutic can be consistent with the principle that the physical integrity of the body should be preserved even if it involves a bodily "mutilation" or intrusion, provided that it promotes the integrity of the whole. Thus, a totally implantable artificial heart might be consistent with physical integrity if it is likely to be effective in preserving life and the risks and side effects are acceptable. Another example would be growth hormone injections for a child with a growth deficiency. Helping a child attain normal stature, it can be argued, promotes the physical integrity of the body, as well as the psychological development of the child. Similarly, breast implants for reconstructive purposes can be consistent with physical integrity, even though they introduce "foreign objects" into the body, and especially if maintaining the "integrity of the whole" includes amelioration of emotional and psychological trauma caused by the mutilating effects of surgery.

Similar arguments cannot be made, however, for interventions aimed at enhancement. Consider, for example, growth hormone or anabolic steroids for enhancement only. Increasing a person's size above normal does not seem to constitute the preservation or promotion of the physical integrity of the body. Moreover, if there are risks to life or health involved in the use of such drugs, they would be risks to the physical integrity of the body, and thus such interventions would be inconsistent with physical integrity. Similar comments apply to other procedures done for enhancement, such as breast implants or genetic modifications, when they involve risks to life or health.

Of course, an intervention's inconsistency with respect to the physical integrity of the body would not be a conclusive argument against it. Other considerations would be relevant, such as the autonomy of persons. Decisions would have to take into account the plurality of values involved. Nevertheless, the concept of physical integrity helps us see why enhancement is more ethically problematic than therapeutic interventions.

In conclusion, a plurality of ethical values will be relevant to emerging issues, whose far-reaching consequences we are not fully aware of yet. A shortcoming of the inviolability-of-persons view is its adherence to strict rules, preventing it from giving due consideration to all relevant values. Thus, it does not provide an adequate framework for resolution of these issues. However, the values that are given special attention by the inviolability-of-persons view are among the important ones to be considered.

References

Ackerman, Terrence F., and Carson Strong. 1989. *A Casebook of Medical Ethics*. New York: Oxford University Press.

Callahan, Daniel. 1969. "The Sanctity of Life." In D. R. Cutler, ed., *Updating Life and Death*, pp. 181–223. Boston: Beacon Press.

Department of Health and Human Services. 1983 "Nondiscrimination on the Basis of Handicap Relating to Health Care for Handicapped Infants." *Federal Register* 48:30846–30852.

Epstein, Franklin H. 1979. "Responsibility of the Physician in the Preservation of Life." *Archives of Internal Medicine* 139:919–920.

In re Guardianship of Gloria Sue Lambert. 1976. No. 61156 (Probate Ct. for Davidson County, Tenn. Ct. App.).

Kelly, David F. 1979. *The Emergence of Roman Catholic Medical Ethics in North America.* New York: Edwin Mellen Press.

McCormick, Richard A. 1981. *How Brave a New World?* Washington, D.C.: Georgetown University Press.

Marshall, John. 1960. *Medicine and Morals.* New York: Hawthorn Books.

Norris, Christina N. 1977. "Recent Developments: Courts—Scope of Authority—Sterilization of Mental Incompetents." *Tennessee Law Review* 44:879–889.

O'Donnell, Thomas J. 1976. *Medicine and Christian Morality.* New York: Alba House.

Pertschuk, Louis P., and Albert S. Heyman. 1965. "The Physician's Responsibility in 'Hopeless Cases.' " *Journal of the American Osteopathic Association* 64:618–619.

Ramsey, Paul. 1978. *Ethics at the Edges of Life.* New Haven: Yale University Press.

St. John-Stevas, Norman. 1964. *The Right to Life.* New York: Holt, Rinehart and Winston.

Strong, Carson. 1987. "The Principle 'Patients Come First' and Its Implications for Parent Participation in Decisions." In W. B. Weil, Jr. and M. Benjamin, eds., *Ethical Issues at the Outset of Life*, pp. 187–209. Boston: Blackwell Scientific Publications.

2

The Substrata of Biomedical Policy: Dichotomies in Somatic Technology

Lynton Keith Caldwell

To understand the conceptual foundation of arguments over biomedical policies and issues, one must look beneath the surface of public affairs to the assumptions and values that shape the lives of people. There is some truth in the saying that "how you stand depends upon where you sit." People view issues from differing points of vantage, thus arriving at differing conclusions regarding the substance of public policies. To the extent that a society is culturally diverse and heterogeneous, arrival at consensus is difficult, especially where deep-seated emotions and values are in conflict. Moreover, in most modern societies belief is dichotomized into commitments to faith or to facts, and to the individual in contrast to the society. These divergences are not always clear or coherent, but they explain the compromises, inconsistencies, and contradictions that appear when policy questions touch upon deeply held values and emotions.

Following this argument, the point of departure for the discourse to follow is *religion*—generically defined. This may seem a strange and inappropriate beginning for a consideration of public policy for biomedical technology. Isn't the issue the applications of science to medicine and the political and legal issues that become pertinent thereto? But before objections are raised, account should be taken of two other considerations that make this point of departure more pertinent and, I believe, fundamental.

Religious Ideology

First, religion, as I conceive it, is a broadly extended and deeply based phenomenon of humanity. Because religion is concerned with the origin, nature, and meaning of life, it is certain to influence the attitudes of people toward the deliberate manipulation of life in the laboratory or hospital, especially toward invasive procedures in the human body. I use the term *religion* generically to include both transcendental religion (e.g., Christianity, including Christian Science) and secular religion (e.g., Marxism or formalized humanism). I understand transcendental religion to be an expression of belief in an omniscient, omnipotent, omnipresent entity (deity) beyond human control, and to which humans owe obedience. I regard religion as separate from ethics, but inclusive of particular ethics, and make no effort to strike a balance between what I regard as the beneficial or harmful consequences of religion. But I would prefer to see public policy for medical biotechnology guided by rational ethics tested by consequences rather than directly by religious faith, whether theological or ideological. But all ethics with which I am familiar have an explicit or implicit basis in assumptions derived from religion. Secular humanism, for example, embraces a broad range of Christian ethics under different rationale and nomenclature.[1]

The second reason for beginning with religion is its influence on popular attitudes toward public policy—especially in democracies on election day.[2] Because the presence of religion in some form (even if inducing irreligion) influences popular evaluations of laws and public policies, its role in public office, legislation, litigation, economic affairs, and education deserve examination. The major political controversies today over public policies for medical biotechnology are rooted in the subsoil of religious conviction. Even controversies that on their surface are economic may be, as Robert Nelson has persuasively argued, religious (in the secular sense).[3]

Attitudes toward the human body have differed greatly among cultures and religions. In the Western world, inviolability of the body appears to be a recent concept, associated with the human rights movement, but not consistently interpreted anywhere. Mortification of the flesh and asceticism have been condoned by governments and regarded by some believers as the apotheosis of religiosity. In view of the callous treatment of human bodies throughout history, why has inviolability of the human body become a topic for consideration today? Why, in view of the intended benefits of biomedical technology for human life, should the inviolability issue arise in policy-making, law, and religious debate? The roots of this issue are neither in science nor in medicine. They extend into the deep substrata of traditional culture. The force that moves opinion here is not science–based nor is it necessarily humanitarian. The initial force (although not always its end) is nonrational moral conviction. Controversy over treatment of the human body reveals deep schisms in modern society. What one may or may not do to or with the human body is only secondarily a biomedical question. Primarily it is a matter of ethics.

If divine intelligence molded the human body out of clay would it not be presumptuous for humanity to attempt to improve upon its omniscient maker? If the creator intended that humans should improve upon divine handiwork, would not this intention be recorded in the sacred scriptures or the legendary accounts of creation? Indeed there are religious sects that hold to the view that only God is perfect and for humanity to presume to emulate God would be sacrilegious. And there are religious groups in scientifically advanced countries that reject medicine as interference with God's will. Where religiously committed parents have refused medical treatment for sick or injured children, "outside" parties have sometimes intervened, asking the courts to order medical care and to remove the children from the custody of obstructive parents.

There are differing perspectives on somatic inviolability inherent in Enlightenment-derived humanism. Unlike religious conviction, instructed by dogma and scripture, humanism is an uncoordinated eclectic set of beliefs focused on humanity as the "measure of all things." Humanist opinion thus inclines toward a liberal view of individual choice regarding invasive medical technologies. But conversely (as a generalization), it may be expected to oppose biomedical procedures imposed upon individuals by society (i.e., government) without, or sometimes even with, individual consent.

Where deeply held differences in religious or quasi–religious ideologies characterize democratic societies, political controversy becomes inevitable. These differences (e.g., over abortion or compulsory vaccination or sterilization) lead toward noncompromise positions. Science–based rationality does not win popular elections. A recent and highly popular American president is alleged to have said that he didn't know whether the creationist or Darwinian theory of humankind's origin was correct. A study supported by the National Science Foundation found that roughly half of the American people rejected the conclusion that humanity evolved from prehuman life forms.[4] "Many a man," wrote John Henry Newman, "will live and die upon a dogma: no man will be martyr for a conclusion."[5]

A problem for public biomedical policy is thus a reconciliation, where possible, between what many people want to believe and contradictory evidence derived from science and/or experience. The challenge to policy for social consensus is less to presidents and legislators, who tend to speak in generalities and cliches, than to administrators in the National Institutes of Health, the Public Health Service, and the Food and Drug Administration, who must deal with specific issues and policies. Fiscal and budgetary agencies have now become concerned with health policies. The costs of medical insurance have risen with new medical technologies and judicial determination of tort liability. Health care has become a national political issue fraught with both ethical and economic arguments.

Faith v. Facts

To avoid entanglement in epistemological controversy, certain assumptions are necessary. At least nine are fundamental to this discussion and to making sense of biomedical issues. Although some people may regard the following distinctions as arbitrary and subjective, they nevertheless seem validated by experience with the workings of the tangible world. Evidence derived from this observable experience may be called "factual"; evidence attributed to intuition or revelation may be called "faith," and it may or may not be validated by demonstrable facts. Of course faith in the validity of our observations—scientific or experiential—is another kind of faith. And so it is not so much faith per se that is at issue in biomedical controversies as is the basis or justification for faith.

Among the assumptions underlying faith in the inviolability of the human body are these:

1. Faith is its own validation. As long as faith persists contrary evidence will be rejected. In science, faith in a theory or method may be withdrawn if invalidated by new evidence.
2. Facts are statements believed or alleged to be true. The facts of religious doctrine (immaculate conception or resurrection of the dead) are unequivocal and unchangeable when sanctified by faith. The facts of science are subject to modification by the weight of evidence. Some may be regarded as axiomatic but none are sacrosanct.
3. Science in the broad sense is the most reliable way yet discovered to ascertain the actual state of affairs in the physical world and the interrelationship among things. But science has limited persuasiveness in emotional issues deeply felt.
4. Knowledge is not wholly obtainable or verifiable by scientific methods; living things show evidence of "knowing" beyond the explanations of science (e.g., *The Wisdom of the Body*).[6]

5. Truth in the conduct of human affairs may be regarded as relative to the interests, situations, and value commitments of its believers—whatever else it may be in science or philosophy.

6. Life is a phenomenon for which no unequivocal definition or explanation exists. Why so improbable a phenomenon exists we do not know, but the science of life is based on the discovery of certain molecular properties common to all living things.

7. Humanity—like all other life forms—is a biological continuum, unavoidably carrying the consequences of its behaviors and its genetic properties into the future.

8. Containment of all known life—physical or spiritual—is bodily structure, but how shaped or by what forces is a matter of conflicting opinion. The attribution of sacral character to the human body is a culture–derived belief. In some societies (e.g., some North American Indians) it was extended to other animals. In Western society the belief has applied only to humans, and then with numerous exceptions and contradictions.

9. Respect for the phenomena of life follows from a thoughtful contemplation of its mystery which is infinitely greater and more enduring than the life of any individual organism. Thus the integrity of life in whatever form should not be impaired without just and rational cause.

These assumptions, or propositions, do not hold for all beliefs, but they provide a rational basis for the formulation of biomedical policy regarding the human body. Their implication is that policy decisions regarding biomedical procedures affecting the human body—and indeed all medical procedures at some point—may encounter a conflict between beliefs regarded as facts and faith. These encounters have often led to awkward compromises or ambiguous judgments affecting, for example, the release of questioned drugs, rules regarding legal abortions, reproductive sterilization, or the funding of research on artificial organs (e.g., an artificial heart).

Of course facts and faith are dichotomies only in a superficial sense. A fact is not necessarily a truth. People, including scientists, may have faith in the veracity of particular facts or in methods of arriving at them. And the faith of people in the correctness of their moral judgments are usually based on perceptions believed to be factual.

A case in point involves the status of a human embryo or fetus. Is the fetus a child or an incipient child? If the former, when does the life of the child begin—at the moment of conception?[7] The Supreme Court of Canada has concluded that the fetus is not yet a person; the Supreme Court of the United States, allowing for judicial ambiguities, has determined that the test of personhood is the ability of the fetus to survive outside the body of the mother.[8] But "Right to Life" anti–abortionists reject this "compromise," the more radical insisting on conception as the beginning of a new life that society is morally bound to protect regardless of the circumstances of conception or the condition of the embryo. Clearly these are incommensurable positions and offer no ground for policy consensus. Drugs or surgical procedures to induce abortion may thus be regarded as violating the body of the fetus, the mother, or both.

A second case involving conflicting interpretations of fact also concerned the status of a fetus. Fetal tissue research and use in therapy was forbidden by President George Bush if the tissue became available as a result of an induced abortion.[9] Biomedical scientists held that tissue from this origin was far more reliable for remedial therapy for several intransigent diseases than is tissue resulting from miscarriages. The government argued that artificial abortion was an illegimate somatically invasive procedure which might be encouraged by the prospect of obtaining fetus tissue in this way. Belief that artificial abortion was immoral and should be illegal caused the presidential administrations of Reagan and Bush to withdraw U.S. contributions to the United Nations Population Fund. That a forced pregnancy was a violation of the body of an involuntary mother was a possibility that the Bush administration declined to consider. The foregoing restriction was, however, lifted early in 1993 by the incoming president, Bill Clinton.

A different type of case involves the mandatory use of personality-altering drugs. In cases involving habitual sex offenders, convicts have been offered the choice of a prison sentence or continuous use of a drug that would suppress their aggressive tendencies.[10] This option has angered some civil libertarians and individualist conservatives, who contend that such an offer constitutes a coerced self–administered violation of the convict's body and personality. These critics argued for an unconditional commitment to prison over the ostensibly immoral choice of causing the convict to violate his own body.

Rapid and unprecedented advances in biomedical possibilities and the persistence of traditional beliefs and values indicate that conflict between faith and alleged fact will be a continuing condition of biomedical policy. But if the substrata of policy affecting the human body is much deeper emotionally than the near-surface rationality, changes must necessarily occur in the concepts and beliefs prevalent in society if biomedical policy is to avoid a contentious and unreconcilable future.

Basic Beliefs and their Policy Consequences

It is no diversion from focus on biomedical issues regarding inviolability of the human body to consider the social forces underlying policy decisions relating to these issues. A factor contributory to failures of such public efforts as the so–called wars on poverty, crime, drugs, and environmental pollution is to attack multilineal problems with linear thinking. Another factor of no less significance is to confuse symptoms with causes. This latter tendency is understandable because the symptoms are generally apparent, whereas the causal factors are not only less obvious but are more complex with ramifications possibly far–reaching but not clearly defined. These are not the kind of factors with which politicians can score points with the public. To probe into basic causes is to risk running into interests that it would not be smart politics to arouse.

Smart politicians, so far as they are able, define issues in terms with which they can cope. They are not inclined to adopt issue definitions that could cause them future embarrassment or require a massive change of popular opinion. Simple explanations that do not require a reorientation of public opinion are preferable politically to explanations that could obtain popular acceptance only through a major effort in societal learning.

Basic beliefs are very often inconsistent, few principles applying to all circumstances to which they are relevant. Tolerance in law or ethics for acts invasive of the human body is circumstantial, and whether the acts are voluntary, involuntary, or coercive depend on the way the action is viewed. Persons undergoing surgery are customarily required to sign consent forms or waivers of liability which are intended to protect physicians and hospitals from law suits. Voluntary acceptance of risk in conventional medical or surgical procedures could be regarded as analogous to accepting the hazards of military or police services. But in fact it is seldom so regarded. Physicians and surgeons seldom enjoy the immunity from accountability for lives-at-risk usually conferred upon military commanders.

Individuals and Society

Since the days of Asclepius, the focus of medical practice has been on the individual body. This is obvious logic for injury or illness affecting individuals. Physicians or medicine men undertake to heal individuals, but the ills of society require other skills and the "health" of society is often a figure of speech about which people disagree. Indeed, the very concept of health has an ambiguity and relativity that applies to both personal and societal health. Analogies between concepts of health in individuals, societies, and environments are as old as philosophy and as recent as holistic medicine and environmental science. For example, there have been studies underway for both human health and ecological or ecosystem health in the region of the North American Great Lakes.[11]

It appears that "violation of the human body" may be indirect as well as direct, not only by nature, but by nonmedical human technologies. For example, impacts of toxic chemicals, atomic radiation, and noise may damage the human body and impair health. Studies in epidemiology and toxicology have accumulated evidence of somatic damage through multiple exposures to humanmade substances released into the environment. Restrictions on cigarette smoking in designated areas are a consequence of biomedical research having social implications. Restrictions on individual behavior for the social good (i.e., other individuals) raise philosophic, moral, and legal issues that are expressed through political contention. Must some individuals, for example, be involuntarily exposed to effects of fluoridation of public water supplies for the social good, or to ultraviolet radiation to save jobs in industries utilizing clorofluorocarbons (CFCs)?

The perceived dichotomy between the individual and society has been institutionalized in universities in the separate identity of schools of medicine and schools of public health. Individuals are primarily concerned with their personal health and with the health of persons about whom they care. The "health of society," if it poses no direct or foreseen threat to them, is seldom a subject of great concern. If, however, they feel threatened by contagious or epidemic disease they may urge social action in personal defense. Social preventives such as quarantine, isolation, expulsion, or compulsory medication (e.g., vaccination) have been sought to protect the individual and thereby also to protect society.

To insist upon the absolute inviolate condition of the human body may entail the sacrifice not only of social well–being but ultimately also of individual health. The early investigations of human physiology involved the surreptitious dissection of cadavers, illegal even in an age that condoned frightful forms of legalized torture and execution. Judeo–Christian ethics has historically shown great inconsistency and illogic in dogma regarding the inviolate character of the human body. The phenomenal advances in science during recent decades appear to have done little to attenuate deeply held doubts and prejudices. And nowhere does opinion appear to be more sharply divided than in applications of the new biotechnology to the human body.[12]

Although objections have been raised to applications of biotechnology in agriculture and animal husbandry, the principal opposition to biotechnology is its use in altering human physiology and personality. Health and safety are the presumed objectives of such actions, but their intent in changing natural (even if pathological) conditions is decried by critics as "playing God." There is a range of objection to invasive medicine, from Christian Scientists who reject nearly all intervention, to people who oppose vaccination, fluoridation, or irradiation, to those who accept most biomedical technologies short of those affecting the natural integrity of the human mind and body. Among the latter, gene therapy, tissue transplants (including organs), and certain surgical modifications of the body (e.g., sterilization) may be regarded as "unnatural" and of dubious morality.

Genetics may turn out to be the most subversive of the sciences. Its therapeutic potentialities are disturbing to many people, especially when human personality may be affected. There has been outspoken, although not uniformly consistent, objections to applying biotechnology (i.e., genetic technology) to the human body and mind. To the many religious conservatives, such action is an impious and arrogating usurpation of the will and work of God. In the opinion of some equalitarian moralists, investigation of the genetics of intelligence is not a proper field for scientific inquiry. Objections have also been raised to genetic screening for any purpose on the ground that possible findings, as in the case also of intelligence, would open the way to discrimination and abuse.

Tissue transplants may be less controversial invasive procedures. But, as previously noted, obtaining organs or fetal tissue for transplant purposes has aroused concern and debate. Contrary to the judgment of medical investigators, the United States government under George Bush temporarily prohibited the use of tissue from induced abortions, alleging that this option might encourage voluntary recourse to abortion. That such tissue transplants might ultimately be used in alleviating or reversing the symptoms of degenerative brain diseases such as Parkinson's or Huntington's syndromes was regarded by President Bush as less important than the risk of possible encouragement of abortion to obtain fetal tissue.

The difficulties of assessing the ramifications of invasive technologies and of attempting to formulate policies for dealing with them do not lie only in our inability to predict outcomes precisely. There is the further and in some senses prior problem of a lack of social consensus about values and goals. It is correspondingly difficult for government officials or medical professionals to assign priorities, or to weigh various desiderata against each other. Clearly, the two problems—lack of knowledge and lack of agreed upon values and goals—affect one another. If we knew for certain what the effects of deliberate genetic interventions would be, it might be somewhat easier to weigh the values of individual freedom and dignity against the values of human improvement. On the other hand, it is conceivable that such better understanding of outcomes might serve to exacerbate value conflicts.

But the problem of values is becoming apparent even with respect to the technologies already at our disposal. As we proceed further in the direction of deliberate planning and technology assessment, there is a need for more careful specification of values. As has been noted, the values issue is especially acute in attitudes toward biomedical methods that alter human potential personalities, or behaviors.

For many years compulsory sterilization of persons believed to genetically transmit severe mental deficiencies was legal in the United States. But under pressure from civil libertarians and human rights activists this practice has been almost altogether outlawed.[13] The prevailing argument is that society has a moral obligation to support and protect the "mentally unfit," or the currently preferred term, "developmentally handicapped." In part, objection to investigating the genetics of intelligence is the apprehension (often unvoiced) that its findings might suggest the social desirability of preventing the reproduction of "defective" humans. In the lexicon of fundamentalist humanitarianism, there are few handicapped humans who are truly "defective"—most are merely "deficient."

Much more common is voluntary sterilization as a method of contraception. A policy issue arises here between persons who regard any surgical sterilization as a morally as well as physically invasive procedure that government should regulate or prohibit and those who oppose regulations that would restrict reproductive freedom—freedom from involuntary pregnancy. In 1978, after six months of public hearings, the U.S. Department of Health, Education, and Welfare issued restrictive rules governing federal participation in sterilization programs.[14] These rules were subsequently tightened in 1982, limiting sterilization where legal to informed consent. Again, as in the preceding issues, the relationship of the human individual to life and society is the underlying factor that determines the position taken by people on the issue.

Suicide and euthanasia have not customarily been regarded as biomedical procedures. Yet today physician-assisted suicides, voluntarily elected, have raised ethical and legal issues. The belief that life, however defined, must be prolonged by all available means has prevented the removal of life-support devices from dying, comatose, or brain-dead patients. Even when urged by family and clergy to withdraw extraordinary life-support measures, courts have frequently ordered the maintenance of life support.[15]

Humanity and Nature

The dichotomy of the individual and society is itself divided into two differing assumptions regarding humanity's place in nature. These positions may be described as "integrationist" and "exceptionalist." The former, taken for granted by most "primitive" people, and recently rediscovered by the environmental movement, assumes the human to be an integral part of nature. Humankind has qualities that have become exceptional in the living world, but humans do not enjoy an exception from the so-called laws of nature. Humankind is an integral part of the biosphere, and even in space, travel must remain encapsulated in an artificial, portable biosphere as a condition of survival.

The exceptionalist assumption places humans outside of nature. Dependence on natural forces (as in space travel) is regarded as domination of nature—making nature serve human purposes. These dichotomies have in other contexts been termed *anthropocentric* (human–centered and able to transcend nature's so–called laws) and *biocentric* (life- or earth-centered). These dichotomies—which are philosophic orientations—interact in biomedical technology notably in their implications for human behavior as it affects human health and social welfare. The separation between medicine and public health reflects the anthropocentric orientation in present-day conventional medicine. The preference for prevention over cure is largely biocentric in character—living in ways to prevent or minimize injury, disease, or the transmittal of disease. The difference between an anthropocentric and biocentric approach to health and medicine is defined by the breadth of their focus. The anthropocentric focus is in the discrete individual with relatively little attention to extraneous environmental factors; the role of medicine is to cure the patient. The biocentric approach looks to conditioning or predisposing factors in the environment (holistic medicine and public health), with greater emphasis on prevention. These differences, of course, are tendencies and are not always sharply defined.

Biomedical Somatic Intervention: The Task of Policy

Possibilities for biomedical intervention in the function and form of the human body have been increasing rapidly. This trend may be expected to continue for an indefinite period unless restrained by human choice. Indefinite expansion does not imply endless expansion of invasive technologies—it means that the limit to possibilities cannot be foreseen. There are doubtless limits to possibilities inherent in nature. But the more probable limitations, short of this barrier, are in political and economic policies generated from what we have termed the "substrata" of biomedical policy.

Socially defined barriers to biomedical research and practice have been and are likely to continue to be selective. Policy limitations are imposed through statutes, regulations, or availability of funding. Informal barriers may also be imposed by peer group consensus or, less often, by administrative disapproval. In some universities both of these latter barriers to research have been raised—notably on studies of the genetics of intelligence.[16] Although work in this area is not now invasive in a physiological sense, its opponents regard it as psychologically invasive. In the investigation of linkages between genetics and antisocial or criminal behavior, civil libertarians fear the use of such invasive therapies. Brain and neural surgery have been seen as ways of preventing behavior that may be regarded as socially undesirable or dangerous but are the ultimate invasion of the human body and personality.

The brain and neural system are critical parts of the body and may be affected by traumas or therapies that show no readily apparent somatic change, although behavioral change may indicate that somatic change has somehow occurred. In view of tragic aberrations in human behavior one might think that preventive and remedial therapies would be welcome. Yet this is obviously not so. There are two reasons for skepticism and rejection. The more rational is doubt regarding the effectiveness of the procedures; less rational is a legacy from the eighteenth-century Enlightenment—a belief that human conduct is environmentally conditioned. From Rousseau to Marx to Freud, environmental influences supplanted the gods and the devil as determinants of human conduct. Conflict with this belief has arisen chiefly in relation to hereditary influences. A more sophisticated and informed understanding of relationships between innate and external influences has developed in society today, but it is not yet widely shared.

If there is a safe generalization regarding biomedical policy, it is that the issues are too diverse to support any substantive generalization. This follows not only from the diversity of the issues but also from those beliefs and assumptions in the psychological substrata that influence the attitudes of people regarding ethics, reason, justice, and the reconciliation of individual and social rights, all of which intermix in human emotional reactions. Advances in biomedical policy may ultimately depend upon finding ways in which human life may be made more satisfying and endurable with those beliefs and biases that would obstruct or deny these benefits.

The following is a brief summary of the issues confronting biomedical policy in overcoming psychological or ideological barriers to bettering the human condition. It should be acknowledged, however, that what I would regard here as betterment may not be so regarded by others. To people who regard life itself as absolutely sacred and inviolate, human suffering and the burden of incurable illness or injury may be preferable to the termination of life by any means and for any reason. The firmness of opinion on biomedical issues involving law and ethics rests upon a foundation of psychological and emotional factors that, in effect, tend to predetermine the way issues are evaluated. Much of the difficulty and frustration of attempting directly to change people's minds results from the greater difficulty in penetrating below opinion to the basic determinants of the way people see life and society. In changing public opinion on biopolitical issues, both overt opinions and their psychological-emotional substrate must be addressed. The task will often be to redirect basic predispositions to changed opinion outcomes.

The decision to use artifical life-support systems, some of which may be very costly, has become a troublesome issue in biomedical policy, particularly so in cases of court–ordered maintenance of life-support for hopelessly impaired or vegetative individuals. Some lawyers, judges, and hospital administrators have insisted that every available measure be taken to keep the body alive as long as possible. The moral conflict here is larger than medical or legal ethics and goes to the heart of people's beliefs about life itself.

The transplantation of living organs or the provision of artificial organs is less an occasion for ethical conflict in principle and more an issue of economics and equity. Prosthetic devices may fall into this category of potential policy differences when cost conflicts with access and equity. None of the means of replacing natural or innate capabilities in their most elementary forms would come into question; there are no serious policy discussions over the availability of eyeglasses, dentures, crutches, walkers, or artificial limbs. The principal barrier to heart bypass procedures and mechanical heart valves are economic. The same seems true with artficial replacement of hips, legs, and arms. Costs raise questions of equity, but otherwise no ethical issue arsis. However, ethical, legal, and economic issues do arise over the use of organ transplants— and as noted in therapies involving fetal tissue. In these cases fear of abuse is largely although not wholly irrational. Fetal tissue might be obtained in unethical ways, and the task of policymakers is to find the formula that will monitor the traffic in living tissues and that will arrive at equitable judgments under conditions of scarcity, perhaps even involving some form of rationing.

Less contentious are the various forms of cosmetic or reconstructive surgery. For the most part, they are intended to improve the quality of life, not to save life. Plastic surgery and corrective surgery on hands and feet do not involve life-and–death issues. For many, face lifts and hair transplants are merely expressions of vanity. Where surgery miscarries, legal liability may become an issue, but biomedical policy per se would not likely be involved. The use of steroids for body building and athletic competition does involve issues of legal and ethical use of biomedical technology.

Biomedical ethics has attracted a growing amount of attention through conferences, institutes, and policy research, and there is a substantial literature on the subject. Yet it is not clear that the fundamental differences in assumptions and values that divide modern society have been effectively addressed, nor that much progress has been made toward social consensus. For example, the right-to-choice—right-to-life conflict over abortion reveals differences in beliefs and values that are unlikely to be resolved very soon by reasonable debate.

Addressing the substrata of biomedical policy is clearly an interdisciplinary task. It is not primarily a biomedical or technological matter; even its ethical and ideological aspects are not the most fundamental issues because they in turn rest upon beliefs regarding the origin and nature of life, and indeed the source and authority of moral values. Thus, a critical task of biomedical policy should be to put forth updated information and develop techniques of forecasting and assessment that could contribute to a more rational biopolicy.

In summary, the substrata of biopolicy exceeds the limits of biology, medicine, ethics, or law. It relates to all of these areas of knowledge, but encompasses much more. One may argue that to resolve present ambiguities, conflicts, and gridlocks in biomedical policy we must move beyond present inclinations toward reductionist and specialist segregation of knowledge, and reconstruct the substrata of our thinking to allow a synthesis among relevant disciplines that will achieve the basis for a consensus on public policy. But this is a highly intellectualized approach that many people today are unprepared to accept. At present, many biomedical policy issues are characterized by strongly held, irreconcilable positions. Popular consensus on policies cannot be achieved unless elements of the ideational, emotional, and basic value substrata of human belief can be reconciled at some common level of comprehension.[17]

How might this be accomplished? There is probably no single way; three possibilities come to mind. The first is the conventional answer: "public education." This includes not only a careful clarification of issue in schooling but also through the other media that inform the public. Obviously this approach will not be taken unless those in charge of these media believe that they have an obligation to assist a rational reconciliation among values. A second source of change could be experience—the demonstrated ability of invasive biomedical procedures to alleviate suffering and to prevent involuntary antisocial behavior. A third might become possible through a new definition of ethical valuees in organized religion. Steps in this direction have been taken in many religious denominations. In all cases time is a factor. Social learning takes time and perseverance. Yet ethics and values do not appear to be innate biological traits. The psychological substrate of biomedical policy has changed over the years and may be expected to change in the future in the course of social learning.

Notes

1. Lewis W. Spitz, "Humanism," *Encyclopedia of Religion*, edited by Mircea Eliade (New York: Macmillan, 1987), vol. 6, pp. 511–515.

2. Thomas C. Weigele, "Organized Religion and Biotechnology: Social Responsibility and the Role of Government," in David J. Webber ed., *Biotechnology, Assessing Social Impacts and Policy Implications* (Westport, Conn.: Greenwood Press, 1990).

3. Robert H. Nelson, *Reaching for Heaven on Earth: The Theological Meaning of Economics* (Savage, Md.: Rowman and Littlefield, 1991).

4. John D. Miller, *The Public Understanding of Science in the United States: A Report to the National Science Foundation* (De Kalb: Northern Illinois University Public Opinion Laboratory, 1991).

5. "Knowledge and Faith" excerpt from *The Tamworth Reading Room* (1841), in Raymond Macdonald Alden, ed., *Readings in English Prose of the Nineteenth Century* (Cambridge, Mass.: Riverside Press, 1917), p. 413.

6. Walter Bradford Cannon, *The Wisdom of the Body* (New York: W. W. Norton, 1932).

7. Bonnie Steinbock, *Life Before Birth: The Moral and Legal Status of Embryos and Fetuses* (New York/Oxford: Oxford University Press, 1992).

8. Daniel Conkle, "Canada's Roe: The Canadian Abortion Decision and its Implications for American Constitutional Law and Theory," *Constitutional Commentary* 6 (1989):299–318; Mary Ann Glendon, "A beau mentir qui vient de loin: The 1988 Abortion Decision in Comparative Perspective," *Northwestern University Law Review* 83 (1989):569–591; and John Hart Ely, "The Wages of Crying Wolf: A Comment on Roe v. Wade," *Yale Law Journal* 82 (1973):920–949.

9. Daniel E. Koshland, Jr., "Fetal Tissue Research," *Science* 257 (June 26, 1992):741. See also Steinbock, *Life Before Birth*, pp. 165–194.

10. Edward A. Fitzgerald, "Chemical Castrations: MPA Treatment of the Sexual Offender," *American Journal of Criminal Law* 18(1) (Fall 1990):1–60 (MPA is medroxyprogesterone acetate, or Depo-Provera); Samuel J. Brakel and Ronald Rock, *The Mentally Disabled and the Law*, rev. ed. (Chicago: University of Chicago Press, 1971); *Skinner v. Oklahoma*, 316 U.S. 535, 62 S. Ct. 1110; 86 *Lawyer's Edition* 1655; and *State of Louisiana v. Michael Owen Perry*, no. 91-KP-1324, Supreme Court of Louisiana, Oct. 19, 1992.

11. Several studies of the biomedical effects of contaminants in the Great Lakes have been underway, e.g., Great Lakes Protection Fund (Health Effects Working Group), International Joint Commission (Council of Great Lakes Research Managers and Science Advisory Board), and Department of Health and Welfare, Canada (Great Lakes Health Effects Program).

12. Robert H. Blank and Andrea L. Bennicksen eds., *Debates Over Medical Authority: New Challenges in Biomedical Experimentation*, vol. II of *Emerging Issues in Biomedical Policy: An Annual Review* (New York: Columbia University Press, 1993); Robert H. Blank, ed., *Biomedical Technology and Public Policy* (New York: Greenwood Press, 1989); and Sandra Panem, ed., *Biotechnology: Implications for Public Policy* (Washington, D.C.: Brookings Institution, 1985).

13. Rosalind Pollack Petchesky, "Reproduction, Ethics, and Public Policy: The Federal Sterilization Regulations," *Hastings Center Report* 9(5) (October 1979).

14. 43 Federal Register F.R. 43. 52171 (Nov. 8, 1978); 47 F.R. 33702 (Aug. 4, 1982); 42 C.F.R. (Code of Federal Regulations) 441.251.

15. *Cruzan v. Missouri*, U.S. 110 S. Ct. 2841 (1990).

16. Most recently at the University of Delaware regarding the work of Linda S. Gottfredson, see "The g Factor in Employment: A Special Issue," *Journal of Vocational Behavior*, edited by Linda Gottfredson, 29(3) (December 1986):293–461. Prominent among investigators of the genetic and biochemical influences on intelligence are Arthur F. Jensen, University of California at Berkeley; Thomas J. Bouchard, Jr., University of Minnesota; and Robert Plomim, Pennsylvania State University. See also articles by Jensen, Rice, and Dobzanski in *Psychology Today* 7(7) (December 1973):79–101.

17. The importance of basic values in the formulation of biomedical policy was acknowledged in the concluding paragraphs of *Implications of Biomedical Technology*, Research Review no. 1 (Cambridge, Mass.: Harvard University Program on Technology and Society, 1968), p. 8.

3

The Church and the Restructuring of Humans

❖

Albert S. Moraczewski

Fiction writers are often successful in forecasting later scientific developments. In his book *Mutation* (1989), Dr. Robin Cook tells the tale of a biological scientist who by a feat of genetic engineering is able to generate a child—his child—with an extremely high IQ. The child performs beyond the father's expectations. However, he had not foreseen that having altered his son's IQ there was no guarantee that there would be a concomitant and proportionate improvement in the boy's ethics quotient (EQ). Ultimately, the boy's ruthless ambition coupled with extraordinary intelligence uncontrolled by a moral sense leads him to an ultimately lethal rampage.

Similar stories may be found in the world's literature. Among these are the various versions of the Jewish tale of the Golem. With the help of secret knowledge and incantations, the knowledgeable Jew was able to form out of clay a creature who would serve to protect the good of the Jewish community. But as it frequently occurs, the human " creator" ultimately uses the creature's power for selfish purposes with the result that it turns on its former master and destroys him and sometimes others (i.e., Singer 1982). A well-known variant of the Golem theme is Mary Shelley's depiction of Baron Frankenstein's monster featured in her 1818 novel, *Frankenstein*.

Today, with the aid of medical technology, physicians are able to intervene in the human body and alter to varying degrees its structures and functions. Psychiatrists and psychologists are able also to modify human behavior in increasingly specific ways with regards to correcting maladaptive behavior patterns. There is also speculation that normal functions such as memory may be improved.

All this vast technological power, which has only recently come into human hands, has raised some vital ethical and theological issues for a number of religious groups. Among others, the Catholic Church has expressed reservations about some of these technical interventions into the *humanum*. For example, a recent document notes that "an intervention on the human body affects not only the tissues, the organs and their functions but also involves the person himself on different levels. It involves, therefore, perhaps in an implicit but nonetheless real way, a moral significance and responsibility" (Congregation for the Doctrine of the Faith [CDF] 1987:3).

In this essay, I will begin with a very brief overview of some of these biomedical interventions. This will be followed by a statement of the basic premises and principles that guide the Catholic Church's reflections on the limits to intervention on the human body; application of these principles to specific biomedical interventions will constitute the third part. The essay will conclude with a look to the future.

Current Biomedical Capabilities

Genetic Engineering

Thanks to recent developments in biological technology, medical personnel are able to match some of fiction's accomplishments and bring about radical changes in living organisms' structures and functions. For more than a decade biotechnology has been able to alter the genome of bacteria so that they can produce biological products of use to humans such as insulin, growth hormone, and interferon. Now, medical scientists have begun the introduction of genes into human cells so as to correct various genetic defects. The first federally approved infusion of genetically engineered cells into a human patient to correct a congenital immune deficiency was carried out at the National Institutes of Health by Dr. W. French Anderson and his colleagues on September 14, 1990 (Weiss 1990:180). More recently, a new engineered gene was injected into a patient's melanoma tumor with the objective of stimulating an immune response, that is, an attack on the tumor itself (Holden 1992:1628).

Surgical Technologies

Using surgical procedures, organ transplantation has become increasingly common in meeting the vital needs of patients whose organs have failed. Currently, organ transplantation includes kidney, liver, heart, lung, corneas, pancreas, bone marrow, and bone or bone fragments.

More problematical in terms of public acceptance has been the surgical alteration of anatomical gender in an attempt to have the body's anatomy in closer conformity to the person's perceived psychological gender. While such changes do not yield a fertile individual, surgical modifications allow some degree of sexual behavior. It has been reported that these gender alterations have yielded satisfactory results for at least some of those who have undergone this sort of radical surgery, while at least one researcher concludes that "neither the case in favor of nor against sex reasssignment surgery has been proven" (Walker 1983:280).

Still another type of surgery, psychosurgery, has not met wide acceptance. This is an attempt to correct maladaptive behavior, generally by severing, more or less selectively, nerve tracts that supposedly subserve certain behaviors. Egas Moniz in 1936 first reported a procedure, leukotomy (leucotomy), known also as prefrontal lobotomy and psychosurgery, as a treatment for mental disorders (Aita 1991:201). While some authors conclude that "in retrospect, psychosurgery was perhaps not as successful as once envisioned (Aita 1991:204), others conclude differently (Laitenen 1988). The difference is that today more precise, stereotaxic methods are used. Accordingly, one author concludes positively:

> Cingulotomy is effective for chronic pain, with addiction and depression, anterior capsulotomy for obsessive-compulsive and anxiety neurosis. . . . Modern psychosurgery does not modify the personality of the patient. On the contrary, it often relieves it from disturbing symptoms of illness. (Laitenen 1988:158)

Reproductive Technologies

Several developments in the area of reproduction have marked the last three decades of reproductive medicine. One group of techniques has been concerned with restricting human fertility. The anovulants and derivatives have done much to alter sexual practices worldwide. It is estimated that oral contraceptives have been used by some 200 million women (Goldzieher 1989:9). Other technologies, of course, are still in current usuage, e.g., intrauterine devices (IUDs), condoms (a return to popularity because of the spread of AIDS and other sexually transmitted diseases),and other barrier-type devices as well as spermicidal agents.

Infertility is a major problem for the 2.4 million couples (U.S. Congress Office of Technology Assessment [OTA] 1988:3). To overcome infertility, a major recent development has been the introduction of several new technologies such as in vitro fertilization (IVF) and gamete intrafallopian transfer (GIFT) (U.S. Congress OTA 1988:123–125). In July 1978 the first child conceived in vitro was born in England. Since that time it has been estimated that more than 10,000 children conceived by means of IVF have been born, while some 169 facilities as of March 1988 (U.S. Congress OTA 1988:311) were offering IVF services. While cloning has been the subject of speculative fiction, beyond the projects using frogs, claims for successes with mammals such as mice have not been substantiated. Because of technological difficulties and an apprehensive public, the possibility of human cloning at present seems technologically too remote to merit any serious consideration for our discussion.

Psychopharmacological Agents

The current widespread abuse of drugs such as cocaine, heroin, and marijuana has raised public concern about the misuse of drugs to a new high. Clearly such drugs do change—albeit in a relatively unspecific manner—the behavior of the user. The writer-philosopher Aldous Huxley, in several of his books lauded the use of various drugs. In *Brave New World* (1950), he extols the merits of the hypothetical drug soma to bring about wonders of peace and contentment. "Now you can swallow two or three half-gramme tablets, and there you are. Anybody can be virtuous now. You can carry at least half of your morality about in a bottle. Christianity without tears—that's what soma is" (285).

In another Huxley work, *The Doors of Perception*, he describes the wonders of the hallucinogen mescaline for bringing about mystical experiences. "But now I knew contemplation at its height, but not yet in its fullness" (41). Departing from his fiction, at a meeting of the New York Academy of Sciences concerned with the new psychotherapeutic drugs resepine and chlorpromazine, Huxley delivered a paper in which he proclaimed a revolution was at hand.

But the pharmacologist will give us something that most human beings have never had before. If we want joy, peace and loving kindness, they will give us loving kindness, peace and joy. If we want beauty, they will transfigure the outside world for us and open the door to visions of unimaginable richness and significance. If our desire is for life everlasting, they will give us the next best thing— aeons of blissful experience miraculously telescoped into a single hour. (Huxley 1957:683)

Life-Conserving Technologies

In addition to the above interventions into the human psyche and soma, modern biotechonolgy has been able to develop a variety of life-sustaining technologies. These are "drugs, medical devices, or procedures that can keep individuals alive who would otherwise die within a foreseeable, but usually uncertain, time period" (U.S. Congress OTA 1987:4). The more important technologies include:

1. cardiopulmonary resuscitation (CPR): "a range of technologies that restore heartbeat and maintain blood flow and breathing following cardiac or respiratory arrest";
2. mechanical ventilation: "the use of a machine to induce alternating inflation and deflation of the lungs, to regulate the exchange of gases in the blood";
3. renal dialysis (hemodialysis and peritoneal dialysis): "an artificial method of maintaining the chemical balance of the blood when the kidneys have failed";
4. nutritional support and hydration (enteral and parenteral): "artificial methods of providing nourishment and fluids" by tubes into the digestive tract or by catheter into the bloodstream;
5. antibiotics: "a large set of drugs used to cure or control numerous bacterial, viral, and fungal infections" (U.S. Congress OTA 1987:4).

This brief summary of the various technological developments that permit radical interventions into the human psyche/soma is not complete without a recognition of their associated problems. Among these are the ethical issues and, more specifically for this paper, the issue of how the Catholic Church views these technological capabilities and achievements. The larger questions may be stated as follows: in light of the Church's teachings, are there any limits to technological interventions that can be performed on a human being? If so, what are they? What is the basis for the determination of such limits?

Relevant Church Teachings

As a general principle, the Church is concerned with *keeping humans fully human*, that nothing should be done to a human being that would violate the respect due to the individual as a member of the human race. The human has, in the Church's view, an intrinsic worth deriving from the Creator and is not conferred by human society, although the latter may confirm and protect that dignity by appropriate laws and ritual. The basis for that stance is the Church's belief that "God created man in his image; in the divine image he created him; male and female he created them" (Genesis 1:27). In addition, the Church holds that God conferred on humans a delegated dominion over creation (at least this part of it): "God blessed them [the humans he created, Adam and Eve], saying: 'Be fertile and multiply; fill the earth and subdue it' " (Genesis 1:28).

But Genesis is silent as to what extent humans were given dominion over *themselves*. Over the centuries since the foundation of Christianity, the Church has developed certain principles by which it dealt with a whole range of ethical questions. Clearly, since the developments in technology are very recent, one should not expect to find in earlier Church teachings statements that are immediately applicable to these new biomedical questions.

Nonetheless, there are some general principles contained in the Church's teachings that can be used in developing more specific principles for use in dealing with these bioethical issues. Among these are the following:

1. Every human being has a right to life.
2. Every human being has a right to the truth, and the freedom to make decisions that concern his or her well-being or life.
3. Every human being has a right to the integrity of mind and body.
4. Human procreation is a sacred event and its inherent dignity and structure is to be respected.
5. Good intentions and objectives do not justify evil means; one may not do evil in order to do good.

Specific Directives

In contemporary times, the Church has issued specific directives that developed, amplified, or particularized some of the above principles. These include:

1. Human life is to be respected from conception to natural death. "The first right of the human person is his life. He has other goods and some are more precious, but this one is fundamental—the condition of all the others. . . . In reality, respect for human life is called for from the time that process of generation begins (SCDF 1974:11–12). "No one can make an attempt on the life of an innocent person without opposing God's love for that person, without violating a fundamental right, and therefore without commiting a crime of the utmost gravity " (SCDF 1980:I,1). "Intentionally causing one's own death, or suicide, is therefore equally wrong as murder; such an action on the part of the person is to be considered as a rejection of God's sovereignty and loving plan" (SCDF 1980:I, 3).

2. The conjugal act is to be fully respected. That is, the act of sexual intercourse between a husband and his wife must be a voluntary act entered into mutually and freely by both spouses who respect both the intrinsic nature and dignity of that act. "The Church . . . teaches that each and every marriage act (*quilibet matrimonii usus*) must remain open to the transmission of life. . . . That teaching, often set forth by the Magisterium, is founded upon the inseparable connection, willed by God and unable to be broken by man on his own initiative, between the two meanings of the conjugal act: the unitive meaning and the procreative meaning" (Paul VI 1968:11–12).

3. The human zygote, embryo, and fetus are to be respected as members of the human race. "Thus the fruit of human generation, from the first moment of its existence, that is to say from the moment the zygote has formed, demands the unconditional respect that is due to the human being in his bodily and spiritual totality. The human being is to be respected and treated as a person from the of conception; and therefore from that same moment his rights as a person must be recognized, among which in the first place is the inviolable right of every innocent being to life" (SCDF 1987:I, 1).

4. A person's bodily and mental integrity must be respected, both by himself and others; no part of the body may be removed or its function destroyed or impaired without proportionate necessity and benefit for the well-being of the whole body. "As far as the patient is concerned, he is not absolute master of himself, of his body, or of his soul. He cannot, therefore, freely dispose of himself as he pleases. The patient is bound by the immanent purposes fixed by nature. He possesses the right to use, limited by natural finality, the faculties and powers of his human nature. Because he is the beneficiary, and not the proprietor, he does not possess

unlimited power to allow actsof destruction or of mutilation of anatomic or functional character.But, in virtue of the principle of totality, of his right to employ theservices of the organism as a whole, he can give individual parts todestruction or mutilation when and to the extent that it is necessary forthe good of his being as whole" (Pius XII 1952:198–199).

Specific Considerations

Genetic alterations. Two distinctions are in order:

1. the difference between acting on somatic cells and on the germ or reproductive cells; and
2. the difference between making alterations designed to correct a structural or functional defect and those directed to improving a normal bodily structure or function.

The present pope, John Paul II, has several times made statements in his addresses that genetic medicine holds out the hope of significant improvement in medical treatment of certain disorders. Yet, while he praised the efforts of scientists working in the field of medicine, it was not without some cautionary statements. In general, he said, it was permissible to correct defects, to employ gene therapy so long that the individual did not experience adverse effects that would be greater then the expected benefit.

The research of modern biology gives hope that the transfer and mutations of genes can ameliorate the condition of those who are affected by chromosomic diseases; in this way the smallest and weakest of human beings can be cured during their intrauterine life or in the period immediately after birth.

While . . . I approve and support your worthy researches, I reaffirm that they must all be subject to moral principles and values which respect and realize in its fullness the dignity of man. (John Paul II 1982:342, 343)

A strictly therapeutic intervention, having the objective of healing various maladies—such as those stemming from chromosomic deficiencies—will be considered in principle as desirable, provided that it tends to real promotion of the personal well-being of man, without harming his integrity or worsening his life conditions. (John Paul II 1983:388)

It is another matter, however, the pope noted, when it is a question of modifying the normal structure and function of the human body-soul unity. While he did not entirely rule out any activity in this area, he did express concern that such attempts not result in any new marginalization of persons or in any way detract from their human dignity.

> It is on the basis of this anthropological view [namely, the identity of man as one in body and soul] that the fundamental criteria have to be found for making decisions of intervention not strictly therapeutic, for example, interventions aimed at improving the human biological condition.
>
> In particular, this kind of intervention must not offer harm to the origin of human life, that is, procreation linked not only with the biological but also the spiritual union of the parents, united by the bond of marriage. Such an intervention must consequently respect the fundamental dignity of mankind and the common biological nature which lies at the basis of liberty; respect, consisting in avoidance of manipulations tending to modify the genetic store [genome] and to create groups of different people, at the risk of provoking fresh marginalizations in society. (John Paul II 1983:388)

With regard to the latter, namely nontherapeutic intervention, one can ask the question, what would be an improvement of the basic structure and function of the human being? When we improve upon something, it usually involves a consideration of its purpose, for example, a better mouse trap, a more efficient automobile, etc. So, if the human is to be improved, how? Perhaps a better memory (better retention, improved retrieval) or quicker intelligence. Other possibilities include a will less inclined to selfishness or misuse of power, or again, greater resistance to disease or to the ravages of old age could be asssets. Yet what might be considered a desirable improvement in one culture or set of circumstances may not be so in another. And who would make the decision as to what qualities to favor? Who would carry out such a program? Would it be voluntary? One can see an immense number of ethical difficulties associated with such an effort to "improve" the human race. The Nazi experiments in eugenics are recent enough that the odious memories remain as a warning to exercise great caution in human experimentation.

The Church sees humankind as having a transcendental destiny, one that extends beyond the grave. Consequently, any judgment about the human is done against the backdrop of that faith. To achieve that destiny the Church holds it is essential that nothing be done by deliberate intervention to the person that would impair the full use of his or her intellectual and voluntary faculties. This is one consequence of the principle of the inviolability of the human soma-psyche unity both in its structure and its function. Hence, any genetic intervention, be it to correct some structural or functional defect (traceable to genes), or allegedly to improve the psyche or some bodily function, must respect the inherent dignity of the human person.

Surgical interventions. Current practice of organ transplantation does not present any fundamental problem for the Church. However, at the beginning of the transplant era, when the issue arose regarding corneal transplantation from a cadaver, Pope Pius II and a number of theologians perceived a problem (Cunningham 1944). Pius found no basic objection to this, but he did voice opposition to the transfer of organs and tissues from a living donor. It must be recalled that Pius XII was writing shortly after the medical atrocities of the Nazi physicians in World War II had become widely known. His objection was also based on the argumentation that was proposed to support such transplantation. Proponents were making the comparison that as an organ was to the whole body so the individual human was to society. Hence, for the benefit of society, a person could donate (perhaps even involuntarily) an organ. The dangers inherent in that concept are too clear. Furthermore, for Pius XII the parts of the human body were strictly for the well-being of that individual who could not divest himself of an integral part of his body for the welfare of another (Pius XII 1956:375–376).

However, subsequent theological discussions were able to find a solution to what could have become a major obstacle for Catholics with regard to the donation and reception of organs and tissues from living donors. A distinction was made between a procedure that would deprive the individual completely of a function versus one that resulted only in a partial loss of a function such as would occur with the transplantation of one member of a paired organ system. Thus, one could donate one of two healthy kidneys on the basis that the one healthy kidney would be able to carry out the necessary renal function. From this viewpoint the deprivation of one kidney—as long as the one remaining could carry out the necessary renal activity—would not be considered a loss of bodily integrity or function. As an act of fraternal charity, one could then donate a kidney to a person who would not live (except perhaps for renal dialysis) without it.

There are, of course, ethical questions regarding the donor and the recipient, such as free informed consent. For certain organs, such as the heart, it is essential that the person is dead before the organ is removed. In any event, if the donor is living then for any organ removed—usually a paired organ—it is vital that the *function* be not impaired. There are questions of equity when it comes to the allocation of scarce resources. But all these issues are also of concern for most ethicists and do not represent any unique concern of the Church.

Psychosurgery. Psychosurgery has some special problems since it is a technique that affects the brain itself, and thus may alter intelligence and the will. Nothing should be done to the patient that would impair the proper functioning of the mind and the will, a basic premise has been reemphasized in a recent address of Pope John Paul II:

> Furthermore, because of his likeness to God, revealed by the human mind, man—as the second Vatican Council affirms—"is the only creature on earth that God has wanted for its own sake" (*Gaudium et Spes*, 24), in such a way that "all that exists on earth must be referred to man as its center and summit"(ibid., 12). Accordingly, the full affirmation of the mind of man, of its functions and capacities, resides the right-duty of mastering creation and itself in conformity with the finalities willed by the Creator (cf. Genesis 1:28). It is the mind, them, which while capable of reaching God, is at the same time the "master" of creation; these are two attributions of incomparable value, to the point of placing it above all other created realities of the visible universe. . . .
>
> In other words, to study the mind we can never neglect the *whole truth about man*, in his close-knit unity as a physical and spiritual being. (John Paul II 1991:10)

While some cognitive functions of the brain can be temporarily suspended, as during sleep and general anesthesia for a surgical procedure, it would not be morally permissible to impede their proper functioning permanently. Yet, as we have seen above, contemporary psychosurgical procedures are more accurately placed by means of stereotaxic procedures. Studies have shown that the procedures used in carefully selected patients and by competent surgeons have in fact yielded good results.

Accordingly, consonant with Church teaching, a few ethical guidelines would need to be observed to protect the rights of the patient (McFadden 1967:283–287):

1. The mental disorder must be such that the individual has notable functional impairment.
2. Other less drastic therapeutic interventions (e.g., pharmacological, electroconvulsive therapy) have been tried and found to be ineffective.
3. The reasonably anticipated benefits are not exceeded by the foreseen adverse effects (such as cognitional or volitional impairment).
4. Appropriate free, informed consent has been obtained.

Gender Reassignment. Another surgical area of interest is so-called gender reassignment. In a condition known as "transsexualism" (or gender dysphoria) the individual experiences a discordance between his or her anatomical sex and self-perceived gender. As some have described it, "I feel like a woman trapped in a man's body" or vice versa. In either case, the surgery aims at making the anatomy match the person's experienced gender. Up to the present, the surgically altered male does not receive any ovaries, while the surgically altered female does not acquire a pair of functioning testes. Yet the ethical acceptability of transplantation of ovaries from a fresh human cadaver to a living recipient has been considered acceptable—on the supposition that it was medically feasible (Healy 1956:142). The removal, however, of normal ovaries or testes from a living donor would not be morally acceptable in light of Church teaching as described above since it would constitute a total loss of the generative function without a compensatory bodily benefit for the donor individual.

The Church to date has not made a specific statement regarding gender reassignment surgery. The basic objection, of course, would be that this is a mutilation; it is the destruction a normally (generally) functioning organ with no proportionate benefit to the *body*. If, on the other hand, it could be shown that indeed there has been a biological error so that the body is discordant with the psyche, then it may be possible to make a case for the surgical alteration on the basis that it would be to correct a defect, to make the individual's anatomy in closer concordance with the person's experienced gender. It has been previously suggested that

> it might be possible for the brain to receive one sexual identification [through the presence or absence of testosterone, for example, during critical periods of the central nervous system intrauterine development] imprint while the reproductive organs develop differently or inadequately because of a developmental error. . . . At this time, however, our knowledge as to which hormones do what to the brain is too fragmentary and insecure to base any clear conclusions about the etiology of gender dysphoria. (Moraczewski 1983:302–303)

Psychopharmacological concerns. Regarding the use of psychotherapeutic drugs in the treatment of a mental disorder or malfunction, the Church has no basic opposition. Of course, due consideration must be paid to the balance between the desired benefits and the adverse effects associated with the drug's action. Ever since the introduction of chlorpromazine (Thorazine) by Daley in France for the treatment of psychoses in 1952, psychiatry has had a powerful tool for dealing with certain types of psychoses. Subsequently, numerous new drugs have been developed for the management of depression, anxiety, panic disorder, phobias, mania, and hallucinations, among other psychiatric conditions. The use of these therapeutic drugs have, all things considered, been considered morally acceptable because their use helps a person variously think, feel, and act more closely in the normal range. These drugs have helped immeasurably to free people from the shackles of their mental disorder. In fact, research over the last forty years has shown that many of the so-called mental disorders have at their base some biochemical malfunction. That is one reason why these drugs can be effective: they interact at the molecular level to modify the actions of the abnormal biochemical events. The specific substancees involved, and the type of biochemical lesion associated with the mental disorder varies. While our knowledge of the precise biochemical mechanisms are too rudimentary at present to determine the exact contribution of biochemical and psychosocial factors, the stigma associated with mental disorders is gradually being dispelled as public appreciation increases regarding the neurobiological bases of many of these conditions.

The use, however, of hallucinogens to induce altered states of consciousness, especially for *recreational* purposes, is more difficult to defend on the basis of the Church's teaching. As was stated above in the discussion of principles, any human action that impairs or destroys a person's rational ability or freedom of the will without a seriously proportionate reason is morally unacceptable. Furthermore, drugs that allegedly bring about a mystical experience are also highly questionable (of course, it would depend on what is meant by a "mystical experience"). It would be difficult to reconcile pharmacological means of inducing an ersatz mystical experience with the experiences and writings of those whom the Church recognizes as authentic mystics (Moraczewski 1967:358–382).

Reproductive concerns. Earlier in this century reproductive concerns focused on controlling excessive fertility. The development of oral contraceptives revolutionized sexual practices for many people throughout the world. With the advent of AIDS, however, there has been a return to the use of condoms and the introduction of female condoms.

To these various practices of artificial birth control, the Catholic Church has been opposed from the beginning. In 1968 Pope Paul VI issued a long-awaited encyclical, *Humanae vitae* in which he restates the Church's position that one should not use any means of controlling birth that separates the procreative and unitive meanings of the conjugal act (since the Church holds that sexual intercourse may only take place between a man and a woman married to each other, that act is often referred to as the "conjugal act"). What is prohibited, then, is the use of a device, chemical agent, or procedure that destroys the natural connection in the twofold symbolism of the one act. The *unitive* meaning stresses that the conjugal act both expresses and reinforces the love and commitment that husband and wife have pledged to each other, while the procreative meaning symbolizes the generative nature of that action; by its biological structure it bespeaks reproduction. The procreative meaning does not require that conception take place, or even require that either or both parties be fecund. Contraception is morally objectionable from the Church's point of view (even if it holds that this is a matter of natural law, perceivable and applicable to all human beings) because such an act destroys the love-procreative unity of the conjugal act. The moral evil of contraception does not require that an actual conception have been impeded; it is sufficient that the couple positively will to prevent a conception and signals that intention by introducing an agent (chemical, physical, or other) whose immediate and direct purpose is to render fertilization and/or implantation most unlikely.

Natural family planning (NFP) methods are permissible because it makes use of the natural infertile periods of the woman. The couple merely abstains from the conjugal act during those infertile periods. There simply is no act whose two-fold symbolism can be sundered. It does not interfere with the natural biological (procreative) consequences of intercourse—if all the requirements for fertilization are present—as do condoms, spermicidal agents, anovulants, and other devices (e.g., IUDs). Nonetheless, to be morally acceptable, the use of NFP methods requires that there be a proportionally reasonable motive for trying to avoid conceiving another child. At the same time, the Church recognizes that there may be circumstances where it would be better to avoid having another child. Thus, Pope Paul VI, in discussing responsible parenthood, states the following principle:

> In relation to physical, economic, psychological, and social conditions, responsible parenthood is exercised, either by the deliberate and generous decision to raise a numerous family, or by the decision, made for grave motives and with due respect for the moral law, to avoid for the time being, or even for an indeterminate period, a new birth. (1968:10)

More recent developments have focused on the management of infertility. In vitro fertilization (IVF) was developed over a period of a decade and resulted in the first live-born child in July 1978. After careful consideration over a ten-year period and consultations with physicians, ethicists, and moral theologians, the Congregation for the Doctrine of the Faith issued a formal statement (CDF 1987), approved by Pope John Paul II, which condemned the use of IVF because the dignity of the new human life would be compromised. The Church holds that a new human being is to be generated within a family (no third-party donors of sperm or egg [oocyte]) as a result of sexual intercourse between husband and wife. Conception must take place within the body of the wife and gestation should take place also within the wife. IVF fails to meet the requirement that fertilization take place in the woman's body; rather, it occurs in a laboratory petri dish and the first twelve to twenty-four hours also take place in an artifical environment, thus placing the very early human embryo at risk. It becomes subject to possible manipulation and ready destruction. For these, and other reasons, the Church is opposed to IVF as a means of mananging infertility.

One of the new fertility methods that may be acceptable to the Church is gamete intrafallopian tube transfer (GIFT) and a very similar procedure, tubal ovum transfer (TOT). In these procedures the oocyte, usually obtained by laparoscopy, is moved from the surface of the ovary to a dish, where it is suspended in a liquid medium. The sperm is obtained by means of a semen sample from a perforated silastic sheath (which permits some of the ejaculate to enter the vaginal tract, a requirement for the moral completion of the conjugal act) used by the couple during the conjugal act. (The Church judges it to be morally unacceptable to obtain the sperm sample by masturbation, for it is the use of the generative powers outside of the conjugal act.) An aliquot of the semen remaining in the sheath is washed. With means of a syringe, one oocyte is carefully drawn into a capillary tube and subsequently a portion of the semen is taken up into the same tube; an air bubble deliberately introduced keeps the sperm and oocyte carefully apart. The contents of the tube are then injected into the fallopian tube. Fertilization, should it take place, therefore occurs in its natural site—the fallopian tube. The embryo, then, is never externalized outside of the mother's body.

Hence, with regards to homologous in vitro fertilization (involving only the husband's sperm and the wife's oocyte it is clear the Church is opposed:

> Nevertheless, in conformity with the traditional doctrine relating to the goods of marriage and the dignity of the person, *the Church remains opposed from the moral point of view to homologous "in vitro" fertilization. Such fertilization is in itself illicit and in opposition to the dignity of procreation and of the conjugal union, even when everything is done to avoid the death of the human embryo.* (CDF 1987:II, B, 5)

However, with regard to GIFT and TOT the Church has not directly and specifically addressed those procedures. Some theologians will argue that the conception of the child depends too much on technology to meet the requirements of *Donum Vitae* (DeMarco 1988:133–135). Others conclude that it is compatible with Church teaching (McCarthy 1988:140–145). For the moment, however, whether GIFT and TOT are concordant with Church teaching remains an open question.

Another reason the Church opposes the externalization of the embryo is that it can be transferred to a surrogate mother. The Church is opposed to such an embryo transfer (ET) because a child should be born of one and the same genetic and gestational mother. In response to whether surrogate motherhood is morally licit, *Donum Vitae* responds:

> *No, for the same reason which leads one to reject heterologous artificial fertilization: for it is contrary to the unity of marriage and to the dignity of the procreation of the human person.* (CDF 1987:II, A, 3)

The court battles that have already resulted between surrogate and genetic mothers point up rather dramatically some of the negative consequences of this procedure.

Another negative consequence associated with the externalization of the human embryo is that the embryo can be subjected to cryopreservation. Some see an advantage in freezing embryos conceived while the mother is still young, i.e., in her early twenties, to be thawed out later and placed in her uterus for gestation (see Edwards and Steptoe 1977). In this manner, a couple may space their children in accordance with their economic and social circumstance, and at the same time conceive a child when the likelihood of chromosomal abnormalities—such as trisomy 21 (Down's syndrome)—would be significantly less. Here, too, the Church has concluded that for the protection of child's rights, it must also protest the practice of cryopreservation of the human embryo:

> *The freezing of embryos,* even when carried out in order to preserve the life of an embryo—*cryopreservation*—*constitutes an offense against the respect due to human beings* by exposing to grave risks of death or harm to their physical integrity and depriving them, at least temporarily, of maternal shelter and gestation, thus placing them in a situation in which further offences and manipulation are possible. (CDF 1987:I, 6)

An embryo can be kept in the deep freeze at the temperature of liquid nitrogen (-196° C.) and stored for months, and even years. This has been done in animal husbandry where frozen cattle embryos have been kept as long as ten years and were still viable. At a suitable time, the embryo can then be defrosted and introduced either in the mother's uterus or that of a surrogate. A recent case of seven cryopreserved human embryos in Tennessee has drawn considerable media attention because the procreative couple subsequently divorced. A public conflict resulted and the court was asked to settle the matter. The man demanded that he not be forced into fatherhood. The court found in his favor and let the hospital, who had temporary custody of the embryos, decide how to dispose of them.

End-of-life Issues. The Church is strongly opposed to induced abortion (SCDF 1974). That should be news to no one. It is also just as vigorously opposed to euthanasia. However, great care must be taken in understanding the Church's position when it comes to a matter of intervention during a terminal condition. While the Church is opposed to direct killing of an innocent person, it nonetheless recognizes that there are times when efforts to maintain a person's life with the help of medical technology may be or become morally optional. In 1957 Pope Pius XII made a fundamental statement with regard to the moral obligation to sustain life:

> Natural reason and Christian morals say that man (and whoever is entrusted with the task of taking care of his fellowman) has the right and the duty in case of serious illness to take the necessary treatment for the preservation of life and health. This duty that one has toward himself, toward God, toward the human community, and in most cases toward certain determined persons, derives from well-ordered charity, from submission to the Creator, and from social justice, and even from strict justice, as well as from devotion toward one's family.
>
> But normally one is held to use only the ordinary means—according to circumstances of persons, places, times, and culture—that is to say, means that do not involve any grave burden for oneself or another. A more strict obligation would be too burdensome for most men and would render the attainment of the higher, more important good too difficult. Life, health, and all temporal activities are in fact subordinated to spiritual ends. (Pius XII 1957)

In those cases in which it is judged that there is an excessive burden relative to the anticipated benefit or in which the treatment (to be either initiated or continued) is without benefit to the indivdual, the treatment can be either discontinued or not initiated and the person allowed to die, but *there cannot be any intent to terminate a person's life* (CDF 1980).

When life-supporting treatment is withheld or withdrawn, death results from the concurrent fatal pathology (which required the life support system in the first place) that has been allowed to run its natural course. The judgment is made on the basis of estimating the proportion between the reasonably expected benefit of the procedure and the burdens anticipated resulting from that procedure in this set of circumstances. If it is estimated that the benefit does exceed the burden, then generally a person would be morally obligated to employ that life-saving technology. If, however, it is deemed that the benefit is exceeded by the burden to the patient or others, then the procedure is considered to be morally optional.

The principle that Pope Pius enunciated was actually a statement of what has been called in recent times the "Principle of Ordinary and Extraordinary Means of Conserving Life," developed in the Church over a period of some four hundred years. During that time a number of theologians attempted to formulate principles that would aid a person in deciding whether he had a strict obligation "to conserve life or whether the obligation was optional" (Cronin 1989).

Conclusion

The Church's position with regard to the limits of intervention on the human being is predicated on its understanding regarding the nature, origin, and destiny of the human race. The Church holds that while God is creator of all that exists, visible and invisible (see the Nicean Creed), all presently existing humans are from a common stock and were made in the image of God (Genesis 1:28). This means that the human race was given a delegated dominion over the creatures of this world (at least) but with accountability to God. The human race thus is a steward, not the proprietor, of this world.

From this perspective, then, humanity is limited as to what it may do to the world and to itself. There is no question that the determination of those limits is very difficult and fraught with ambiguity. Nonetheless, the Church believes strongly in the limiting principles as delineated and applied in the preceding discussion. As stated in the beginning of this essay, the Church wants to keep humans fully human. Nothing may be done to one or many that would degrade or denigrate the individual. His life is sacred and his bodily and mental integrity must be safeguarded. Hence, those activities aimed at a human being must not compromise his freedom nor his capacity to know; his cognitive and voluntary faculties must be protected. Any invasion of his being requires his free and informed consent. Actions intended to remedy or correct a defect and directed to restoring normal function as much as possible would be permissible, but those directed toward "improving" upon the normal would require extremely careful review to ensure that fundamental human rights are not violated.

The Church can look to the future with guarded optimism. Increased knowledge and the wise control of nature can lead to human betterment. This thought is reflected in the words of Pope John XXIII:

> For it is indeed clear that the Church always taught and continues to teach that advances in science and technology and the prosperity resulting therefrom, are truly to be counted as good things and regarded as signs of progress of civilization. But the Church likewise teaches that goods of this kind are to be judged properly in accordance with their natures: they are always to be considered as instruments for man's use, the better to achieve his highest end: that he can the more easily improve himself, and in both the natural and supernatural orders. (John XXIII 1961:246)

The cautionary note is not really inhibitory of scientific and technological progress but serves to recall to mind that such advances are to serve authentic human freedom and happiness:

> The first reason for disquiet concerns the essential and fundamental question: Does this progress, which has man for its author and promoter, make human life on earth "more human" in every aspect of that life? Does it make it more "worthy of man"? There can be no doubt that in various aspects it does. But the questions keep coming back with regard to what is most essential—whether in the context of this progress man, as man, is becoming truly better, that is to say more mature spiritually, more aware of the dignity of his humanity, more responsible, more open to others, especially the neediest and the weakest, and readier to give and to aid all. (John Paul II 1979:8)

Finally, the Church views true progress in science and technology as part of Divine Providence. The idea that science and technology are not in competition with God is part of the Church's teaching as formalized by Vatican Council II:

> Far from considering the conquest of man's genius and courage as opposed to God's power as if he set himself up as a rival to the Creator, Christians ought to be convinced that the achievements of the human race are a sign of God's greatness and the fulfillment of his mysterious design. With an increase in human power comes a broadening of responsibility on the part of individuals and communities: there is no question, then, of the Christian message inhibiting men from building up the world or making them disinterested in the good of their fellows: on the contrary, it is an incentive to do these very things. (Vatican Council II 1965:34)

References

Aita, John F. 1991. "Psychosurgery: A Retrospective" *Nebraska Medical Journal* 76:201–204.

Congregation for the Doctrine of the Faith. 1974. *Declaration on Procured Abortion.* Boston: Daughters of St. Paul.

Congregation for the Doctrine of the Faith. 1980. *Declaration on Euthanasia.* Vatican City: Vatican Press.

Congregation for the Doctrine of the Faith. 1987. *Instruction on Respect for Human Life in its Origin and on the Dignity of Procreation.* Braintree, Mass.: Pope John Center.

Cook, Robin 1989. *Mutation.* New York: Putnam.

Cronin, Daniel S. 1989. "The Moral Law in Regard to the Ordinary and Extraordinary Means of Conserving Life." In Russell E. Smith, ed., *Conserving Life.* Braintree, Mass.: Pope John Center.

Cunningham, Bert J. 1944. *The Morality of Organic Transplantation.* Washington, D.C.: Catholic University of America Press.

DeMarco, Donald T. 1988. "Catholic Moral Teaching and TOT/GIFT." In Donald G. McCarthy, ed., *Reproductive Technologies, Marriage and the Church.* Braintree, Mass.: Pope John Center.

Edwards, R. G., and Steptoe, P. C. 1977. "The Relevance of the Frozen Storage of Human Embryos." In *The Freezing of Mammalian Embryos.* CIBA Foundation Symposium 52.

Goldzieher, Joseph W. 1989. *Hormonal Contraception.* Dallas: Essential Medical Information Systems.

Healy, Edwin F. 1956. *Medical Ethics.* Chicago: Loyola University Press.

Holden, Constance 1992. "Another Gene Therapy First." *Science* 256:1628.

Huxley, Aldous. 1950. *Brave New World* New York: Harper.

Huxley, Aldous. 1954. *The Doors of Perception.* New York: Harper.

Huxley, Aldous 1957. "The History of Tension." *Annals of the New York Academy of Science* 67:683.

John XXIII. 1961. *Mater et Magistra.* Washington, D.C.: National Catholic Welfare Conference.

John Paul II. 1979. "Redemptor Hominis." *L'Osservatore Romano* (March 19).

John Paul II. 1982. Address to study group of the Pontifical Academy of Sciences. English translation in *Origins* (November 4):343.

John Paul II. 1983. "The Ethics of Genetic Manipulation." Address to the participants of the World Medical Conventions. *Origins* 13(23):386–389.

John Paul II. 1991. "The Human Mind." Address to the participants at the Fifth International Conference organized by the Pontifical Council for Pastoral Assistance to Health Care Workers. *Dolentium Hominum* 16:10–14.

Laitenen, L. V. 1988. "Psychosurgery Today." *Acta Neurochirurgica* Supplement 44:158–162.

McCarthy, Donald G. 1988. "Response [to DeMarco]." In *Reproductive Technologies, Marriage and the Church.* Braintree, Mass.: Pope John Center.

McFadden, Charles J. 1967. *Medical Ethics.* 6th ed. Philadelphia: F. A. Davis Co.

May, William E. 1988. "Catholic Moral Teaching on In Virtro Fertilization." In Donald G. McCarthy, ed., *Reproductive Technologies, Marriage and the Church*. Braintree, Mass.: Pope John Center.

Moraczewski, Albert S. 1967. "Mescaline, Madness and Mysticism." *Thought* 166:358–382.

Moraczewski, Albert S. 1983. "Gender Dysphoria—A Theological Note." In Mark E. Schwartz, Albert S. Moraczewski, and James A. Monteleone, eds., *Sex and Gender—A Theological and Scientific Inquiry*. St. Louis: Pope John Center.

Paul VI. 1968. *Humanae vitae*. New York: Paulist Press.

Pius XII. 1952. "Allocution to the First International Congress of Histopathology." In *The Human Body*. Boston: St. Paul Editions, 1979.

Pius XII. 1956. "Allocution to a Group of Eye Specialists." In *The Human Body*. Boston: St. Paul Editions, 1979.

Pius XII. 1957. "Address to an International Congress of Anesthesiologists." In *The Pope Speaks*, 4(4):393–398.

Singer, Isaac Bashevis. 1982. *The Golem*. New York: Farrar, Straus, and Giroux.

U.S. Congress Office of Technology Assessment. 1987. *Life-Sustaining Technoligies and the Elderly*, OTA-BA-306. Washington, D.C.: U.S. Government Printing Office.

U.S. Congress Office of Technology Assessment. 1988. *Infertility: Medical and Social Choices*. OTA-BA-358. Washington, D.C.: U.S. Government Printing Office.

Vatican Council II Documents. 1965. *Pastoral Constitution on the Church in the Modern World*, edited by Austin Flannery. Boston: St. Paul Editions, 1975.

Walker, Paul A. 1983. "A Contemporary Perspective on Gender Dysphoria." In Mark E. Schwartz, Albert S. Moraczewski, and James Monteleone, eds., *Sex and Gender—A Theological and Scientific Inquiry*. St. Louis: Pope John Center.

Weiss, R. 1990. "First Human Gene-Therapy Begun." *Science News* (September 22).

4

Postmodernity and Limits on the Human Body: Libertarianism by Default

H. Tristram Engelhardt, Jr., and Kevin Wm. Wildes

Clinical and research biomedicine have been shaped by the technological developments of the last forty years and, for the foreseeable future, they will continue to be formed by these developments. As biomedical technologies realize new possibilities for medicine, the limitations on human existence itself are also challenged. Biomedical technology opens the doors to novel possibilities for curing illness, prolonging life, and even altering the most basic structures of human life. In so doing, these technologies create new choices for almost every aspect of human life, from conception to death. Many of the technological developments in biomedicine, in which the body has become not only the locus of medical intervention but the source of materials, raise questions about how the human body should be treated. For example, many hold that the body has a "special meaning" (Hastings Center 1985) or "sanctity." The implication is that there are certain ways in which the body should be viewed and used. However, these intuitions and claims about the body are not endorsed by all. Indeed, people often have radically different intuitions about the proper use of the body. The question then becomes how to choose among these competing beliefs.

In the first part of this paper we will argue that the postmodern crisis over secular moral authority renders general secular appeals to intuitions about the "sanctity," "special meaning," or "inviolability" of the human body at best confused and ambiguous and at worst meaningless. In the second part we will develop the implications of the postmodern condition for understanding the human body in health care policy. In the midst of moral pluralism there remains a thread of guiding rationality for resolving moral controversies between moral strangers regarding the body. Moral discourse at this level relies on the authority of moral agents and the discourse is purely procedural and empty of content. The final section of the paper will highlight the emptiness of the general, secular understanding of the body by viewing the body within the understanding of a particular community.

Living in a pluralistic society, we are confronted by a multitude of moralities rather than a single moral narrative. The only defensible moral position, in such a context, is libertarian. Since one cannot assume that others share the same moral values, rankings, and premises in resolving moral controversies, and since secular reason cannot discover a contentful moral vision that all parties are rationally compelled to accept, then one must rely on the moral authority that comes from the agreement between individual moral agents. The libertarian conclusion is not a covert appeal to the value of liberty, for such an appeal would beg the question. If God is not heard by all in the same way, and reason cannot discover a contentful morality, then one must rely on the consent of those involved in a dispute if one is to act with moral authority. Controversies around such issues as ownership and use of the human body (e.g., use of blood products, participation in experimentation, assisted suicide) can only be resolved, on a secular level, by the agreement of the parties involved.

The Postmodern Predicament

The term *postmodern* has had a wide currency in contemporary intellectual circles but suffers from its diverse, and rather vague, usage. In this essay it is used to understand a cluster of sociological, cultural, and philosophical difficulties confronting secular moral philosophy.

The sociological dimension of postmodernism in our society is in the fact that there is a widespread diversity of moral opinions and sensibilities. There is no longer a grand moral narrative in the West (Lyotard 1984). Bioethics is instructive here in that one has only to recall its many controversies to encounter such a plurality of moral visions and values in contemporary Western culture (e.g., abortion, euthanasia, the use of limited health care resources). This pluralism of moral values reflects a profound change in Western culture. Western culture has gone from a culture homogeneously Christian and often intolerant of other views to being a morally pluralistic culture which expects a diversity of moral judgments about foundational issues. As a result, societies have ceased to share sufficient contentful premises to resolve contentful moral controversies.

However, the crisis of postmodernity also poses epistemological issues for moral philosophy. The conceptual difficulty for a postmodern moral philosophy lies in justifying the initial choice for moral judgments. If one understands "secular" as a morally neutral framework (Engelhardt 1991), then the choice of a particular theory of morality poses the difficulty of choosing a starting point. One might hope that moral content can be discovered by reason without appeal to a particular ideology, religion, or culture. Bioethicists have tried various theoretical justifications of moral philosophy; there have been numerous attempts to develop a system of moral judgment in biomedicine (e.g., Singer 1979; Veatch 1981; Daniels 1985; Pellegrino and Thomasma 1981; Grisez and Boyle 1979). Yet each theory faces two basic difficulties. The first is to justify its foundational starting point. Each theory of normative morality must presuppose some structure on which to base its appeal (e.g., consequences, duty, nature) (Brody 1988). However, it is not at all clear why one element of moral experience should be chosen over others as the basis for the structure of moral reasoning. Indeed, one of the criticisms of moral philosophy, at least from a feminist perspective, has been regarding its assumptions about the nature of reason (Gilligan 1982; Carse 1991).

Resolving this dilemma, however, will not address the second difficulty: each theory needs a particular content. Without a content (e.g., some ranking of values, or discount rate in order to compare present and future preferences) the theory will remain universal but be unable to deal with concrete dilemmas. For example, the first principle of the natural law ("Do good and avoid evil") (Aquinas 1948:I–II, 94, a.2) needs content if it is to guide practical reason. One must specify a ranking of goods if a moral theory is to aid men and women in resolving moral dilemmas. Indeed, theories often build in ways in which goods are ranked (e.g., the mechanism of preference utilitarianism, the basic goods of human flourishing, the correct lexical ranking of principles). However, with the adoption of a particular ranking of values a theory becomes particularized. Unless individuals share the same ranking of values they will not be able to agree on the proper resolution of a moral conflict. There is as a consequence an overabundance of answers to the foundational questions about moral reason.

Some have tried to avoid this difficulty altogether by invoking middle-level principles without appealing to a foundation in any particular theory (Frankena 1973; Beauchamp and Childress 1989). Middle-level principles, however, are themselves fraught with problems. First, there is the difficulty of determining what any of the principles, mean. One suspects, for example, that when Beauchamp and Childress claim to have agreed on the meaning of their four middle-level principles one is witnessing a sleight of hand. For a preference utilitarian, like Beauchamp, "autonomy" will be understood as the liberty to satisfy preferences. For a deontologist, like Kant, autonomy is concerned not with the pursuit of heteronomous desires but with acting in accord with the demands of reason imposed by the moral law. Childress, even though he does not endorse a Kantian deontology, relies upon right-making and wrong-making criteria that are independent of consequences. So while both Beauchamp and Childress speak of "autonomy," the term is a placeholder for different meanings in radically different moral languages. In different moral "languages" the same word, or moral term, can have different meanings, depending on the context and assumptions that frame their use.

These general difficulties become apparent in the bioethics of the body. Much of the effort to regulate and constrain the use of the human body is embedded in a moral language of "sanctity," "dignity," "justice," "integrity," and "solidarity." The meanings of these terms can only be given their weight within a moral narrative. When bioethicists appeal to different principles in order to evaluate, restrict, or condemn the uses for the human body, they are speaking from a *particular* moral view. They are mistaken to think that, while people may use the same terms, the terms have the same meaning.

A second attempt to offset the difficulties of a postmodern moral theory has been through a revival of moral casuistry. Jonsen and Toulmin (1988) offer a historical account of casuistry and maintain that it can resolve moral controversies in a pluralist, postmodern secular world. Unfortunately, they do not develop how this secular casuistry would meet the challenges it faces. Traditional casuistry was built upon the analysis of particular cases and their resolution within a concrete moral tradition. Within that tradition certain cases and their resolution could be regarded as paradigmatic for moral dilemmas because of their place within a very particular moral ethos. The difficulty with a secular casuistry is that there is no way to decide which cases are to function as the paradigm cases. One cannot affirm one history or tradition of analysis without losing the generality sought.

Often the proponents of casuistry or middle-level principles respond that there is sufficient "agreement" in contemporary culture to resolve moral controversies by consensus. But one must be explicit as to what is meant by "agreement." When people "agree" on the resolution of a moral controversy the agreement can range from a course of action (e.g., because of the financial, social, or political advantages of concurrence) to a "deep" agreement over the reasons why the resolution should be chosen. Of course, one can reach an agreement on the choice of a course of action without agreeing on the reasons for justifying the choice. However, without an agreement on the reasons for the choice of an action there is little hope for generalizing beyond the case at hand. For example, people agreeing to stop artificial feeding and hydration to a PVS (persistent vegetative state) patient may do so for many different reasons. One may reach this conclusion because there is general disutility in continuing the treatment while another thinks that continued treatment would be a burdensome, extraordinary means as well as an idolatry of physical life. One can also imagine two people entering a hospital so that one of their kidneys can be transplanted to someone in need. While one may act out of altruistic impulses, the other may do so in order to be paid. When we include the reasoning behind a case, one comes to see that there are often radically different approaches. A disagreement over an action's justification will make it difficult to extend that agreement to other cases.

The postmodern predicament leads to a recasting of traditional moral authority and hence the resolution of moral dilemmas.If one cannot appeal to a particular universally accepted concept of God or an understanding of moral rationality, or an understanding of nature in order to ground bioethics, there is only one source remaining: the authority of the moral agents involved. If one cannot discover an authoritative moral vision to ground moral judgments, then one must appeal to persons as the source of moral authority. When we meet outside a particular understanding of morality, we have only each other to appeal to in order to resolve moral disputes and to frame the fabric of moral interactions. Absent agreement on "external," objective moral standards, the only moral standards possible are those derived from consensus among individuals as moral agents.[1] If one is to resolve moral dilemmas peaceably in a pluralistic society, without recourse to force or coercion, and with an authority that can be justified in a secular world, then that moral authority can only be derived from the agreement between people as moral agents.

Moral strangers can then use each other only when they act with commonly conveyed moral authority. Those who use others without consent lose a commonly justified basis for protest when they are met with punitive or defensive force. Limited democracies draw upon the morality of mutual respect to provide protection from and punishment for the violation of individuals (e.g., murder, rape, burglary) as well as to ensure the enforcement of recorded contracts. In addition, they are able to create, through consent and using common resources, endeavors such as basic health care systems. But private resources and peaceable agreements with others will create areas of free choice. Rights to privacy play a crucial role in any secular state but not because of any positive value they may possess. Rather they mark out the limits of the plausible moral authority of the state to intervene in the peaceable consensual actions of individuals.

The Body

Recent technological developments have opened up discussions over the "ownership" of human cells and tissues (OTA 1987), the use of genetic material (Engelhardt and Wildes 1991), as well as questions regarding the proper limits of therapeutic interventions.

In a pluralistic society, with its competing views of the good life, there can be no canonical notion of how one ought to treat the body. Individuals must then rely on the authority of the agreement between themselves rather than on the authority of a shared moral vision, tradition, or account. While one may disapprove of certain uses of the body, as many hold the practice of prostitution to be immoral, there is no general secular moral authority to show such actions to be immoral. One must regard the practices within a particular moral narrative to understand its immorality. As long as proper permission is obtained and agreements are kept, it will not be possible to show that something wrong has occurred without appealing to a particular account of sexuality or the proper use of the body. In a secular world one may lament the behavior of others, but lack the secular moral authority to condemn much less prohibit such actions.

The question is then why such prohibitions exist in a secular culture. One finds an interesting clue in the general justification for the prohibition of the sale of organs developed in *Organ Transplantation* (DHHS 1986). In rejecting the commercialization of organ donation, the task force said that society's moral values "militate against regarding the body as a commodity" (DHHS 1986:96). It went on to cite a report from the Hastings Center:

> The view that the body is intimately tied to our conceptions of personal identity, dignity, and self-worth is reflected in the unique status accorded to the body within our legal tradition as something which cannot and should not be bought or sold. Religious and secular attitudes make it plain just how widespread is the ethical stance maintaining that the body ought to have special moral standing. The powerful desire to accord respect to the dignity, sanctity, and identity of the body, as well as the moral attitudes concerning the desirability of policies and practices which encourage altruism and sharing among the members of society produced an emphatic rejection of the attempt to commercialize organ [donation and] recovery and make a commodity of the body. (Hastings Center 1985)

The view expressed here that the body is intimately bound to our conception of ourselves seems true enough. The difficulty is that when one tries to give content to notions such as "dignity," "sanctity," and "solidarity," one is committed to a particular moral point of view.

One way to understand the claims of the Hastings Center and DHHS task force reports is to see them as providing "bits and shards" of a once intact tradition (MacIntyre 1981:10). Appeals to "sanctity," "integrity," and "altruism" are the remnants of the once-powerful, widely accepted Judeo-Christian moral vision,which gave structure and coherence to an objective morality. The sanctity of the body was grounded in its relationship to a creator God and appeals to altruism. But it is not clear how, in a secular culture, one is to ground such claims. Indeed in a secular society there is no way to distinguish, morally, the different uses of the body as long as the uses are justified in the proper moral authority of the agent. From giving one's body to another in marriage to the life of prostitution there is no way, on a secular level, to make out moral claims about the propriety or impropriety of such uses of the body as long as they are consensual.

Various forms of indentured servitude—entering the military or a religious order—are all relationships which transfer to others, in whole or in part, rights that one has over one's self. Outside of concerns about how agreements are made or kept, secular moral discourse must pass over such relationships in silence.

Postmodernity thus leaves us without a univocal account of how to live our lives or to use our bodies. Birth, sexuality, health and well-being, disease, disability, and death receive concrete meaning within particular moral imperatives. They tell men and women how to reproduce. They instruct regarding what forms of sexual activities are permissible, laudable, perverse, and condemnable. They indicate what kinds of interventions in preventing birth are allowable and which are forbidden. If the moral vision, tradition, or narrative has the robust anxiology and metaphysical character of a religious account, it will even give an interpretation regarding the ultimate meaning of life, suffering, and death.

It is only within a particular narrative that one can determine whether particular uses of the body are to be praised, condemned, or regarded as morally neutral. Thus, within traditional Judeo-Christian understandings of sexuality and the body, prostitution is seen to be morally evil, though Babylonian temple prostitution regarded such as praiseworthy. Indeed, it is impossible to understand what should count as exploitative use of another's body unless one restricts such a sense of exploitation to identifying cases in which individuals consent to have their bodies used against their value commitments, albeit with their consent.

Postmodernity thus both gives an account of why moral controversies regarding the proper use of body parts are interminable, as well as why people presume, contrary to fact, that they can indeed be concluded in general secular terms. On the one hand, to be able to show by sound rational argument that any particular use of the body is exploitative when individuals agree and the choices they make are in accord with their values, one will need to be able to appeal to particular canonical contentful premises about human dignity, sanctity of the body, or the proper use of human body parts. Consider, for example, two views of exploitation with regard to the sale of organs. Those who oppose such sales may argue that one exploits the poor by enticing them to sell their organs to the rich, which sales they would not engage in were they not poor. Those who support such sales might argue that the rich in developed countries exploit the poor in the developing world to satisfy their moral feelings by forbidding the poor from coming to the considered judgment that their best interests are served by selling their organs. Whose view regarding exploitation should triumph? One needs a canonical understanding, a canonical narrative or moral vision, about how individuals should deport themselves to determine which exploitation is the real exploitation.

On the other hand, when one lives within a particular secular or religious moral narrative, one may forget that others do not in fact share it. It becomes axiomatic that others should agree that a particular understanding of human dignity, sanctity, or the proper use of human organs is canonical. This temptation may be less among those of religious commitment, who understand that the grace of true belief comes from God, prayer, and fasting, not from rational arguments. Those embedded within particular secular ideologies are more likely to forget the particular historically conditioned character of the moral premises they endorse.

One may also fail to recognize that in general secular terms much will simply be permissible that one knows to be wrong, since the only way to determine how one should use another's body is to determine whether that individual has agreed to the use. Here an important caveat must be underscored: to permit is not to endorse. One is often committed to holding that, in general secular terms, people have a right to do that which others may know is wrong. That is, one will not in general secular terms be able to justify coercive intervention, but one will know that the behavior engaged in is seriously morally disordered. Those of us who are committed to a correct and contentful moral understanding embedded within a particular religious view will know that many uses are highly morally opprobrious. It is simply that the wrongness cannot be shown in general secular terms, that is, outside of the grace of a commitment to a contentful moral narrative with all of its particularity, but also with all of its content. When one talks to moral strangers and attempts to justify moral policy regarding the use of persons' bodies and parts in ways that they can understand as morally binding, one will by default be libertarian. This libertarianism is not grounded in any celebration of license or caprice, but in a recognition of the limits of secular moral reasoning.

Moral Friends

This analysis of the pluralistic moral discourse is not a plea for the destruction of the visions of particular moral communities. Rather, it is the recognition of the limits of secular moral reason and the importance of a particular moral community. Moral communities are the places of substantive moral discourse. Such moral communities come in great varieties. They range from those based on particular ideologies (Marxism, Cambridge Liberalism) to those based in God's revelation. Within communities one often finds moral discourse concerning the human body. One such community that has reflected extensively on the proper uses of the human body is the Roman Catholic Church.[2] This community's tradition provides a good example of moral discourse. The community shares a common moral sense (e.g., "the sanctity of life") articulated in moral principles (e.g., "No direct taking of innocent human life") and structures of moral authority (e.g., confessors) to interpret moral dilemmas. Roman Catholicism has a particular view of the human person and the sanctity of the human body that stands in contrast to a secular moral discourse. Within the vision of this community the body is understood as "God's masterpiece in the order of the visible creation" (Monks of Solesmes 1960:71–72). It has a glory not only here and now, but it will "enjoy immortality in the glory of heaven" (Monks of Solesmes 1960:71–72). Man is "not the owner of his body, not its absolute lord." Man's power over his body is, although limited, direct (Monks of Solesmes 1960:55–56). Within the context of its own moral narrative the tradition has developed principles about the proper use of the body. These principles are derived from the intrinsic function of the body parts (Monks of Solesmes 1960:53–54). In this view, the use of one's body is limited by the "natural finality" (purpose) of the member or organ. One also finds approval, given by Pope Pius XII, for compensation for the provision of organs (Monks of Solesmes 1960:381–382).

The point is that an understanding of the proper use of the body is always a particular understanding. It presumes a particular narrative that explains appropriate and inappropriate use of the body and body parts. It assumes that there is a canonical understanding of values, a subsequent ranking of values, a role for personal choice, a role for obligations to others, and a correct discount rate for time. One can not in any contentful fashion understand how to use the body in a vision from nowhere. And that vision has costs. It rules that certain choices are in and others out. Living one's life and using one's own body and the bodies of others within such a moral vision is thus quite different from how one can understand such choices when one meets moral strangers or attempts to articulate a policy for their peaceable collaboration in terms that are mutually understandable.

Conclusion

With the continued technological development of biomedicine, attempts to regulate the use of the human body by the power of the state will continue. One thinks, for example, of the closing section of *Donum Vitae*, which argued that the state has the duty to regulate and control reproductive medicine according to the *particular* moral point of view articulated in that document (Congregation for the Doctrine of the Faith). Many in a liberal democracy would not only find the views of *Donum Vitae* unacceptable but would also find the use of state authority to enforce this view morally objectionable. However, many of these same people want the state to prohibit the commercialization of body parts, for example, because of their *particular* moral intuitions about the body. They do not seem to recognize that they have no better justifications, in general secular terms, for their position than does the Congregation for the Doctrine of the Faith. The particular views of the proper use of the human body are just that: *particular*. For a secular state there is no *moral* justification for the deployment of state authority to impose a particular moral point of view.

Notes

1. Certainly the authors of this paper believe that objective standards of morality do exist. The conceptual difficulty is epistemological in that there is no "view from nowhere" which enables us to know which are the correct standards. While philosophers have attempted to ground objectivity in the idea of "supervenience" this seems, to the authors, to be a secularized version of God's grace.

2. These citations from Roman Catholic sources should not mislead the readers; the non-Jesuit author of this article is an Orthodox Catholic.

References

Aquinas, Thomas. 1948. *Summa Theologica*. Westminster, Md.: Christian Classics.
Beauchamp, T., and J. Childress. 1989. *Principles of Biomedical Ethics*. 3d ed. New York: Oxford University Press.

Brody, B. 1988. *Life and Death Decision Making*. New York: Oxford University Press.

Carse, A. 1991. "The 'Voice of Care': Implications for Bioethical Education." *Journal of Medicine and Philosophy* 16:5–28.

Congregation for the Doctrine of the Faith. 1987. "Instruction on Respect for Human Life in its Origin and on the Dignity of Procreation: Replies to Certain Questions of the Day." *Origins* 16:697–711.

Daniels, N. 1985. *Just Health Care*. New York: Cambridge University Press.

Department of Health and Human Services. 1986. *Organ Transplantation: Issues and Recommendations*. Washington, D.C.: U.S. Government Printing Office.

Engelhardt, H. T. 1991. *Bioethics and Secular Humanism: The Search for a Common Morality*. London: SCM Press.

Engelhardt, H. T., and K. W. Wildes. 1991, "The Artificial Donation of Human Gametes." In W. A. W. Walters, ed., *Human Reproduction: Current and Future Ethical Issues, Bailliere's Clinical Obstetrics and Gynaecology*. London: Bailliere Tindall.

Frankena, W. 1973. *Ethics*. 2d ed. Englewood Cliffs, N.J.: Prentice Hall.

Gilligan, C. 1982. *In a Different Voice: Psychological Theory and Women's Development*. Cambridge, Mass.: Harvard University Press.

Grisez, G., and J. Boyle, J. 1979. *Life and Death with Liberty and Justice*. Notre Dame, Ind.: University of Notre Dame Press.

Hastings Center. 1985. *Ethical, Legal and Policy Issues Pertaining to Solid Organ Procurement: A Report on the Project on Organ Transplantation*. Hastings-on-the-Hudson, N.Y.: Hastings Center.

Jonsen, A., and S. Toulmin. 1988. *The Abuse of Casuistry*. Berkeley: University of California Press.

Lyotard, Jean-François. 1984. *The Postmodern Condition*. Translated by G. Bennington and B. Massumi. Manchester: Manchester University Press.

MacIntyre, A. 1981. *After Virtue*. Notre Dame, Ind.: University of Notre Dame Press.

Monks of Solesmes. 1960. *The Human Body*. Boston: Daughters of St. Paul.

Office of Technology Assessment (OTA). 1987. *New Developments in Biotechnology: Ownership of Human Tissues and Cells*. Washington, D.C.: U.S. Government Printing Office.

Pellegrino, E., and D. Thomasma. 1981. *A Philosophical Basis of Medical Practice*. New York: Oxford University Press.

Singer, P. 1979. *Practical Ethics*. New York: Cambridge University Press.

Veatch, R. 1981. *A Theory of Medical Ethics*. New York: Basic Books.

5

A Tortuous Dilemma: Maternal Inviolability Versus Fetal Medicine

Clifford Grobstein

As we approach a new millennium there is growing concern about the expanding powers of medical technology (for example, the ability to read and modify genetic codes) and the impacts this may have on human rights (for example, maintaining one's identity against possible meddling by others). Not least among such concerns are those that center on interactive impacts upon maternal and fetal influences operating jointly during the course of pregnancy. The initiation, persistence, and intensity of such interactive tension derives from the ancient and still-current practice of internal fertilization followed by intrauterine gestation, thus generating an intimacy between mother and offspring throughout the pre-embryonic, embryonic, and fetal stages of human development.

As an example of the resulting dialectic, surgery to alleviate a life-threatening fetal genetic defect may require incisions not only through the maternal abdominal wall but into the uterus itself. The procedure is not without substantial discomfort and can even threaten the life of the pregnant woman. Is the anticipated fetal benefit at least equal to (or preferably even greater than) the substantial surgical risk to the mother? By what calculus can so complex and difficult an interaction be evaluated and even-handedly resolved? Also what role should the pregnant woman's preferences play in making the decision?

Our contemporary dilemma has its roots millennia ago in an epoch when protomammals first came into existence. These early mammalian forebears were the initiators of internal gestation of offspring—an evolutionary "decision" that provided protection to vulnerable young by secluding them within a maternal "incubator." The strategic decision was consequential and advantageous in many ways and, in the process, undoubtedly contributed mightily to mammalian evolutionary success, including contemporary human dominance of the earth and its biota.

Now with the advent and rapidly expanding applications of fetal medicine, conflicts of interest inevitably arise between mothers and intimately dependent offspring. Physicians find themselves simultaneously, and sometimes unexpectedly, involved with two interdependent patients that can present a serious dilemma. For example, which of the two has the higher priority for attention and advantage if therapeutic risks and benefits are not similarly distributed between the two? Can a surgeon expose and treat a fetus—already sequestered in the uterus—without imposing significant risk on the mother? May circumstances arise in which maternal welfare is jeopardized—if not completely sacrificed—to assure fetal benefit? May the life of either the offspring or the mother sometimes be traded off to increase the chances for survival of the other? Who is to make decisions under these circumstances and according to what ethical considerations?

The fact is, of course, that the contemporary record of medical intervention as a component of patient care is replete with such difficult situations, many of which have never been satisfactorily resolved. Complicating this problem is the obscuration of the lines between experimentation and therapy, raising the question of whether we are dealing with subjects or patients. Equally to the point at this juncture, the available record by no means resolves all such concerns—either about the appropriateness of the proposed procedures or their rationales. Rather, the persistent questions point to an overall policy dilemma—the issue being whether any such ambiguous attempts should be initiated without previous recommendations based upon careful study and analysis utilizing new and special kinds of assessment.

Implicit in such an assessment must be an overall assumption that ethically based inviolability of the human person should never be breached without the sanction of a carefully defined and specified process and multiperson authority. Such a procedure must function as a check and balance at a level above that of the parties at interest. A clarification of this stipulation is especially critical at this time when major advances in biomedical science are vastly expanding medical capability to provide benefits via increasingly bold interventions in both their objectives and processes.

The general direction thereby emphasized is toward new institutional structures to assess human values newly challenged by the dynamics of expanding clinical opportunity. New ethical guidelines are needed to cover what is now an obviously rapidly growing and transforming clinical terrain. Unless they are flexible enough to be updated constantly, however, these guidelines will run the risk of strangling what are clearly legitimate and beneficial medical innovations. In order to minimize possible naive "overkill," we will have to reevaluate our whole approach to making choices on such matters.

One such approach already under way involves therapeutic intervention to relieve life-threatening fetal deficiency at specific genetic sites. The approach seeks to exploit advances in genetic engineering, particularly involving activities and functions of DNA. Little more than a decade ago such an idea was greeted with almost hysterical protest, and such measures were regarded by critics as a certain road to disaster. With the greater experience and knowledge of today, but still maintaining appropriate caution, the concept is not only acceptable but is viewed as an entirely reasonable and attractive option to be pursued.

How should the DNA be delivered so as to be incorporated usefully into the embryonic genome? Might it instead be incorporated randomly into the maternal genome, thereby producing a pathological state in the mother instead of normalizing her offspring? Such a possibility must certainly be considered and guarded against, first by studies in other mammals and then cautiously in carefully monitored human subjects. Until this possibility is ruled out through these prior studies, routine clinical applications should not proceed.

A key question at this stage is whether intervention is justified if it can improve the fetal prospect but only at the cost of substantial maternal risk. Under these circumstances which patient is entitled to first consideration—the deficient fetus or the otherwise entirely normal mother?

Suppose that at a pretreatment conference the responsible physician forecasts probable death for the fetus without intervention but calls attention to substantial maternal risk if intervention is attempted. The distraught mother desperately wants to save the offspring but the equally distraught father is more concerned about the risk to his partner. What relative value should be assigned to the several parties involved, and upon termination of the conference whose should be the final decision?

First, consider the responsible physician who believes the fetus can be saved by a "doable" procedure although the procedure is still being investigated and admittedly is risky for both mother and offspring. The physician is not put off by the uncertainty but is, in fact, motivated by it since he is assembling cases for subsequent publication in what will be a widely read clinical research report. Moreover, while the medical imperative is to save a life whenever possible, incident risk is certainly to be considered but as a cost to be borne and gradually reduced as experience grows.

Second, the novel therapeutic approach cannot be attempted without consent of the mother—she is, after all, the patient in the usual medical sense. In the scenario provided she is very anxious to do everything possible to ensure success of the pregnancy because she is in her forties and already showing signs of reduced fertility. She has listened carefully to the medical advice, understands the risks, but also is impressed by the rising success rate already experienced.

Third, the prospective father is distinctly more cautious. This is his second marriage and he already has two children from his first marriage. While he is not averse to having another child he is more concerned with the welfare of his second wife for whom he has deep affection. Moreover, his religious beliefs incline him to feel that matters of life and death, particularly in utero, are better left to divine rather than medical or personal decision.

The scenario thus provided has been deliberately structured as background for discussion of the following recently emergent features of biomedical policy:

1. Scientific and associated technological advance is now the principal driver of the changing clinical scene. Effects will continue to register, and adjustment on the part of all parties involved will continue to be required.
2. The embryo-fetus in utero will increasingly be a prime therapeutic target, whether via surgery, controlled nutrition, drugs, or genes.
3. The embryo-fetus *ex utero* (ectogenesis) is already foreshadowed by fertilization and blastocyst formation in vitro (IVF).
4. Technological advances in other areas (e.g., space exploration and colonization) are likely to fortify the case for more equal sharing of parental obligations—more readily attainable via at least partial ectogenesis.
5. Thus, advances in developmental technology, of which IVF and gene transfer may be forerunners, are likely to progress despite various risks and ethical concerns.
6. What is needed under these circumstances is a perceptive and sound mechanism for evaluation of each innovation and for the creation of policy that will minimize risk and maximize favorable outcomes.
7. Various mechanisms that might lead in this direction have been established. In the United States a congressionally established effort was curtailed by the political effects of the abortion controversy. However, a national board recently established jointly by the American Fertility Society and the American College of Obstetricians and Gynecologists may be able to provide suitable leadership.

6

Fetal Interventions: The Biomedical Politics of Maternal/Fetal Rights

Cynthia R. Daniels

During the 1980s a number of cultural, political, legal, and technological developments converged to bring the fetus into public consciousness as an independent and autonomous being. In law and popular culture, the fetus emerged as *physically separate* from the pregnant woman, and as *willful*, having interests, concerns, and needs which may conflict with the pregnant woman's. In the public mind, the fetus came to be seen as a "tiny person" housed within the pregnant woman's body, a vulnerable child/citizen with rights and interests to be protected by the state.[1]

While the characterization of the fetus as a fully formed person was not new, technological and legal developments during the 1980s contributed to unprecedented attempts to mediate and control the internal "relationship" between the pregnant woman and the fetus.[2] As the fetus grew larger in pregnancy, so too grew the public interest in the woman. Fueled by such sentiment, the state could literally seize the pregnant woman's body as public property, restricting her access to work, regulating her sexual relations with her husband, jailing her for drinking or for failing to follow doctor's orders, or forcing her to undergo major surgery against her will (Daniels 1993).

By 1992, 167 pregnant women had been criminally prosecuted for fetal drug delivery, for in vitro child neglect or abuse, or for manslaughter in cases where pregnancies ended in stillbirth (Paltrow 1992). Hospital authorities in twenty-four states had sought court orders to force pregnant women to undergo medical treatments, such as forced cesarian sections, maternal blood transfusions, or fetal medical treatments like intrauterine transfusions. In all but three cases, those court orders were granted and two court orders were actually approved for the hospital detention of two pregnant women (Kolder 1987). The 1980s also witnessed the reemergence of fetal protection policies in the workplace, where women might be excluded entirely from certain forms of work based on the potential threat to fetal health posed by workplace conditions (Daniels 1991).[3]

While most of these attempts to criminalize, restrict, or regulate the behavior of pregnant women have been successfully challenged in the courts, the very attempt to undermine women's rights at so fundamental a level tells us something important about the ways in which women's association with reproduction continues to be used as the basis of attempts to undermine women's status as liberal citizens.

Understanding the *animation* and *personification* of the fetus in law and popular culture can help to clarify the sources of this threat. The increasing cultural, political, and legal distance between the woman and the fetus has provided the ideological space for the state to attempt to mediate the social and biological relationship between the pregnant woman and fetus. Indeed, the idea that pregnancy was a *relationship* and not a simple *condition* affirmed the fiction of the fetus as an independent "person" caught in a dependent but not always friendly relationship to its "host" mother. Even when attempts to prosecute pregnant women were unsuccessful, such cases could still contribute to a public culture which cast women as "anti-mothers" and fostered new forms of public vengeance against women. These political and legal developments generated a new kind of reproductive politics for women, one which focused not on the right to reproductive choice and abortion but on the duties and obligations imposed upon women who continued their pregnancies.

The kind of public coercion fueled by fetal rights cases throughout the 1980s was completely without precedent in American law. What contributed to so dramatic a shift in the law? What spurred this virtual revolution in popular culture? A number of critical developments converged in synergistic fashion to contribute to the emergence of the idea of fetal personhood. First, a legal ideology emerged in the 1980s that endowed the fetus with independent "rights" against its "host" mother. Second, new technological developments allowed the public to literally "see" the fetus in utero through ultrasound and intrauterine photography. Technologies that allowed women to have greater control over their pregnancies also made it possible for *others* to control pregnancy as well. Third, capitalizing on such developments, a powerful anti-abortion movement waged a major media war against abortion by presenting the visual image of the fetus as a fully formed "preborn baby." The fetal rights politics to emerge in the 1980s was generated both by forces which empowered women as well as by forces which sought to institutionalize new forms of masculine control over the female body.

The Fetus and the Law

It was not long ago that the idea that maternal interests and fetal interests could be legally opposed was completely without precedent in American law. Having no separate legal status under common law, the fetus did not gain rights as an individual until it existed outside of the mother's body. Any recognition of fetal interests was construed purely as an extension of the interests of the mother.

The earliest fetal rights case was *Dietrich v. Northampton*, brought in 1884 by a woman in Northampton, Massachusetts who fell as a result of a defect in the town highway and subsequently miscarried a four- to five-month-old fetus. She sued the town for damages in tort court. Writing for the court, Oliver Wendell Holmes argued that the unborn fetus had been lost "before he became a person." The case, he argued, depended upon the question of "whether an infant dying before it was able to live separated from its mother could be said to have become a person recognized by the law as capable of having a *locus standi* in courts." Legal action, he argued, was dependent upon the child having acheived "some degree of quasi independent life" as well as the ability to "live separated from its mother." Holmes denied any award to the woman on the basis fact that the fetus was "a part of the mother at the time of the injury"(*Dietrich v. Northampton* 1884).

For fifty years following the *Dietrich* decision, the law recognized only limited rights of the fetus, and in these cases, granted such rights only after the fetus had been born alive. As one justice put it, the unborn child "is not regarded as a person until it sees the light of day" (*In Re Peabody* 1959). The earliest deviation from this legal standard came in the form of inheritance cases, recognizing for limited legal reasons, the "existence" of the fetus before birth. A fetus could inherit property upon its birth even though the fetus did not technically exist as a person at the time of death of its benefactor (see Johnsen 1986).

While the courts provided such limited inheritance rights for a fetus throughout the early twentieth century, the paradigm set by *Dietrich* generally viewed the fetus as a part of the woman's body and not a separate person having rights and interest of its own. While such a paradigm maintained the legal unity of woman and fetus, it was also limited in a number of important ways. For instance, it provided no means by which parents could recover damages for injuries inflicted on a fetus before birth, even after the "live birth" of the child. The *Dietrich* case, for instance, failed to compensate the pregnant woman herself for her true loss.

Beginning in 1946, the *Bonbrest v. Kotz* case allowed a father to recover for fetal harm caused by a doctor during delivery, establishing the existence of limited rights for the parents of the fetus before birth. The case broke precedent with *Dietrich* but still maintained that the fetus gained no separate recognition until it passed the point of viability, very late in pregnancy. In addition, such rights were conferred upon the fetus only after it was "born alive." Other cases established the rights of parents to compensation for prenatal injuries in cases involving physical assault on the pregnant woman or in cases involving injuries from automobile accidents.

In 1960 the *Dietrich* paradigm was further eroded by a pivotal case that allowed parents to recover for injuries inflicted on the fetus *before* the point of viability. *Brennan v. Smith* granted recovery for a fetus harmed in an automobile accident. While prenatal injuries experienced in the moments just before birth were more easily established in law, the *Brennan* case clearly affirmed the rights of a fetus before it was "viable" or capable of living outside of the mother's womb. As the court stated,

> the viability distinction has no relevance to the injustice of denying recovery for harm which can be proved to have resulted from the wrongful act of another. Whether viable or not at the time of the injury, the child sustains the same harm after birth. (*Brennan v. Smith* 1960)

As technological advances made it possible to prove a causal link between injuries sustained in early fetal development and medical problems experienced by the child after birth, the impetus to hold those responsible for such injuries became more and more compelling. Why should women not be able to sue in cases where physicians, chemical corporations, or employers harmed fetal development due to their negligence? In fact, some analysts now suggest that such rights exist for the "preconceived" as well—that parents may sue for damages, for instance, in cases where birth defects are caused by parental exposure to mutagenic substances, such as Agent Orange, not only before *birth*, but before *conception* (see Parness 1985).

Another major contribution of the *Brennan* case was the court's statement that "the child has a legal right to begin life with a sound mind and body" (*Brennan v. Smith* 1960). This affirmed not only the right of the child to sue for damages, but the right of the child to be *protected* from negligence or harm in utero. This was a precedent whose far-ranging consequences would emerge only later in the 1980s.

The spirit of legal decisions in the late 1970s, while endowing the fetus with rights independent of the mother, viewed injuries to the fetus as synonymous with injuries to the mother (or father). Court cases such as *Brennan* were motivated by a desire to give parents the power to recover for prenatal harm. The precedent set by *Brennan* and affirmed many times over throughout the 1970s provided pregnant women with a powerful legal tool for recovering damages from third parties (including abusive husbands) who, through criminal or negligent behavior, threatened the health of their wanted child. The right of the child (and parents) to sue for compensation due to prenatal injuries is now recognized by law in almost every state, but this right is still generally contingent upon the live birth of the child. That is, the parents can sue for damages on behalf of the child after the child becomes a "person" at birth. Such cases, while recognizing the additional interests of the pregnant woman, still did not affirm the separate legal personhood of the fetus.

As long as fetal rights remained contingent upon live birth, and as long as the spirit of the law remained focused on the injustice done not only to the fetus but to the mother, the establishment of fetal rights posed no threat to pregnant women's autonomy. Such cases did not endow the fetus with rights separate from the pregnant woman but rather recognized the fact that the woman was pregnant. The law assumed the fetus was an inseparable part of the pregnant woman's body and sought simply to compensate the child and parents for negligent or criminal behavior.

Conservative advocates seized on the legal opportunity to expand the grounds for fetal rights. In promoting the idea of fetal rights, Jeffery Parness, a conservative legal scholar, cites many stories of legal injustices done to pregnant women and their unborn children. Presented in these writings are stories where pregnant women lose their wanted children due to the recklessness of drunken drivers, the violence of muggers or rapists, the careless mistreatment by doctors, or the willful negligence of corporations who poison women with toxins or require them to work in unsafe workplaces.

> Because states bestow upon the fetus and other unborn virtually no criminal law protection from intentional infliction of nonfatal injury by a third party, great injustices may prevail. The assailant who repeatedly strikes an expectant woman, intending to damage and actually damaging the fetus, can often only be prosecuted for crimes against the woman. Assault on the fetus does not constitute a separate crime.

As a result, Parness argues, "the interests in protecting potential life are not fully vindicated" (1985:140).

Parness also promotes the establishment of fetal rights before birth by relying heavily on cases where pregnant women miscarried after severe beatings by their husbands. Because of the "live birth" rule, these women had no way to recover damages for the loss of their pregnancy. In these cases, he points to the inadequacy of the law:

> Thus, Smith from the California case of *People v. Smith* apparently could not have been prosecuted for criminal abortion had he acted in Illinois, because he only beat his pregnant wife with his fists for an hour, kicked her in the stomach, shouted that he did not want her fetus to survive, and said, "Bleed, baby, bleed." (Parness 1985:135)

Similarly, in the cases of *Hollis v. Commonweath* (in Kentucky) and in *Keeler v. Superior Court* (in California) men who caused the intentional loss of their "unborn children" by severely beating their wives late in pregnancy could be prosecuted only for assault on the woman and not for the death of the fetus.

There were clearly problems with the law as it stood, both for pregnant women themselves and for those who would later affirm the rights of the fetus against the rights of women. While the law could compensate parents for prenatal injuries, it ironically could not compensate them for prenatal death. Injuries sustained in utero were legally recognized if they were severe enough to cause permanent injury to the fetus after birth, but not if they were severe enough to cause the loss of the pregnancy, because the fetus only became a legal "person" at birth.

Given the ability of modern technology to "save" the fetus before birth, conservative advocates argued that the "born alive" rule was outmoded, archaic, and no longer served a useful purpose. Why, Parness asks, should the destruction of fetal life one moment before birth be so different from the murder of an infant moments after? As he argues, the legal system "too often treats differently the actor whose culpable conduct terminates the existence of a nine month old fetus and the actor who causes the death of an infant which had existed independently of the mother for an instant" (Parness 1985:131).

The answer to such injustice was to close the gap between the "born" and the "unborn." "Feticide" laws, such as an Iowa statute that prosecutes for murder anyone who "intentionally terminates a human pregnancy after the end of the second trimester of pregnancy," conservative advocates argued, could help to protect not only women's rights to compensation, but also the legal integrity of "preborn life" (Parness 1985:133).

A dramatic shift in opinion began to emerge in the courts during the 1980s as a result of pressures brought by such advocates. Exactly one hundred years after the Massachusetts courts set precedent in the *Dietrich* case by denying the independent rights of the fetus, Massachusetts again set precedent in precisely the opposite direction by affirming for the first time in legal history, the "personhood" of the fetus before birth. In 1984 the Massachusetts *Commonwealth v. Cass* case recognized the fetus as a "person" when a fetus died as a result of injuries caused by an automobile accident. Since then, at least ten states have enacted laws allowing the prosecution for homicide of those who "murder" a fetus.[4] Since 1984 there has been a dramatic increase in cases involving prosecution for fetal homicide. Nearly every newspaper story detailing the murder of a pregnant woman now addresses at least the possibility of prosecution for the homicide of the fetus as well. Dozens of states have enacted "feticide" laws, giving the fetus full legal status as a person under criminal and tort law (see Parness 1985 and Johnsen 1986, 1989 for full legal citations).

While discarding the live-birth rule, most states still do not grant such rights to a fetus until it has reached the point of viability. That is, one can be prosecuted for the "murder" of a fetus only once it has reached the point where it could have, in theory, existed separately from the woman, generally after about the twenty-third week of gestation. *Roe* (*Roe v. Wade* 1973) had denied the state's interest in fetal life before the point of viability and had affirmed the right of the woman to terminate a pregnancy before the third trimester. While *Roe* was important in affirming the state's right to "protect" the fetus after the point of viability, it effectively prevented the development of fetal rights before viability.

The Supreme Court's *Webster* decision, which upheld a state provision granting the fetus "all the rights, privileges, and immunities available to other persons, citizens, and residents of the state," has made it increasingly possible for the fetus to be construed as gaining independent legal rights before viability (*Webster v. Reproductive Health Services* 1989). *Webster*, therefore, holds important implications not only for women's rights to abortion but also for a whole range of state policies that may "protect" the fetus from "abuse" from the earliest moments of pregnancy.

As long as third parties remained those who would endanger the health of pregnant women themselves—from abusive husbands and incompetent doctors to negligent employers and violent criminals—the provision of rights to the fetus did not threaten but rather increased the rights and powers of women. As Dawn Johnsen, legal counsel for the National Abortion Rights Action League (NARAL) argues, "Holding third parties responsible for the negligent or criminal destruction of fetuses is therefore consistent with, and even enhances, the protection of pregnant women's interests" (Johnsen 1986:603). But soon to emerge on the legal and political scene was a movement to cast women themselves as the "criminal actors" who posed the gravest threat to fetal health through their ignorance, negligence, or their own criminal behavior. As the language of the law shifted attention from the loss experienced by the parent/mother to the loss "experienced" by the fetus, it created the "legal fiction" of the fetus's existence separate from the woman's body (Johnsen 1989).

The Cultural Construction of Fetal Rights

The development of fetal rights was related to the development of both scientific and cultural images of the fetus as a person. A number of technological advances contributed to the development of the image of the fetus as an independent and autonomous being, among them the use of ultrasound and intrauterine photography, the advent of fetal surgery, and the development of neonatal technologies to save premature infants. Each of these made the fetus more visible, and made it appear as if there was no significant difference between the "unborn" and the "born" child.

The idea that the fetus was *separable* from the woman was based not only on attempts to wrest reproductive control from women, but also in technological innovations that made it possible for the fetus to exist outside of the woman's body. As Emily Martin has observed, "Human eggs, sperm, and embryos can now be moved from body to body or out of and back into the same female body. The organic unity of the fetus and mother can no longer be assumed, and all these newly fragmented parts can now be subjected to market forces, ordered, produced, bought and sold" (Martin 1987:20). Ironically, many of the same technologies used to aid women with fertility problems were used to challenge women's control over their bodies once they became pregnant. And since many women's fertility problems could be traced to delayed childbirth, the use of fetal technologies to wrest control from women could be construed as a form of punishment for women who had made the choice of career over family earlier in life.

Ultrasound

Ultrasound technology, developed during the 1960s and now widely used during pregnancy, provided the visual imagery of the fetus as a "tiny baby" housed inside the pregnant woman's body. With the help of technicians and physicians, potential parents came to see the fetal image as the image of the newly formed baby. Ultrasound imagery was distinct enough to suggest the similarities between the fetus and the baby (through the shadowy though distinct images of head, hands, knees, fingers, and toes), while it was vague enough to mascarade the dramatic differences between the fetus and the newborn infant (the lack of developed brain cells, central nervous system, or lungs).

The fetal imagery produced by ultrasound technology created a great imaginary drama of fetal development—a drama pursued as much by expectant parents as by health practitioners eager to display their latest technological wizardry. Ultrasound images of "baby's" first picture coupled with dramatic intrauterine photography in films and documentaries to reveal the "lifelike" images of the fetus at earlier and earlier stages of development (see Nilsson 1976).

The pregnant woman becomes transparent as the technology "passes through" her to visualize the hidden fetal body. Visual images rarely acknowledge the presence of the pregnant woman and so the public may more easily dismiss or forget the true location of the fetus. The development of fetal imagery has led to the transformation, at a most fundamental level, of how we think about the pregnant woman's body. As Petchesky has observed, fetal technologies have disrupted "the very definition, as traditionally understood, of 'inside' and 'outside' a woman's body, of pregnancy as an 'interior' experience" (Petchesky 1987:65). With the aid of visual technologies, fetal development became an event for public viewing. Once this very private, internal process became publicly visible, it opened up the possibility, as well, of the public control of pregnancy. The very "publicity" of pregnancy and fetal development entailed certain risks as well as rewards for women.

Neonatal Technology and the Question of Viability

The fiction of the fetus's independence from the woman's body was further enhanced by technological advances that have made it possible to save very premature infants. Questions about fetal viability fueled fantasies about the ability of the fetus to survive outside of the woman's body not only in the last stages of pregnancy, but from the first moments of conception.

In *Roe v. Wade*, the Supreme Court established the interest of the state in the fetus at viability, defined as the point at which the fetus is "potentially able to live outside the mother's womb, albeit with artificial aid" (*Roe v. Wade* 1973 at 160). Once the fetus has the potential for "meaningful" (and not just "momentary") life outside of the mother's womb, the state presumably has an interest in preserving that life, even if it conflicts with the woman's right to privacy.

A woman's right to privacy has thus been contingent upon the shifting definition of fetal viability. *Roe* originally defined viability at twenty-eight weeks, but recognized that it may occur as early as twenty-four weeks of pregnancy. Rather than setting a strict time limit on abortions or establishing some "measure" of viability, like fetal birth weight, it left the question of viability up to the woman's physician. Currently, fewer than 1 percent of all abortions are performed after twenty weeks of gestation and only 10 percent are performed between the thirteenth and nineteenth weeks (Paltrow 1986:24).

How then is viability defined? Is a fetus viable if it has a 10 percent chance of survival? If it survives only for a few days, weeks, or months but has no chance of long-term survival? If it is inflicted with severe handicaps that will ensure a life of pain and suffering? Before actual birth, the measure of viability is purely hypothetical. How then do we "measure" the viability of a fetus?

The earliest point at which a fetus has been documented to survive is twenty-three weeks (see Williams 1989). As one physician, Dr. Avery of Brigham and Women's Hospital in Boston, has reported, about half of all babies born after twenty-four weeks survive and about one-tenth of those born after twenty-three weeks survive, but "the odds of survival become infinitesimal before twenty-three weeks" ("Survival of the Fetus" 1989).

Cultural images have encouraged the perception that the fetus can survive at a much earlier age. Ronald Reagan once stated that premature infants had been born "even down to the *three month* stage and have lived to . . . grow up and be normal human beings." Supreme Court Justice Sandra Day O'Connor suggested in a dissenting opinion in one abortion rights case that "fetal viability in the first trimester of pregnancy may be possible in the not too distant future" (both as quoted by Paltrow 1986:15).

Despite such cultural imagery of fetal survival, the primary determinant of survival is fetal lung capacity, which typically develops at twenty-three to twenty-four weeks. Technological advances have been unable to pass the biological "line" set by lung development and so twenty-three weeks is generally believed to be the lower limit on fetal survival. Those who envision fetal survival before this point rely on the hope that massive technological intervention might be possible at earlier stages through the development of an "artificial womb," but, in general, this is currently thought of as scientifically (and financially) unfeasible.

Nevertheless, cultural perceptions of the survivability of the fetus at ever earlier stages of development have encouraged the perception of the fetus as an independent person from the earliest stages of pregnancy. Images in the media of two-pound "miracle" babies encourage the belief that the first- and second-trimester fetus is simply a physically complete but *smaller* version of the newborn infant, a tiny "person" inside the womb. Anti-abortion activists, such as Dr. Bernard Nathanson, have encouraged this view: "Significant advances in science and technology in the past four years, such as realtime ultrasound scanning, fetal medicine, intrauterine surgery, and in vitro fertilization have all confirmed beyond a reasonable doubt that prenatality is just another passage in our lives." Nathanson argues that abortion advocates have simply not come to grips with advances in modern technology, as they "cling to their flat earth credo" (Nathanson 1983:2). Fetal personhood here is presented not as a moral, religious, or philosophical question, but as a technical and medical one. Science has simply "revealed" the humanness of the fetus.

Fetal Surgery and the Fetus as Second Patient

The idea of the fetus's independence has also been encouraged by the development of technologies for fetal surgery. As Bernard Nathanson has characterized it, the physician can now come "eyeball to eyeball" with the fetus (Nathanson 1983:132). Through modern technology, Nathanson adds, "one can see the six-week-old infant clearly. We can even study the face, fingers, toes—in fact, the entire young child" (134).

The speed with which new technologies changed the medical view of pregnancy was quite remarkable. Ultrasound, the technology that first made fetal diagnosis and treatment possible only came into widespread use in the mid-1970s. By the mid-1980s, the testing and treatment of the fetus as patient had become an accepted part of prenatal technology. Ultrasound allowed physicians to diagnosis a whole range of the most obvious physical disorders. But more importantly, it gave physicians a window through which they could "see" the fetus. This visualization of the fetus made a whole range of fetal therapies possible (Hubbard 1982).

With ultrasound providing the visual guide, physicians could insert a long needle into the uterus of the pregnant woman to remove amniotic fluid and diagnose genetic defects, such as Tay-Sachs disease, Down's syndrome, trisomy 13, and sickle-cell anemia. With the development of the "fetoscope," a long, thin optical probe with which they could literally see the fetal body, doctors could draw fetal blood samples from tiny blood vessels and diagnose conditions like thalassemia, a form of acute anemia, which can cause the death of the fetus before birth, or certain illness and death after. Diagnosis of genetic disorders gave potential parents increased control over pregnancy. In cases where genetic disorders were untreatable, expectant parents could opt for abortion. Fetal medicine spoke to the desperate needs of women at high risk for genetic disease, women who had perhaps already undergone stillbirth or had delivered babies who suffered with disease and died shortly after birth. Fetal diagnosis promised to empower pregnant women and potential fathers with knowledge of disorders early in pregnancy so that they could end the pregnancy without experiencing the distress of postnatal death. Such diagnosis quickly became accessible to a wide range of women as processes like amniocentesis became a routine part of prenatal care.

But the ultimate point of diagnosis for those physicians pioneering the field was not termination but treatment. In cases of fetal anemia, physicians could inject fresh blood into the fetal abdomen where it was absorbed by the fetus (Kurjak 1985). No longer did the physician have to medicate the woman to treat the fetus, for now medications could be delivered directly into the fetal body. Obstetricians treated fetal goiter, for instance, which could obstruct the trachea and cause asphyxiation and death, by injecting medication into the amniotic fluid where the fetus could ingest or absorb it (Davidson et al. 1991).

During the 1980s, these less intrusive techniques for fetal treatment had been fairly successful (and less controversial) than those to come. Such treatments posed little or no risk to the pregnant woman herself, except for the increased risk of spontaneous abortion or infection that came with any medical penetration of the uterus. In the early 1980s, Dr. Michael Harrison and his colleagues at the University of California at San Francisco began experimenting with fetal surgery, inserting a needle directly into the fetus to shunt urine out of the bladder in cases of urinary-tract blockage or to drain excess fluid from the brain in cases of hydrocephalus. By 1987 the team had developed the techniques needed for full fetal surgery (Kolata 1990).

For fetal surgery, an incision is made into the woman's uterus, the aminiotic fluid is removed and kept warm, and the fetus is partially removed so that surgery can be performed directly on the fetal body. The fetus is then placed back into the woman, the fluid replaced, and the incision repaired. As the physicians from the earliest fetal surgery team have reported, preterm delivery remained the limiting factor "because successful correction of the fetal pathophysiology requires time for organ development in utero—the best possible intensive care unit"(Longaker et al. 1991:740). The fetus thus needs time to continue to develop lung capacity before the lungs are needed at birth. In all of the first seventeen documented cases of fetal surgery, maternal outcome was good, producing little or no long-term effects on the pregnant woman. Nevertheless, all of the seventeen women who underwent fetal surgery went into early labor. Of these first seventeen cases, one fetus had to be aborted and twelve others died at or shortly after birth. Of the four who survived, one is living with renal failure, one died in a nursery accident (and so no "recovery" information is available), and two remain alive and healthy (Longaker et al. 1991). Despite these limitations, the survival of the first few children to be born healthy after undergoing major surgery in utero has been perceived as a technological breakthrough. As one physician, Dr. N. Scott Adzick at the University of California, San Francisco Medical Center stated, "Fetal therapy is here to stay" ("The Tiniest Patients" 1991:56).

Each of these technological developments was seized on by the media as well as by anti-abortion advocates in their own campaign to promote the fetus as a person. Perceptions of fetal technologies merged with a powerful anti-abortion movement to create the public spectacle of fetal personhood. While these technologies could not themselves endow the fetus with independent life, they could suggest the ways in which such imagery might be used to shift the power of procreation and pregnancy away from women.

Anti-Abortion Rhetoric and Imagery

The anti-abortion movement successfully coupled technological innovations with the powers of modern discourse to provide the visual animation of fetal life. Together, these forces provided powerful weapons in the debate over fetal personhood. By endowing the fetus with independent life, the movement to monitor and control women's reproductive decisions was given a powerful impetus.

Visual imagery presented by the anti-abortion movement reinforced the identification of the fetus as a baby. Photographs used in anti-abortion campaigns focused on the specific fetal body parts that most resembled the newborn infant—the tiny feet of a ten-week-old fetus, the thumb approaching the mouth of the four-month-old "unborn child." The image of the tiny feet at ten weeks was used repeatedly in literature, billboards, on buttons, and in media campaigns to suggest the "humanness" of the fetus from the earliest moments of conception. "This is what your feet looked like when you were only ten weeks old" reads the caption from one anti-abortion pamphlet. "Perfectly formed? Yes! You even had fingerprints then" (as quoted by Condit 1990:88).

Such images sought to *personify* the fetus, to suggest visual metaphors that established a complete identification between "preborn life" and the full-grown human being. Through such imagery, the anti-abortion movement sought to promote the full animation of the fetus as a person. It was a strategy that was as successful as it was dramatic. As Celeste Condit suggests in her fascinating study of the discourse surrounding the abortion rights debate, "Personification here worked most effectively. The fetus was not only a person; it was *you*" (1990:86). The image of the tiny feet operated as a synecdoche, a rhetorical device used to encourage one to see a part (the feet) for the whole (the fetus/baby). This tactic removed from the visual image any suggestion that the fetus was unformed, dependent, or lodged within the pregnant woman's body. As Condit observes, an "accurate, full picture of a young fetus includes features not associated with adult human beings—the placenta and the umbilical cord, and, in a six-week fetus, even a 'tail.' With these and its ungainly face and head, off-balance and poorly formed, a young fetus looks like a wretched creature, bloody and undernourished" (Condit 1990:88–89). In fact, at eight weeks the fetus is so ill-defined that it would be difficult for an uninformed observer to recognize it as anything human at all.

In the public representation presented by the anti-abortion movement, the focus is not on the woman but the uterus. The uterus is not a part of the woman but is the fetus's "sanctuary." The woman is not pregnant but is an "expectant mother," a mother whose child has already been "born" at conception but not yet released from the womb. As in the famous anti-abortion film, *The Silent Scream*, the woman becomes the "maternal environment" that either nurtures and feeds the "preborn child" or threatens the child with "imminent extinction and death" (*The Silent Scream* 1985).

The animation of fetal life through such imagery did more than just personify the fetus. As the fetus emerged as a person, the pregnant woman began, literally, to disappear from view. In much of the promotional literature of the anti-abortion movement, the fetus is *visually severed* from the mother, presented as an autonomous free-floating being, attached tenuously to the "mother ship" by the umbilical cord. As Dr. Bernard Nathanson describes it, the fetus is a "person floating freely in a fluid environment . . . as free of gravity as any astronaut in space orbit." When the amniotic sac is broken in labor, "he feels the pull of gravity for the first time, like an astronaut re-entering the earth's relentless embrace" (1983:139). But, as Barbara Rothman has suggested, in this metaphor the pregnant woman becomes "empty space."(Rothman 1986:114) As the fetus has gained visual autonomy, the woman in the picture has begun to disappear, to reemerge later as a threat to the fetus's health, as a barrier to fetal life, as alien to the fetus's interests.

Bernard Nathanson, a prominent antu-abortion advocate, casts the conflict between the woman and the fetus at the most fundamental microbiologic level by arguing that the woman's body resists the very implantation of the fertilized egg from the first moment of fertilization, recognizing the conceptus as *not of itself*:

When a pregnancy implants itself into the wall of the uterus at the eighth day following conception the defense mechanisms of the body

... sense that this creature now settling down for a lengthy stay is an intruder, an alien, and must be expelled. Therefore, an intense immunological atttack is mounted on the pregnancy by the white blood cell elements, and through an ingenious and extraordinarily efficient defense system the unborn child succeeds in repelling the attack. In ten percent or so of cases the defensive system fails and the pregnancy is lost as a spontaneous abortion or miscarriage. *Think how fundamental a lesson there is for us here: Even on the most minute microscopic scale the body has trained itself, or somehow in some inchoate way knows, how to recognize self from non-self.* (Nathanson 1983:151; emphasis added)

The lesson here is also highly political: at even the most fundamental microscopic level, Nathanson suggests that there is a battle going on between the woman and the fetus. From the earliest moments of life, the pregnant woman rejects and threatens the fetus. The fetus must defend itself against the woman. By implication, the continuation of fetal life requires that it force itself against the social and biological impulses of the woman to expel it, neglect it, or otherwise threaten the life not only of the fetus but even of the fertilized egg. Highly politicized characterizations of the biological processes of reproduction thus inform our understanding of the maternal-fetal relationship at a most fundamental level.

Where once there was an assumed biological and emotional unity of mother and child—a powerful maternal bond—now there is a deeply fundamental conflict between the pregnant woman and fetus, a conflict that must be mediated and regulated by outside forces in order for the fetus to survive. With the biological unity between woman and fetus broken, men, who before could exert little control over women's procreative power, could now begin to control pregnancy itself.

With pregnancy made a public event, the power of men to influence and control pregnancy was enhanced. Images of the fetus as autonomous from the woman were built upon ancient assumptions of the fetus as "male seed"—as a tiny being implanted into the womb by the man. Aristotelian philosophy endowed the sperm with the power of life, as the agent that "ensouled" the fetus. The pregnant woman just provided the *place* for conception; the man provided the *potent seed* (Rothman 1989:248). Cast in these terms, the power of procreation is shifted from the woman to the man. Current debates over fetal rights again reflect the view that the fetus is owned by someone other than the pregnant woman, who simply acts as the "host" for the man's unborn child.

The science of reproduction deeply reflects gender assumptions—assumptions about power, rights, and ownership of the fetus and, by extension, the pregnant woman's body. The devaluation of women's contribution to conception and pregnancy has, for centuries, provided the basis for men's control of women's reproductive power (O'Brien 1981).

The marriage of anti-abortion ideology with the development of fetal technologies has led to a powerful cultural movement which has given the fetus meaning and life outside of the woman's body. The fetus, temporarily "cradled" in the mother's womb, would become the seed of male power and control over women's bodies. By the early 1980s, this characterization was clearly reflected in science, popular culture, and the law.

The State's Interest in "Potential Life"

The technological possibility of early fetal "separation" from the mother has moved the state's interest in the fetus earlier and earlier into pregnancy, suggesting that the state has an interest in fetal development from the earliest stages of life. What is the basis of the state's interest in the fetus? Fetal rights advocates argue that the Supreme Court's decision in *Roe v. Wade* sanctioned and legitimated the state's direct interest in the fetus in the third trimester of pregnancy. In *Roe*, the Supreme Court recognized and approved the state's "important and legitimate interest in protecting the potentiality of human life"(*Roe v. Wade* 1973). While affirming the woman's right to privacy in the first trimester and the joint interests of the woman and state in the second, *Roe* explicitly affirms the dominance of the state's interest in the third trimester, once the fetus has passed the point of viability.

The abortion debate has been cast in terms of a balancing act between women's rights to privacy and the state's interest in preserving fetal health. While not explicitly protected under the U.S. Constitution, the right to privacy is fundamental enough in the Anglo-American legal tradition that the violation of this right must be justified on substantial legal grounds. That is, the woman's right to privacy "trumps" the right to fetal health until the fetus reaches the point of viability. But once the fetus is endowed with "personhood" the balance changes dramatically. The fetus's right to life is then balanced against the woman's right to privacy—a contest in which women's rights are almost always subordinated.

In an ironic (or strategic) twist of politics, some conservative advocates argued that it was women's right to choice that paradoxically affirmed the state's right to regulate and control pregnant women. The state had an obligation to ensure not only women's choice of abortion in the early stages of pregnancy but also the healthy birth of wanted children later in pregnancy. Robertson ironically referred to this as the "bittersweet nature" of women's reproductive freedom, which confers upon women the right to "bring or avoid bringing a child into the world," but also entails the loss of her legal autonomy from the point of viability and perhaps even from the point of conception. The potential conflict between woman and fetus

> gives rise to the seemingly paradoxical result that a woman has an unrestrained right to control her body until the fetus reaches viability and then suddenly loses this right once she decides to carry the child to term. At that point, if the well-being of the potential child is at stake, she loses her autonomy, and her body may be invaded and treated for the child's sake. (Robertson 1983:463)

Once a woman decides to keep a pregnancy, she gains certain responsibilities to ensure the healthy birth of that child.

> A woman is free not to conceive or, even though her actions destroy the fetus, to terminate the pregnancy altogether up to the point of viability, and she can terminate the pregnancy beyond the point of viability if its continuation threatens her life or health. Conflicts over management of the pregnancy arise only after she has decided to become or remain pregnant. Once she decides to forgo abortion and the state chooses to protect the fetus, the woman loses the liberty to act in ways that would adversely affect the fetus. (Robertson 1983:437; citations omitted)

What is the nature of her loss of liberty? Robertson's answers are quite clear. If fetal health were at risk, she could be forced to undergo surgery. If she were "mentally ill," she could be civilly committed. If she were an anorectic teenager, she could be force-fed. If she were working in a toxic workplace, she could be forced to quit her job. If she were a drug addict or alcoholic, she could be incarcerated simply for the "crime" of being pregnant and addicted. As Robertson characterizes it,

> These obligations may require her to avoid work, recreation, and medical care choices that are hazardous to the fetus. They also obligate her to preserve her health for the fetus' sake or even allow established therapies to be performed on an affected fetus. Finally, they require that she undergo prenatal screening where there is reason to believe that this screening may identify congenital defects correctable with available therapies. (Robertson 1983:445)

At the point of viability, the woman's body literally becomes the body of the state, at which point the woman loses her most fundamental rights to resist state intrusion. As Robertson most explicitly argues, "she waived her right to resist bodily intrusions made for the sake of the fetus when she chose to continue the pregnancy" (Robertson 1983:445). While women may have the freedom to control their bodies, that freedom is circumscribed by the obligations they incur to the fetus. These obligations may be imposed upon the woman not only from the point of viability, nor even from the moment of conception, *but from the point of her fertility*. What if a woman engages in behavior early in pregnancy, like working in a toxic environment, smoking cigarettes, or drinking or using illicit drugs, which clearly threaten fetal health before viability? Some of these restrictions have been upheld by the courts, some have been struck down. All of them suggest the extent to which a woman's right to bodily integrity is *contingent* upon the state's "higher interest" in the fetus.

Women's self-sovereignty is thus increasingly threatened by scientific, legal, and cultural constructions of the fetus as an autonomous being located within the pregnant woman's body. As the state interest in the fetus moves earlier into pregnancy, it becomes clear that a woman's right to bodily integrity is never absolute. It is traded against (and often traded away) by a woman's right to reproductive "choice."

Such threats to women's autonomy have been vocalized not only by a small religious or anti-abortion minority, but by liberal legal scholars, like Alan Dershowitz of Harvard University Law School. In one editorial, Dershowitz argues precisely for the limitation on women's rights during pregnancy. "Now I am not a "fetal-rights" advocate. I favor *Roe v. Wade*. I believe that a pregnant woman should have the right to choose between giving birth or having an abortion. But I am a human-rights advocate, and I believe that no woman who has chosen to give birth should have the right to neglect or injure that child by abusing their collective body during pregnancy" (Dershowitz 1989:V,5). While opposing what he calls the "totalitarian" proposals of many fetal-protection advocates, Dershowitz nevertheless adopts the logic and language of fetal advocacy and defends the restriction of women's rights in what he sees as the most extreme drug-abuse cases. A woman does not have the right to "inflict a lifetime of suffering on her future child, simply in order to satisfy a momentary whim for a quick fix." The rights of the woman are contrasted to the rights of the baby, or as Dershowitz characterizes it, "your right to abuse your own body stops at the border of your womb."[5]

By linking the maternalist affirmation for life with the masculinist use of coercive state power, fetal-rights advocates have constructed an extremely compelling case for fetal rights. Proponents of fetal protectionism clearly understand the coercive uses to which state laws can (and should) be put. As Parness states, "One major goal of the criminal law is to deter specific antisocial acts. Accordingly, criminal law utilizes the threat of punishment as a means of promoting proper social conduct. The aims of rehabilitation, education, and retribution are also sometimes served by the criminal law." Statutes promoting the respect for the unborn must provide *"punishment that looms large in the minds of those who might act negatively toward the unborn. . . .* The publicity accompanying the trial, conviction, and sentencing of criminals educates the public concerning the proper distinctions between good and bad behavior"(Parness 1985:117; citations omitted; emphasis added).

Fetal Rights Cases Today

It is within this cultural context—with a fetus animated with life and victimized by neglect, ignorance, or abuse—that public and legal tides began to turn against the rights of women and for the rights of the fetus "housed" inside the pregnant woman's body. Indeed, much of the literature began to envision the fetus as "trapped" within the pregnant woman, as a victim of her excesses and freedoms.

The pregnant woman became the vessel that transported the fetus in its journey toward birth. The woman, in proper domestic fashion, "houses" the fetus, "feeds" it, and then "releases" it when it has reached the age of birth. But a child that is housed by the mother can also be made "homeless" by her; a child that is fed by the mother can also be "poisoned" by her. The power of the pregnant woman to nourish and contain the fetus became then a power that could be appropriated by others and used against her.

As the fetus gained ideological, legal, and political independence from the woman, it came also to be seen as "public property," to be treated independently by doctors, protected in utero by the courts, and retrieved by the state, if necessary, after birth. The alienation of the woman's body from the fetus thus provided the grounds for the subordination of women's legal rights and the control of women's behavior during pregnancy by a whole range of social actors, from medical practitioners, lawyers, and bartenders, to husbands, bosses, and state agents. It is on this philosophical ground that justifications were built for the whole range of fetal rights cases that emerged during the 1980s and 1990s.

Despite the great political and cultural momentum in favor of fetal personhood, few of the current legal attempts to restrict or criminalize the activities of pregnant (or fertile) women have been successful. In the spring of 1990, in a forced cesarian section case in which the pregnant woman, Angela Carder, died, the U.S. Court of Appeals for the District of Columbia upheld the right of pregnant women to refuse medical treatment (*In Re*

A. C. 1990). In the spring of 1991 the U.S. Supreme Court unanimously struck down a company policy (at the Johnson Controls Corporation) that restricted the work of fertile women on the grounds of fetal protectionism (*UAW v. Johnson Controls* 1991). And in the summer of 1992 the Florida State Supreme Court reversed the lower court's prosecution of Jennifer Johnson for delivering drugs through her umbilical cord to her fetus (*Johnson v. State* 1992).

While one may be heartened by the power of women, their lawyers, and their allies to turn back attempts to restrict women's behavior on the grounds of fetal rights, one must also acknowledge that the forces that gave rise to these cases continue to animate fetal politics. Despite the U.S. Court of Appeals strong ruling in the Angela Carder case, thirty-five of the forty-six states that currently have living-will laws explicitly restrict the right of pregnant women to control their right to die when they are both severely ill and pregnant. In twenty states pregnant women are disqualified without exception from the right to die as soon as they become pregnant, even in cases where they have fully executed living wills (Hoefler and Kamoie 1991). While the Johnson Controls decision was a unanimous one, the court did leave open the possibility that a workplace policy that restricted only pregnant women, and not all fertile women, might be acceptable to the court. The decision also failed to address the larger political question of why women (or men) should be forced to choose between their reproductive health and their ability to earn a living wage.

While most attempts to criminally prosecute drug- or alcohol-addicted pregnant women have failed, they have failed strictly on statutory grounds because they rely on state laws designed not to prosecute pregnant women, but to prosecute drug dealers or parents who abuse or neglect their children. Efforts have been made in at least eighteen states to enact fetal abuse laws, to subject pregnant addicts to additional criminal penalties for drug use, to require health care providers to test pregnant women for drugs, or to report or commit pregnant women to state authorities if they admit illegal drug use (Moss, Guerrero, and Kolbert 1991). Like criminal prosecutions to date, these laws will disproportionately affect those women who most use public facilities and who are more often assumed by state or medical authorities to be "chronic" abusers of drugs—women of color and poor white women (Roberts 1991). When more appropriate fetal-abuse laws are passed—and such proposals now stand before many legislatures—criminal prosecutions will succeed.

The significance of public controversy over fetal rights cannot be contained to current legal discourse, but fuels as well a public culture that may more easily endorse subtle forms of social control over women. The legal,

technological, and cultural developments discussed here, which have personified and animated the fetus, will continue to generate attempts to cast
women as unreasonable or irrational actors who, in the end, are unworthy
of the dignities, rights, and responsibilities of full citizenship.

Notes

1. This article is excerpted from *At Women's Expense: State Power and the Politics
of Fetal Rights* (Cambridge, Mass.: Harvard University Press, 1993), which analyzes
more fully the politics of fetal protectionism in the 1980s and 1990s and addresses
the broader theoretical questions raised by "fetal rights" cases for women's standing as liberal citizens.

2. For excellent reviews of the history of characterizations of the fetus in a variety of historical and cultural contexts, see Rhode 1989; Luker 1984; Petchesky 1984;
Tribe 1990.

3. A study in one state in 1989 found that 50 percent of the chemical and elec-
tronics companies employing 500 or more workers excluded women from some
forms of work based on the potential risk to fetal health (Daniels, Paul, and Rosofsky 1989).

4. These states are California, Illinois, Iowa, Michigan, Mississippi, New Hampshire, Oklahoma, Utah, Washington, and Wisconsin. For specific penal codes, see
Johnsen 1986:602, n. 14.

5. One is tempted to ask Mr. Dershowitz if men's right to abuse their bodies
stops at the border of their testicles, given the evidence of the reproductive damage
done by men's alcohol abuse (and the consequent harm inflicted on children born
prematurely or with low birth weight or birth defects as a result).

References

In Re Angela Carder. 1990. 573 A 2d, 1235, DC.

Bonbrest v. Kotz. 1946. 65 F.Supp. 138.

Brennan v. Smith. 1960. 157 A.2d. 497.

Commonwealth v. Cass. 1984. 467 N.E. 2nd.

Condit, Celeste. 1990. *Decoding Abortion Rhetoric*. Urbana: University of Illinois Press.

Daniels, C. R. 1991. "Competing Gender Paradigms: Gender Difference, Fetal
Rights and the Case of Johnson Controls." *Policy Studies Review* 10(4):51.

Daniels, C. R. 1993. *At Women's Expense: State Power and the Politics of Fetal Rights*.
Cambridge, Mass.: Harvard University Press.

Daniels, C. R., M. Paul, and R. Rosofsky. 1989. "Family, Work and Health Report."
Massachusetts Department of Public Health.

Davidson, Kim M., D. S. Richards, A. D. Schatz, and D. A. Fisher. 1991. "Successful
In Utero Treatment of Fetal Goiter and Hypothyroidism." *New England Journal of
Medicine* 324(8):545.

Dershowitz, Alan. 1989. "Drawing the Line on Prenatal Rights." *Los Angeles Times* (May 14):V, 5.

Dietrich v. Northampton. 1884. 138 Mass.

Hoefler, James, and Brian Kamoie. 1991. "The Right to Die: A Developmental Analysis of Case Law and a Comparative Analysis of Statutes in the American States." Paper delivered at the annual meeting of the Northeastern Political Science Association.

Hubbard, Ruth. 1982. "Legal and Policy Implications of Recent Advances in Prenatal Diagnosis and Fetal Therapy." *Women's Rights Law Reporter* 7(3):201–208.

Johnsen, Dawn. 1986. "The Creation of Fetal Rights: Conflicts with Women's Constitutional Rights to Liberty, Privacy, and Equal Protection." *Yale Law Journal* 95:599–625.

Johnsen, Dawn. 1989. "From Driving to Drugs: Governmental Regulation of Pregnant Women's Lives After Webster." *University of Pennsylvania Law Review* 138:179–215.

Johnson v. State of Florida. 1992. No. 77,831.

Kolata, Gina. 1990. *The Baby Doctors: Probing the Limits of Fetal Medicine.* New York: Delacorte Press.

Kolder, Veronica E. B., J. Gallagher, and M. Parsons. 1987. "Court-Ordered Obstetrical Interventions." *New England Journal of Medicine* 316(19):1192–1196.

Kurjak, A., ed. 1985. *The Fetus As Patient.* New York: Excerpta Medica/Elsevier Science.

Longaker, Michael T., Mitchell S. Golbus, Roy A. Filly, Mark A. Rosen, Sophia Chang, and Michael Harrison. 1991. "Maternal Outcome After Open Fetal Surgery: A Review of the First Seventeen Human Cases." *Journal of the American Medical Association* 265(6):737–741.

Martin, Emily. 1987. *The Woman in the Body.* Boston: Beacon Press.

Moss, K., G. Guerrero, and K. Kolbert. 1991. "Legislative Update on Drug Use During Pregnancy." American Civil Liberties Union memorandum, September 16.

Nathanson, Bernard. 1983. *The Abortion Papers.* New York: Frederick Fell.

Nilsson, Lennart. 1976. *A Child Is Born.* New York: Delacorte Press/Seymour Lawrence.

O'Brien, Mary. 1981. *The Politics of Reproduction.* New York: Routledge and Kegan Paul.

Paltrow, Lynn. 1986. "A Review of Advances in Reproductive and Neonatal Technology As They Relate to Abortion Rights." *Reproductive Rights Law Reporter* (October 30):24.

Paltrow, Lynn. 1992. "Criminal Prosecutions Against Pregnant Women: National Update and Overview." Reproductive Freedom Project, American Civil Liberties Union, New York.

Parness, Jeffrey. 1985. "Crimes Against the Unborn: Protecting and Respecting the Potentiality of Human Life." *Harvard Journal on Legislation* 22(97):97–172.

In Re Peabody. 1959. 5 N.Y.2nd 546, 158 NE2nd 844, 186 N.Y.S.2nd 269.

Petchesky, Rosalind. 1987. "Foetal Images: The Power of Visual Culture in the Politics of Reproduction." In Michelle Stanworth, ed., *Reproductive Technologies: Gender, Motherhood and Medicine.* Minneapolis: University of Minnesota Press.

Roberts, Dorothy. 1991. "Punishing Drug Addicts Who Have Babies: Women of Color, Equality and the Right to Privacy." *Harvard Law Review* 104(7):1419–1482.

Robertson, J. A. 1983. "Procreative Liberty and the Control of Conception, Pregnancy and Childbirth." *Virginia Law Review* 69(3):405–464.

Roe V. Wade. 1973. 410 U.S., 162.

Rothman, B. K. 1986. *The Tentative Pregnancy.* New York: Viking.

Rothman, B. K. 1989. *Recreating Motherhood.* New York: W. W. Norton.

The Silent Scream. 1984. Film produced and directed by Jack Duane Dabner. Anaheim, Calif.: American Portrait Films.

"Survival of the Fetus." 1989. *New York Times* (April 18):C1.

"The Tiniest Patients." 1991. *Newsweek* (June 11).

United Auto Workers v. Johnson Controls. 1991. No. 89–1215 U.S. S. Ct.

Webster v. Reproductive Health Services. 1989. 109 S. Ct. 3040.

Williams, J. Whitridge. 1989. *Williams Textbook of Obstetrics,* 18th ed. Edited by F. Gary Cunningham, Paul C. MacDonald, and Norman F. Gant. Norwalk, Conn.: Appleton and Lang.

7

Our Most Important Product

George J. Annas

EDITOR'S NOTE: The following minutes from an October 1993 meeting of a top secret federal interagency group known as Perfect People 2020 (PP2020) were mistakenly provided to the author following a Freedom of Information Act request. When the mistake was discovered, the U.S. Attorney General, Janet Reno, attempted to recover the document, alleging that its dissemination would violate national security interests. All names are pseudonyms. A federal judge reviewed the document and personally excised all material that could affect national security. The author has assured me that what follows is representative of both the entire document and the overall research strategy of PP2020. Footnotes and references were added by the editor for clarification. The group apparently meets once every five years to assess their progress.

Minutes (PP2020)

The meeting began at 1800 hours on October 31, 1993 and opened with a general discussion of project goals in view the events of the past five years. All present agreed that with the end of the Cold War the overall goals of Perfect People 2020 (PP2020) should be modified. From its inception after World War II, the group's primary goal had been to develop the perfect soldier, one who could survive illness, injury, or capture, and continue to function effectively as a fighting man. In the mid-1960s the group agreed to also work toward developing the perfect astronaut for space flights. Although progress has been made toward attaining both of these goals (see below), the group agreed that they are too narrowly defined. Instead, the group adopted as its new goals the same goals that are currently being implicitly pursued by noncovert researchers in America's academic medical centers: human immortality and the genetically perfect human. As one member put it, Dan Callahan himself probably didn't realize how right he was to compare medical care with space exploration: "No matter how far you go, there's always farther you can go" (Callahan 1990).

It was argued that there may soon be no further need of PP2020 since it now appears that the public is willing to accept virtually *any* experiment on a human being that promises either to lengthen life or to alter or eliminate defective genes. A 1992 March of Dimes public opinion poll, for example, found that although 86 percent of Americans know "little" or "nothing" about gene therapy, 89 percent approve its use in both therapy and research.

It was also noted that although the 1947 Nuremberg Code requires protecting both the rights and the welfare of human subjects, most contemporary researchers and bioethicists seem to approve of any experiment in which *either* the welfare of the subject is protected by prior peer review or the rights of the subject are protected by requiring informed consent to the experiment. In the case of terminally ill subjects, the researcher's assertion of trying to "save the life" of the subject seems sufficient in virtually all instances so that even seemingly bizarre experiments can be justified as "treatment."

It was agreed that the trend of characterizing all research as therapy is one PP2020 should support. We will therefore continue to financially support both ACT-UP and the *Wall Street Journal* as long as they continue their campaign to blur the distinction between experimentation and treatment, by insisting that individuals suffering from incurable diseases should have access to any drug or procedure they want regardless of its proven safety or efficacy. In this regard, the group members have been strongly supporting the FDA's development of both "compassionate use" and parallel track exceptions to their drug licensing regulations, and will continue to do so. [*NATIONAL SECURITY DELETIONS*]

Discussion of Past Experiments

There was considerable debate over which experiment or series of experiments the various divisions of PP2020 have sponsored should be considered prototypes for future work. Dr. Green expressed some consternation with the Institute of Medicine's publication of an exposition of our World War II mustard gas and lewisite studies on U.S. Navy personnel (Institute of Medicine 1993). As a member of the IOM panel, he had managed to steer the study away from its human experimentation aspects, but in the end Jay Katz convinced the panel to document the use of U.S. service personnel as guinea pigs in "gas chambers" in which they were exposed to mustard gas without their knowledge or consent, and which they were forbidden to ever discuss. As *Nature* rightly reported, U.S. soldiers were used as "experimental animals" by their own government (*Nature* 1993). Luckily, it seems no one cares. The mustard gas chamber experiments thus still provide the group with its prototypical model in that they are done on completely controlled populations without their knowledge or consent, by government employees or military personnel who are sworn to secrecy, and on subjects who have no legal redress to damages. This is also how we were able to expose more than 250,000 U.S. troops to nuclear explosions in the early 1950s to study the effects of radiation on the human body, and expose hundreds of U.S. servicemen to LSD to determine the drug's effect on their minds and behavior. As discussed in more detail at the last meeting, the group was both surprised and pleased that the U.S. Supreme Court ruled in 1987 (*United States v. Stanley* 1987; Annas 1992) that the victims of these experiments could not sue the federal government for compensation for the harm caused them even though these experiments were in direct violation of the Nuremberg Code. [*NATIONAL SECURITY DELETIONS*] The U.S. courts also proved very helpful and supportive of our efforts in Operation Desert Storm when they approved of our scheme to use experimental drugs and vaccines on our troops without their consent, although we did agree to have the protocols reviewed at the Department of Defense prior to commencing the experiments. The group did not speculate on how soon we can count on another shooting war, but group members all agreed to have new experiments ready to go in the event that the opportunity arises in the near future. It was the consensus that, whenever possible, members of the military should be used as experimental subjects whenever healthy volunteers are required.

The other candidates for most promising prototype were more closely related to the new goals of PP2020. Perhaps the most spectacular was the 1971–1984 experiment involving David, the so-called bubble boy. He lived almost his entire life in a sterile bubble and provided a tremendous amount of information for both our space travel and our immortality studies. Dr. Blue expressed (as he had five years ago) astonishment that the American public accepted this experiment—he had wanted it conducted in secret. It is Dr. Blue's view that if it is societally acceptable to raise a human being in a laboratory—to live a completely artificial life—then "anything goes" in American experimental medicine already, and PP2020 is unncessary. Other members of the group thought we just got lucky with the bubble boy. We can justify experiments on our troops on the basis of national security and the military mission, but who would have though we could raise a child to be used as an experimental animal, confined to a plastic cage, and denied all direct human contact, even with his mother? Instead of considering his bubble a cage or a prison, for example, most Americans (those who thought about it at all) considered it a life-saving device. The singer Paul Simon also unwittingly helped with his song lyrics about "miracles and wonders," with its examples "the boy in the bubble and the baby with the baboon heart," thus instantly transforming these experiments into cultural artifacts.

The Baby Fae experiment was not sponsored by PP2020, but the group (strongly) approved of the experiment as it created tremendous public interest in and support for xenografting. This has led to additional experiments on adults, including baboon liver transplants at Pittsburgh. Dr. Yellow expressed the view that permanent xenografting was still very premature (and may remain so until our transgenic pig is perfected), suggesting that PP2020 encourage researchers to perform xenografts only as bridges to human organ transplants. Although the use of a pig liver as a bridge last year got some bad press, the group considered that experiment a scientific success and will continue to fund xenograft work across the country.

The xenograft project's short-term goal is to produce a virtually infinite supply of replacement organs so that the life span of chosen individuals can be significantly extended. In the long term, all members of the group believe that artificial organs will be the ultimate replacement parts; the overall goal (discussed below) must be production of a totally artifical body that will act as a permanent enclosure to protect the human brain. [*NATIONAL SECURITY DELETIONS*] The general assessment of the artificial heart program was that it was on track. Dr. Magenta was congratulated all around for his exemplary work on the Institute of Medicine's artificial-heart assessment panel, which endorsed continued research on the artificial heart in the face of criticism from the National Institutes of Health (NIH).

Some of the most exciting work is currently being done in the field of cryonics. We have established that the human embryo can be frozen and thawed out later for implantation without damage to the resulting child. This work has won wide public support and the group believes that most of it will continue with existing private funding.

We have also been extraordinarily successful in launching the Human Genome Project (HGP) as a cover for our genetic engineering project. We were successful in getting the HGP to fund our friends the bioethicists. No group in America has been as helpful to our programs as the bioethics community, and they deserve our support. Our old goal of producing a grass-eating human who is resistant to radiation and chemical- and biological-warfare toxins now seems achievable by the year 2010.

We will also continue to support experiments on embryos with identified genetic disorders, such as cystic fibrosis, to see if these genes can be suppressed or replaced. In this regard the work of Dr. Puce with NIH's Recombinant DNA Advisory Committee has been very effective. The consensus was that, at least in genetics if not in all areas, we will not have to force our experiments on the population—the American people can be made to demand genetic perfection as their right with simple advertising. Cosmetic surgery advertising provides a useful model here. Experimental medicine really is a consumer good.

Dr. White noted that the public has already begun to demand the right to whole-body cryopreservation. A California male, dying of a brain tumor, went to court to seek a declaratory judgment that he had the legal right to be frozen prior to death. Although the judges failed to grant his petition, his request got lots of publicity, and was even featured on the television series *L.A. Law*. It won't be long until our own private foundation (established to cryopreserve individuals and attempt to revive them in the future) will be open for business. Although the group decided not to initiate legislation on this issue now, we will support individuals or groups that do so in the future. We will also continue our support for all state "aid in dying" referendums, with a view toward amending them to include predeath cryopreservation.

New and Continuing Projects

L103. There was some sentiment to shutting down our citizen-monitoring projects, which have been concentrated on the development of unremovable devices. When the state of New Jersey canceled its parole program using ankle monitors in late 1992, it was a blow to the future of these devices. Nonetheless, our new concept of an employee "smart card ID," which the employer can use to monitor where the employee is, with whom, and for how long, got solid reviews. The project will continue. Dr. Green has also been involved in the Clinton Health Care Task Force, and has become its main consultant on designing a national health care "smart card." His plan (which the group adopted) is to get everyone's complete medical records on these cards to help with continuity of care. Of course, for our purposes, there will have to be a central data bank to store and update everyone's medical histories (so that lost and stolen smart cards can be replaced), and this will provide us with all the medical data available in the U.S. to perform epidemiological studies. There has been virtually no public outcry against this idea and it is hoped that by the next time the group meets we will be able to formally pronounce informational privacy a dead issue in the United States. Dr. Green will also work with the genetics subgroup to incorporate an individual's entire genome onto the smart card when this technology becomes available. Once medical privacy is seen as an unnecesssary luxury, genetic privacy will not be maintainable.

Dr. Black asked for group approval to begin his project to implant nonremovable monitoring devices at the base of the brain of neonates in three major teaching hospitals (L103B). The implantations would be done by nurses trained by our agents. The devices would not only permit us to locate all the implantees at any time, but could be programmed in the future to monitor the sound around them and to play subliminal messages directly to their brains. The experiment was approved, subject to review in five years. [NATIONAL SECURITY DELETIONS]

L195. Dr. Lemon reported that his organization was having trouble recruiting surrogate mothers for his genetic experiments. He proposes setting up a new institute (akin to Will Gaylin's neomortuary in which the bodies of the recently deceased were mechanically maintained so that their organs could be harvested) that would house women patients in persistent vegetative states. The uteruses of these women would be hormonally prepared and used to incubate embryos that were genetically altered. This would have many advantages, the clearest being that when the children are born, they would have no parents who knew or cared about them. Thus, we could continue our genetic engineering experiments on the children without having to worry about consent or unwanted publicity. Until our artificial uterus is constructed (and this project [A18] is way behind schedule), this seems a viable option. The members generally agreed, although required that the facility be located outside the United States and have a self-destruct mechanism that could be activated by the chair at any time. [NATIONAL SECURITY DELETIONS] Long-term plans call for the genetic alteration of all female embryos (a sonic mutator that can be placed in prenatal clinics is under consideration) to eliminate or disable the fallopian tubes. This will, of course, require that these women (eventually all women) use in vitro fertilization (IVF) to have children, which will in turn give us access to their embryos. The long-range plan is to screen all human embryos, and perhaps enhance their characteristics. Defective embryos would be discarded. Our project to crossbreed a chimpanzee and a human [A35] was eliminated as no longer necessary. The living offspring will be sacrificed.

L206. Work on the "magic pill" (a pill that an adult could take that would enhance cell function in order to maintain perfect health until all the cells of the body suddenly collapse and the person dies instantly) continues without success. Our hope is to create a pill that high school students could take that would insure them good health until about age sixty, at which time they would die suddenly without costing society any money to pay for their final illness. It is likely that if we succeed in developing the pill, we will want to introduce its active ingredients into early human embryos (perhaps at the 8-to-16-cell stage) so that humans are programmed for "perfect" health and a quick death.

L396 and 397. A lively discussion followed the suggestion that we also shut down the human gill-adaptation program (GAP) and the human wing-adaptation program (WAP). These programs are designed to use human fetuses that are aborted alive as subjects for grafting gill slits and wings. So far the results have been terrible, although one fetus did survive more than an hour under water and the gills did function. Therefore, we know it can be done. None of the grafted wings has functioned. Since the ocean will have to be used for human habitation within two or three centuries, it was decided that GAP should continue. WAP will be shelved until GAP is successful. The bionic wheel project [A26] was also suspended, although artificial wheels have been successfully attached to two Department of Veterans Affairs patients who were double amputees. The general feeling in the room was that although the bionic wheel will be much more efficient for space travel, the astronaut will much prefer to walk on the destination planet.

Coordination

There was basic agreement that all projects for the next five-year period should be coordinated by one of two leaders: a principal investigator for immortality (PII) or a principal investigator for the perfect human (PIPH). The first project will concentrate on cryonics. It will perfect ways to freeze and store embryos, fetuses, and live (but near-death) children and adults. In addition, this project will continue its development of a totally artificial body that can serve as a receptacle for the human brain. It was recognized that in the absence of renewable brain tissue, immortality of the individual will have to rely on computer technology: dumping the entire content of the human brain onto a computer disk, and then updating copies of that disk during the life of the continuing (new?) artificial body—computer-driven entity. To help move this project along, the existing portions of the project will be shifted away from the goal of creating the ultimate fighting machine to creating the immortal citizen. [*NATIONAL SECURITY DELETIONS*]

The second project will devote all of its efforts for the next five years to

1) the detection and cure of genetic diseases in the early human embryo; and 2) the enhancement of human characteristics in the early human embryo. We will be looking to genetically engineer a taller, stronger, smarter, and more beautiful human with a longer life span. We will be kept informed of all developments at all labs sponsored in whole or in part by the NIH/Department of Energy Human Genome Project.

Public Relations

The group then discussed the possible reaction to PP2020 by President Clinton (if he finds out about it). Dr. Peach noted that since World War II only Truman (who started the program) and Kennedy (who found out about it a week before he was assassinated) ever learned of PP2020. It is unlikely Clinton will ever hear of it. If he does, he will likely respond with initial horror. The group predicted a typical "Frankenstein reaction" in which the president says we are overstepping ourselves, fooling with things that belong to God and not to man, and that we should end the project before its results turn on us and destroy us the way Frankenstein's monster eventually destroyed him and his family.

Dr. Velvet then played a surveillance tape of a 1984 conversation between the Secretary of Health and Human Services, his speechwriter, and an unidentified doctor. [*Author's note: The transcript of the following tape was obtained by the author from a member of PP2020 two years ago, and this member speculates that Dr. Velvet's unit (the surveillance unit) purposely planted the minutes of the PP2020 meeting in the FOI files as a payback for this earlier disclosure, a speculation that seems reasonable.*]

IN SERVICE: HEALTH DEPT/EXE 3.1.84 VOICE-ACTIVATED TAPE FILE 84: HEAL75932EX

> SECRETARY: I need something good for openers with the Senate Finance Committee. Those guys wanted a management-whiz type in this job, not a practicing physician. They're stuck with me for now but they probably don't like it much.
>
> SPEECHWRITER: There's a lot of paranoia in the country that the whole works is going down the tubes—that the average guy's got nothing to say because of a gigantic bureaucracy in Washington that has lost touch with everything but power. Individuality is out, conformity is in. The art of medicine is going to hell. Medical ethics is being transformed into business ethics. What the country needs is someone to tell them about the good things progress has

given us. Here's my plan. Everyone's half crazy worrying about 1984. We get 1984 this and 1984 that, it's enough to make you throw up. You put it on the line. Here we are in 1984. Orwell predicted this and that; well, it hasn't happened. In fact, as far as our medical and scientific community goes, we've continued to work to foster individual freedom and initiative. You pledge that you will foster this tradition, and the benefits of medical progress will be available to all citizens.

SECRETARY: Spell it out for me. It's been a long time since I've read *1984*.

SPEECHWRITER: Orwell envisions this highly structured society, the ultimate totalitarian dictatorship with "Big Brother" at the helm. Big Brother broadcasts his constant messages and watches his subjects by means of telescreens in every room and every public place. The citizens' activities are directed by slogans that tend to negate thought process and the language is constantly being simplified to eliminate thought altogether. The principal slogans are "War is Peace," "Freedom is Slavery," and "Ignorance is Strength." All books have been destroyed and the news is completely managed. If Big Brother wants to change history, he merely rewites the newspapers in his archives—the only permanent record in existence. People who don't conform to the wishes of the government are imprisoned, tortured, brainwashed, and released only after their will to resist has been completely destroyed. It is total government founded on fear.

SECRETARY: What does all that have to do with the United States? Other than the use of slogans, I don't see any parallel. And what's wrong with "Health is Happiness" anyway?

SPEECHWRITER: That's the point, chief. *1984* has been blown way out of proportion. People shouldn't be worried about it; everything is under control. Take Orwell's concept of "doublethink," the ability to hold two contradictory beliefs simultaneously, and accept both of them. The good party member does this at all times. Thus when the party alters history or changes its interpretation of an event or belief, there can be an immediate acceptance of the new line. Doublethink has the advantage of divorcing thought completely from reality, letting one live in an imaginary world. In such a world citizens do not attempt to influence or change the real one. Fact reversal becomes a prime tool of government. The Ministry of Peace concerns itself with war, the Ministry of Truth with lies and propaganda, the Ministry of Love with torture, and the Ministry of Plenty with starvation.

VISITING DOCTOR: I get it. Like our Department of Defense is really a War Department; our Department of Agriculture is working to keep land out of production; and hell, our own Health Department is really concerned only with disease.

SPEECHWRITER: Let's forget the doublethink. How about *1984*'s main slogan, "Big Brother is Watching You." Now that's the guts of the book, and we don't have anything like that.

SECRETARY: I'm glad you're not in my planning department. Back in 1978 HHS awarded a contract to develop a cheap and efficient computer that could be used by physicians. Within another decade all physicians and hospitals who get payments from Medicare or Medicaid—and that's about 90 percent of them—will have to use this computer to enter complete patient history, diagnosis, and each and every test and result. We'll keep it all confidential, of course, but we'll be able to profile every doc in the country. We'll know the names and conditions of all his patients, his patterns of practice, his diagnostic techniques, his frequency of surgery for certain indications, and his success rates. The computer will also be linked to public health and law enforcement agencies to permit instant reporting of gunshot wounds, child abuse, drug abuse, VD, and the like. And if it's the only thing I do as secretary, I'm going to put the marginal practitioners out of business: those docs who don't know the difference between mono and leukemia, or those who still routinely treat sore throats with chloromycetin.

VISITING DOCTOR: Wait a minute. They could do that in the book, but this is the United States. You don't have the power to restrict the practice of private physicians.

SECRETARY: I'm going to let you spend a week with my legal staff. They'll tell you a thing or two. Congress has the power to turn all licensing authority over to my department. We're developing a set of implementing regulations right now that would permit our own quality assurance panel to pull the license of any physician in the lower 5 percent of the nation on any of about 500 categories that measure quality of care on a combination process-outcome scale. We're also going to be able to draw a computer map of the country based on medical specialty and population density and tell doctors where they can and can't practice.

VISITING DOCTOR: [Inaudible]. I thought we were going to use positive incentives, education and all that.

SECRETARY: That didn't work. I want to put the fear of the Lord in them. That works every time. The next phase will be to allocate all expensive medical treatments by computer.

SPEECHWRITER: Gee, chief, maybe the *1984* bit's no good. How about *Brave New World*? Huxley saw it about 600 years in the future, although he later changed that estimate to a century or so. It involves control of the population by a combination of genetic engineering, operant conditioning, and psychotropic drugs. Anyone who doesn't conform is labeled as sick and is treated. Unlike *1984*, where the goal is power, the goal of *Brave New World* is to maximize happiness. Instead of mind-altering drugs being illegal, their use is encouraged. The analogy he uses is life in a large insect community, like a beehive or anthill, where liberty is unnecessary and all work for the collective good. Now we've got nothing like that on the drawing boards, and the senators might get a kick out of looking at how Huxley went wrong in imagining man's future.

SECRETARY: They might. That is, if I could keep myself from thinking about our embryo development experiments and the Armed Forces Behavior Modification Program (top secret, of course), which makes basic training look like a cub scout jamboree weekend. As for drugs, Huxley's got it right: a drugged citizen is a happy citizen.

SPEECHWRITER: Maybe there's something in Zamiatin's *We* that you can use. That book is based on a mission to subjugate the inhabitants of other planets to mathematically faultless happiness.

SECRETARY: That's it! Forget *1984*. Our theme will be *1999*. You know, after that space program that used to be on TV. Americans love technology. They love to talk about space gadgets, ray guns, and creatures from other planets. My theme will be space-age technology in medicine and how we can retain and retrain the family doctor to be a super-healer. You know, a sort of Dr. McCoy from *Star Trek* for every citizen. Hell, I might even hold out the prospect of bringing back home visits—by telescreens, of course.

There was a brief discussion of the implications of the tape, and the meddling in health policy by neophyte appointees. It was noted that under virtually any version of Clinton's health reform proposals the centralization of all medical records in a federal computer bank will be probable; thus, the scenario envisioned by the past secretary of Health and Human Services in which we can monitor the daily activities of physicians will soon be a reality. This is beside the point of our own experiments, but the data bank itself could prove invaluable and Dr. Green will make sure that our group's projects have access to it. It was also noted that the character of Beverly Crusher of *Star Trek: The Next Generation* is the proper model now and that the TV space programs had done a terrific job of preparing the American population for novel experiments. Too bad we didn't sponsor any of them.

Some concern was expressed over the decision taken at the last meeting to cancel the "soma experiments" [L284–289] on the basis that the underclass in the U.S. was already using far more mood-altering drugs voluntarily than we could ever hope to enduce them to use through our methods. On the other hand, the short supply of these drugs, especially heroin and cocaine, has greatly contributed to the crime rate in the cities. PP2020 agreed to financially support groups dedicated to decriminalizing the use of mind-altering drugs. It was agreed that William F. Buckley, Jr., should receive any financial support he needs to continue his drug decriminalization campaign, as should the ACLU.

Discussion then returned to dealing with the president should he discover the existence of PP2020.

Our response should be that, unlike Frankenstein, we are not lone rangers. We are not working for ourselves, but for the good of the human race. We are not out for our own glory (all our work is secret and even the scientists and physicians we fund do not know our real names), but for the glory of America. Moreover, all of our projects have built-in self-destruct mechanisms and can be destroyed before anything we create can destroy us.

It was easier to justify our work when we could just say, "The Russians are doing it, and we have to beat them to it." On the other hand, we can now use the real reason: immortality and genetic perfectibility are *the* most important frontiers in science, and we either go forward and try to conquer them or we stagnate at our current level and ultimately perish. If that doesn't work, we'll tell him we're shutting down and continue business as usual. Experimentation is too important to leave to the commander-in-chief.

The meeting came to a close at midnight.

References

Annas, G. J. 1992. "Changing the Consent Rules for Desert Storm." *New England Journal of Medicine* 326:770–773.

Annas, G. J. 1993. *Standard of Care: The Law of American Bioethics*. New York: Oxford University Press.

Annas, G. J., and S. Elias, eds. 1992. *Gene Mapping: Using Law and Ethics as Guides*. New York: Oxford University Press.

Annas, G. J., and M. Grodin, eds. 1992. *The Nazi Doctors and the Nuremberg Code: Human Rights in Human Experimentation*. New York: Oxford University Press.

Callahan, Daniel. 1990. *What Kind of Life: The Limits of Medical Progress*. New York: Simon and Schuster.

Callahan, Daniel. 1993. *The Troubled Dream of Life*. New York: Simon and Schuster.

Committee to Evaluate the Artificial Heart Program, Institute of Medicine. 1991. *The Artificial Heart: Prototypes, Policies and Patients*. Washington, D.C.: National Academy Press.

Institute of Medicine. 1993. *Veterans at Risk: The Health Effects of Mustard Gas and Lewisite*. Washington, D.C.: National Academy Press.

Lawrence, R. J. 1985. "David the 'Bubble Boy' and the Boundaries of the Human." *Journal of the American Medical Association* 253:74–76.

Najarian, J. S. 1992. "Overview of In Vivo Xenotransplantation Studies: Prospects for the Future." *Transplantation Proceedings* 24:733–737.

Nature. 1993. (February 11):479.

"1984 and Beyond, a Symposium." 1979. *American Medical News* (January 26):1–13.

President's Commission for the Study of Ethical Problems in Medicine. 1982. *Splicing Life: The Social and Ethical Issues of Genetic Engineering with Human Beings*. Washington, D.C.: U.S. Department of Health and Human Services.

Remington, C. L. 1972. "An Experimental Study of Man's Genetic Relationship to Great Apes by Means of Interspecific Hybridization." In J. Katz, ed., *Experimentation with Human Beings*, pp. 461–464. New York: Russell Sage.

Sargent, P., ed. 1976. *Bio-Futures: Science Fiction Stories about Biological Metamorphosis*. New York: Vintage.

Thomas, G. 1989. *Journey into Madness: The True Story of Secret CIA Mind Control and Medical Abuse*. New York: Bantam.

United States v. Stanley. 1987. 483 U.S. 669.

U. S. Congress, Office of Technology Assessment. 1993. *Protecting Privacy in Computerized Medical Information*. Washington D.C.: U.S. G.P.O.

Welsome, E. 1993. "The Plutonium Experiment." *The Alguquerque Tribune*, November 15–17.

8

The Prospect of Human
Genetic Engineering

Robert L. Sinsheimer

I want to look to a future time, well after the Human Genome Project is completed—when all of the human genes are known, their detailed interconnections have been elaborated, and the complex working of the human genome simulated on a computer. To a time when even the intricate interactions of genome and environment—of nature and nurture during development—are becoming clear. And to a time when the potential of selected gene or gene group replacement in the egg or sperm or somatic cell is well realized.

The advent of genetic engineering—derived from an understanding of the molecular bases of genetic structure and function—provides the potential for the design and redesign of living matter to human purpose. And living matter includes homo sapiens.

To what use will humanity put this capacity—this ability to define the future human genomes? And how will such a power affect the nature of humankind? The answers to such questions are not clear. This paper is an attempt to explore some facets of this conundrum.

There *will* be a conundrum. For once knowledge—the potential—is available—and since we know the path to this knowledge, in a sense it already is—then the decision *not* to deploy such knowledge is in itself as conscious, as fateful, as any specific manner of its use.

Constraints

There will be constraints upon the scope of genetic engineering, both biological and social. Just as the laws of physical and chemical interaction limit the structures and materials we can form of inanimate matter, so surely will the principles and the requirements of biological organization constrain the forms of animate matter we may design and produce. Design choices made early in development must constrain later options.

However, evolution suggests that many choices are available. The fossil record tells us that many body plans other than those now extant are possible. In their time these failed the harsh test of natural selection, but with human nurture or under specified conditions, such forms might flourish. Nor has three billion years necessarily exhausted evolutionary possibilities.

Genetic engineering may be somatic—to affect only the treated individual—or genetic—to affect the treated individual and his/her/its descendants. The uncertainties associated with all initial attempts will likely restrict such efforts, at least in humans, to somatic therapy.

"Genetic engineering" need not be understood necessarily to involve the direct modification of DNA sequences. In the course of evolution, organisms have developed a variety of means for the *control* of gene expression. The diversity of differentiated cells in the more advanced species illustrates the potential latent in such patterns of control. Indeed, simple variation in the timing of specific gene expression during embryonic development is thought to have played a major role in some steps of evolutionary change.

Known means of control include specific gene activators and repressors and transcription factors, variation in the "strength" of promoters or enhancers or terminators, methylation of key cytosine residues, modification of histones at key sites, and structural changes, condensation and decondensation, of chromatin. Others likely remain to be discovered.

Modification of control could in principle be accomplished by external provision of appropriate chemical or biological agents, such as hormones, growth factors, or "antisense" RNA. Such agents might be needed only during a critical period of development, or until puberty, or throughout life. Conversely, to be effective, such treatments may well have to be applied during fetal development, which would require elaboration of the requisite technology.

Initially, genetic engineering will be technically limited to discrete, single-gene functions—as in the relief of human diseases traceable to specific gene defects—or to the modification of specific physical traits, such as height or pigmentation. But with time, more complex, multi-gene traits will likely become amenable to genetic modification.

And, of course, there will be societal and cultural constraints that may well be the most determinative. Because these will derive from cultures yet evolving, often in the process of swift change, they are the most difficult to anticipate. In Western cultures, at least, our attitudes toward "endangered species" or the use of "body-enhancing drugs" (even those that occur naturally in the body) suggest a predilection to preserve the biological world as we have inherited it and know it, a policy of conservation. One might thus anticipate a social hesitance to consider the introduction of novel or significantly modified species—including homo sapiens.

Genetic engineering presumably will be most effective if applied prior to conception or early in development. Such action will clearly amount to human experimentation without the "informed consent of the subject." To what extent will society permit such experiments? What would happen to the experimental "failures"? What assurance of success would be required? Who would assume, or be assigned, responsibility?

Indeed, the acquisition of the knowledge necessary to perform such experiments successfully would seem to be a major hurdle to the achievement of human genetic engineering. Animal models and computer simulation will be of assistance, but are not likely to be definitive. The experiments of nature, natural human variation, will likely provide the best evidence for the potential and prognosis of genetic redesign.

The implications of hazard may well long confine human genetic engineering to the relief of those genetic defects known to be certain to produce a grievous outcome. Here the justification for attempts, even if hazardous, to alleviate the condition is self-evident. Extension of genetic engineering beyond such circumstances will depend upon societal values and motivations (economic, political, military) of a future era.

Social Effects

One very likely consequence of the greater understanding of the human genome will be a much deeper and surer comprehension of the extent to which individual characteristics are biologically determined or, alternatively, are culturally malleable. Simple observations, pedigree studies, and especially comparisons of human twins have provided evidence of major biological influence upon physical characteristics, personality traits, even intellectual or artistic capacities. However, lacking direct ties to specific genes, such correlations have remained amorphous and controversial. Definitive genetic understanding, accompanied by known functional cause-and-effect relationship will surely markedly shrink the areas of controversy.

A broader and firmer recognition of biological determination will surely impact upon the individual sense of personal responsibility. Democratic social systems rely ultimately upon an acceptance of personal responsibility. The consequences of diminution of that core value are difficult to foresee. In democratic societies we have always struggled to reconcile our ideals of human equality with the reality of genetic inequality—of unequal luck in the genetic "lottery." It has been a historic fact that we are not born with equal capacities, physical or mental. In our society, of course, various genetic endowments can lead to very different lives—and rewards. Until now this fateful allotment has been outside human control, much as the tides or the seasons.

Genetic inequality has always been both the Achilles heel and the bulwark of democracy. The Jeffersonian ideal that "all men are created equal" is belied by the inexorable results of the genetic lottery. But the potential for the demographically unpredictable appearance of talent has provided the rationale for many democratic institutions.

But what if the genetic lottery were no longer inexorable—if chance were replaced by calculation?

If—and when—it becomes possible to predetermine various physical or mental characteristics, who will do this? The parents, the community? And who will bear the responsibility? And how will this impact upon the coherence and integrity of the society, upon the individuals who will know that their very inheritance was a product, not of chance, but of calculation? This must change our basic conception of the human condition. Different societies and cultures may well view this issue in very different ways.

And then what of the progeny—those whose genetic qualities have been preselected? How will they cope with genetic predestination? How will they view their lives, their parents, their community?

How might parents manage this ability to select the genetic traits of their children? And how will the community—the family, the group, the nation, the planetary society—exert its influence, protect its interests, foster the "common good."

Parents often seek to perpetuate certain "family traits"—physical appearance, literary or artistic or analytical or athletic skills, personality features such as perseverance, caring, adventurousness, boisterousness, "bookishness," whether the child is active or reflective, etc. In our time their ability to do so has been limited by the genetic lottery associated with mating. Within those limits, society has generally given parents great freedom to guide their children's paths—to launch them on tennis or swimming or ice skating or musical careers at an early age—and to foster predilections toward a profession, law or medicine or journalism or science. The widespread conflicts of adolescence bear witness to the limits of such parental predetermination. Indeed, personality traits conducive to acceptance of such guidance might become a primary objective.

Such effective imposition of parental choice might need a communal counterweight to preserve societal balance. A simple example would be to retain equal numbers of males and females (if this were desired). A balance of athletes and scholars, of artists and entrepreneurs, etc., might somehow need to be maintained.

In this future time, the necessity to limit procreation will have long since justified state intervention in this area of human life. And with state intervention may, expectably, come a concern with quality as well as quantity. For human societies have surely evolved in forms adapted to make use of the genetic diversity found in our population. Any marked shifts—extensions or diminutions or new imbalances—in that diversity would require societal adaptation, planned or unplanned.

Philosophical Questions

In a sense the history of civilization has been the record of the struggle between the urge to self-expression and the restraints imposed by the community—which in turn are necessary so that self-expression can flourish beyond that needed for mere survival. In early societies, slave power provided affluence for a few, which greatly enlarged their scope of self-expression. In our technological age, machine power has done the same for a much greater number. Genetic engineering will open a wholly new dimension of the age-old struggle between individual will and communal need.

Science-fiction authors have proposed that genetic engineering would convert human society to a genetically designed, functionally differentiated caste or "hivelike" system. But these scenarios overlook the potential of computer-controlled machines that could better perform the menial, reiterative tasks assigned in these scripts to the lower castes or precisely programmed hive members.

These scenarios also assume complete control of the entire human genome to be molded and shaped to rigid specifications. In fact, of course, knowledge about and manipulation of small, functionally discrete segments of the genome will long precede any possibility of global genetic redesign.

Our common evolution, our shared, if resigned, acceptance of the outcomes of the genetic lottery have long reinforced the concept of human brotherhood. With the exception of rare genetic "sports," human diversity has remained within accustomed bounds—and over the generations the lottery has evened out the genetic pedigrees and allowed individual talents to arise randomly throughout society.

The diversity of the human species has been a source of great cultural richness. It is also a source of societal fragmentation. Democratic societies exist in a state of tension that seeks to allow cultural variety to flower, yet avoids social disintegration. Will human genetic engineering expand or contract genetic diversity?

To what extent does our sense of our common humanity stem from the unspoken realization that we are each the hapless, unwitting product of that genetic lottery—that, in truth, "there but for the grace of God go I"?

The "human condition" is about to change. We are one of the last generations to know our form of humanity. Humankind is about to evolve to homo cyberneticus. Many will likely prefer that we eschew such an adventure, such an undefinable break in the course of human history. The known is more comfortable than the unknown. In evolution and indeed in human history, however, the inevitable forces of competition have always overcome the tendencies to inertia. Will that pattern continue as we move from the natural world that bore us into the synthetic world created by our own intellect?

9

Manipulating Human Life: Is There No End to It?

Daniel Callahan

The title of this essay, and the question it raises, is meant to be ambiguous. In asking whether there is any "end" to the manipulation of human life, I actually intend to pose three questions. The first, and the easiest, is whether we are likely to see any cessation of efforts to manipulate human life, by which I mean attempts to change, improve, and modify that life, whether by genetic, surgical, pharmaceutical, or other medical means.

There is only one plausible answer to that question: no. Unless we human beings run short of medical ingenuity—not likely—or run out of unhappiness with some aspect or other of our lives—an even less likely eventuality—we can assume a continuing effort to manipulate our very nature. I suspect we would do so even if we concluded that, on balance, it was a bad idea. There would always be the lure of finding a way to do it better, to avoid the errors of the past, to give it one more try. Just one. And one more. Just as the desire for knowledge is part of our human nature, as Aristotle pointed out long ago, it seems no less part of our nature to take arms against the sea of troubles which that same nature, in its mental or physical manifestations, washes over us.

The second and third questions are more difficult. The second is whether it is a good and defensible activity to endlessly manipulate human life. To ask "is there no end to it?" is to ask whether there *ought* to be some end to it, some point at which we might decide that we have gone far enough, that point—if we could know and discern it—at which the aggregate harms begin to outweigh the aggregate benefits, the evils greater than the goods? Or that there ought to be an end to it because it entails evils of a kind that ought not to be tolerated, whatever the apparent overall gains or entailing means that are unacceptable no matter how noble and good the ends?

The third question is meant to recall, and to then ask again but in a revised form, an ancient question about our human *telos*: is there some goal—a utopian purpose in our manipulation, or some as-yet-unrealized inherent human end—toward which we could say the manipulation is aiming, wittingly or not? Does there lurk out there, short of heaven but in some kind of platonic form, an ideal human life, one toward which our manipulations might or could converge?

An immediate puzzle arises once these questions have been posed. If I am correct in assuming that human beings are likely to continue manipulating human life even if the results are bad, does it not become irrelevant to ask whether there *ought* to be some end to it? Isn't that second question beside the point? Not necessarily. At a minimum, the existence of some belief or feeling that there is and should be some point beyond which we should not go can introduce a healthy attitude of caution. We will at least look before we leap, even if we do not look very much. We already make gestures in that direction in our various regulatory activities to control and monitor medical advances. The regulations are a tribute paid to our sense of uncertainty about how far science should push, but also a form of official sanction that progress should be pursued. Moreover, however intolerable regulations may be at times, they are nowhere near as intolerable as a flat ban on biomedical research would be. The former may be intolerable; the latter is unthinkable, at least in our culture.

But there is another, and more serious, reason for asking whether there *ought* to be some end to the manipulation of human nature. Do we know where we are going? Do we know what biomedical innovations will improve the human condition? Do we know, that is, just what it is that would make us happy and flourishing as human beings? Do we have in mind, even if implicitly and inchoately, some end toward which our medical manipulation is tending, some ideal outcome?

I do not know that anyone would claim there is such an outcome, even though it is easy enough to find utopian dreams and fantasies in great number. These include, for instance, the conquest of the degenerative diseases of old age and the chronic illnesses of all age groups, a radical extension of average life expectancy, the compression of morbidity, the eradication of genetic disease, and the creation of new genetic possibilities, and so on.

What is striking about such medical dreams in the scientific literature (as distinguished from science-fiction writing), however, is not their projection of some generally improved human state or human nature. They appear instead more as a one-by-one, incremental set of improvements, focused on this or that discrete condition or malady, but not on all of them together as a unified goal for the medical enterprise. Each medical specialty has its own hopes and fantasies, but there is no overarching vision that collects all of them together and sets a unified goal (such as, for instance, the elimination of all bodily pain and psychological suffering).

If, then, there is no single, unified goal toward which medical research and intervention are in fact aiming—and thus by implication no general standard by which to measure whether the overall progress is real or illusory—a different kind of question can then be raised. If we do not know where we are going, and perhaps can not know, can we agree on where we should *not* be going? If we accept continuing intervention as inevitable, that is, can we specify some kinds of intervention as harmful and unacceptable? Is there some level of inviolability that we should recognize as setting an outer limit to our efforts in improving the human condition?

This question can be answered in two very different ways, according to what I will call the conventions of modernism and traditionalism. The conventions of modernism are essentially consequentialist: our medical interventions should not go in those directions that increase the likelihood of more harms than benefits. Those conventions, however, set no absolute or intrinsic standards of benefits or harms, nor are they altogether precise about what counts as a benefit or harm. We are free instead to pursue our preferences, admonished only to respect individual freedom and autonomy, to avoid doing physical or psychological harm to others, to preserve by good husbandry the collective human future (especially genetically and environmentally), and to seek an equitable distribution of the fruits of medical advancement.

Traditional conventions move in a different direction. They have sought to find some intrinsic or inherent standards of appraisal and judgment. This has sometimes taken the form of attempts to define an essence of human nature; that would then give us a standard by which to judge whether that nature was being enhanced or harmed by medical or scientific interventions. At other times the emphasis has fallen on efforts to define some actions that would be intrinsically harmful or degrading, actions that would violate in some fundamental way the very notion of what it means to be human. At still other times the emphasis has fallen on an effort to use our emotional repugnance toward this or that intervention, our spontaneous intuitive responses, as the foundation for condemnation.

While the emphasis falls in different places, each of these conventions of traditionalism shares the conviction that, at some point, medical manipulations or interventions could cross some line that should not be crossed.

The determination of that line can not be reduced to a calculus of harms exceeding benefits. It would be, in contrast, a line that should not be crossed even if it offered the promise of some great benefits.

How are we to choose between these two conventions? I want to argue that neither of them is satisfactory, and that a third alternative needs to be developed. In what follows I want to offer criticisms of both conventions, but also ask what we might want to preserve from them, and then sketch another way we might go in the future. I will first, and probably too pre-emptorily, take on the convention of consequentialism.

Consequentialism, whether in its utilitarian or other forms, has an obvious attraction. It holds that our actions have effects, good and bad, and the measure for those actions should be whether the good results outbalance the bad. There is a commonsensical quality about that argument; it is a way human beings routinely deal with many matters of uncertainty. It seems all the more reasonable when dealing with new and innovative medical manipulations. We can hardly know in advance with any certainty whether our manipulations will either achieve their intended aims; or, if they do so, whether they will satisfy the desires or interests that led us to undertake them; or, moreover, whether they will do so without producing undesirable and unforseen side effects. It seems eminently reasonable, therefore, to both make an advance judgment about the likelihood that a manipulation will work, both in the sense of achieving its intended goal and also leaving us satisfied that the goal was worth achieving.

Yet consequentialism has some profound problems, and all the more so with those medical interventions and manipulations that take human life in new, wholly unexplored directions. Some of the objections are old and familiar. By what standards do we judge whether the consequences of an action are good or bad? Are those standards intrinsic and nonconsequentialist, or are they themselves also consequentialist? If the former, where are we to find them? If we think (following a main line of utilitarian thought) that the standard of judgment is to be found in satisfying our preferences, can we judge whether our preferences are good or bad? Should we have such preferences? If consequentialism is a purely formal standard, empty of content, then it will give us only the illusion of moral guidance. But if it has some real substance, that substance would have to rest on something more solid than a maximizing of our pleasures or preferences—something that would have to look suspiciously like the intrinsic standards sought by conventional traditionalism.

All of these shortcomings are magnified with medical interventions, particularly those that could decisively change the human condition. I have in mind here, for example, significant genetic manipulations with unforeseeable effects on future generations, or dramatic changes in life expectancy, affecting our notions of the life cycle or intergenerational relationships and obligations. The problem here is that we have no available record of human history, or even any good theory, to know just what those changes might mean. We cannot therefore find any solid ground from which to make reasonable judgments about future consequences. If the past record of efforts to extrapolate from present knowledge and experience to long-term results is any guide, we are as likely to be wrong as right in our judgments, not much better off than flipping a coin.

Even worse, it is wholly impossible to determine what the aggregate, or synergistic, consequences of numerous simultaneous interventions will be, e.g., genetic manipulations taking place at the same time as life expectancy is increasing, in turn taking place at the same time as cultures and expectations are changing, and all this on top of environmental changes, affecting the background conditions of all the other alterations. No form of cost-benefit analysis, or futuristic calculi, can handle so many variables in any reliable way.

I can only conclude that conventional consequentialism can not possibly tell us either where to go or where to stop. Of course we should pay attention to consequences, and try to calculate them as best we can. But consequentialism can not provide us with any solid guidance—at best hints and warnings, at worst the illusion of wisdom but none of the substance.

Does conventional traditionalism offer a more promising route? In a fine essay on the marketing of transplantable organs, Leon R. Kass sensitively explores the use of our "untutored repugnance," as a standard for drawing a line over which our desire to save and improve human life should not step (Kass 1992:69). Why, he asks, does he find the idea of selling organs, of making them a market item, "so offensive," even if he can at the same time see how a case could be made for such an arrangement? He concludes that the notion of a market in organs, even if it draws on some basic Western principles, is repugnant because those principles "painfully collide here with certain other notions of decency and propriety, pre-modern and quasi-religious, such as the sanctity of man's bodily integrity and respect owed to his mortal remains" (Kass 1992:68). In the face of "rational expertise and policy analysis," we should pay attention to "notions that are expressed and imbedded in our untutored repugnance at the thought of markets in human flesh"(Kass 1992:69). Immanuel Kant's rejection of the sale of body parts, two centuries earlier, on grounds of its intrinsically degrading nature, invokes the same sense of repugnance (Chadwick 1989).

This is an appealing direction in which to go. There is no doubt that most people do feel a sense of repugnance at some forms of medical manipulation and at least a profound, though often unarticulated, uneasiness about others. Only the most doctrinaire of rationalists, not to mention the least self-perceptive, would dismiss out of hand our feelings of moral repugnance and uneasiness. They are *a* guide (if not *the* guide) to our conduct, an indispensable point of departure for moral judgment (Callahan 1991). Yet there are also some serious problems here. It is, first of all, not clear that there are any utterly "untutored repugnances," that is, repugnances that have not been instilled by the culture in which we are imbedded, or repugnances that do not have some rational (even consequentialist) basis.

Even the seemingly universal repugnance against cannibalism (to which Kass oddly likens organ transplantation) seems to me understandable as a primitive and collective judgment that human community would be impossible if humans looked upon each other's bodies as sources of nutrition. It would bespeak a strange idea of a common life, much less an ideal common life, and it would introduce a thoroughgoing mutual insecurity. The repugnance we feel is nothing less, I suspect, than a deeply tutored cultural insight, even if we have not noticed the tutoring, not something springing full blown from some genetic or other hidden biological source.

Whether that is true or not, we must always be ready to question what we find repugnant, if only to affirm even more strongly the importance of honoring the repugnance toward what should repel us and to keep its force morally viable. But we must also ask: toward what ought we to feel repugnance? A feeling of repugnance is not, as such, a self-evidently valid guide to moral conduct. It can be right, and illuminating, or wrong, and misleading. We should have learned from our own lives in particular, and human history in general, that what we sometimes earlier took to be an untutored, self-evidently valid repugnance was simply wrong, and in some cases disastrously so. No one who grew up in the south, as I did, can readily forget our own error in thinking that our palpably felt hostility toward the mixing, much less the intermarriage, of the races was a matter of "untutored repugnance," the natural order of things. It was painful to learn that it had been instilled and tutored, all the more deceptively because rarely articulated directly.

It is noticeable, in fact, that the language Kass uses to characterize those concepts that he believes should serve as moral guides has a distinctly social, rather than narrowly psychological, flavor to it. "What, then," he asks, "is the fitting or suitable or seemly or decent or proper way to think about and treat the human body, living and dead?"(Kass 1992:70). We find an answer to this question, he suggests, by considering the meaning of the body, a meaning that encompasses the integrity and wholeness of the body; and it will be the violation of that integrity that will elicit repugnance, a repugnance that will, for instance, have to be overcome to accept surgery. It is not clear in Kass's analysis, however, whether our felt repugnances are a result of our societal notions of what is fitting and seemly, or whether it is the untutored repugnances that shape our notions of them— or whether there is some reciprocal relationship between them (which strikes me as most plausible).

In any case, Kass's own analysis suggests that it is not an "untutored repugnance" but an implicit analysis and rational judgment that lies behind the repugnance. For just that reason, then, it is open to us to understand more deeply just how far, and with what validity, we should trust our repugnances and the implicit rationales behind them. The ways in which they get translated into our common life is by socially conveyed senses of "seemly," "decent," "proper," and the like, terms of social art, not purely terms describing emotions. Our "untutored repugnances," therefore, are probably neither wholly untutored in their origins nor do they long remain without a translation into the modes of social discourse. This means we must pass judgment on both the repugnance we feel—should we feel it—and on the way it gets brought into our common life by means of the social tutoring of what is proper and seemly.

The necessity of judgment is also unavoidable because there will be occasions when our repugnances come into conflict with each other. Kass himself concedes that, repugnance or not, he would "probably make every effort and spare no expense to obtain a suitable life-saving kidney for [his] own child"(Kass 1992:68). Oddly enough, he does not explain *why*, "regardless of all [his] arguments to the contrary," he would do so. I surmise that the reason is precisely the existence within him (and most everyone else) of a repugnance against the idea of allowing someone to die when there lies at hand the means to save the life of that person. I would also surmise that this is not an untutored repugnance, but one that emerged historically with the advent of medically effective means to save life, and which has now become buried deep in our psychic lives and cultural institutions.

What I primarily want to suggest, however, is that our repugnances will not necessarily be wholly consistent with each other; they will on occasion come into direct conflict. We must then decide how to choose among them, asking which ones are comparatively more or less compelling under what circumstances—and, once that is done, to educate ourselves and others about what is "proper" and "seemly." On the whole, it seems fair to say, it would now appear improper and unseemly to most people to allow someone to die out of a felt repugnance at the idea of an organ transplant. We would feel, as Kass's admission of what he would do were it his own child seems to imply, a positive duty to put aside the feeling of repugnance at transplantation (and even the sale or purchase of an organ) in order to save the life; or, put differently, to allow the repugnance at the prospect of a lost life to take precedence over the repugnance against transplantation, even a commercialized transplantation.

What I want to draw from this analysis is not a case against the importance of our feelings of repugnance, or against the importance of tutoring ourselves as a community on what is seemly and proper. I only want to claim, hardly in a controversial way, that our repugnances must, at some point, be examined critically. They do not carry their own validity with them. At the same time, a morally strong culture will have to depend heavily on its shared repugnances, those that have withstood examination (even if not by everyone and even if the justification is more implicit than explicit), and which have been socially translated into the moral practices, attitudes, and character traits that we will call fitting and proper.

But how are we to carry out such an examination? By what standards are we to measure our repugnances and, beyond them, what our supposed elders and betters tell us is fitting and seemly? Are we not back where we started: by looking to their consequences, or by looking still more deeply for some kind of certain measure of what is inherently repugnant or intrinsically degrading?

I have come to think such a search will be in vain, or even if partially successful will not tell us enough to be all that helpful. Just as Descartes was wrong to think we could find some perfect starting point for human certainty, we are likely to be wrong in thinking we can find some self-evidently inviolable line we ought not to cross in manipulating human life. There are still some perfectly valid old lines that should not be crossed, but affirming them does not take us very far into our "brave new world." We can all agree readily enough, for instance, that we should not kill one innocent person to save the life of another (hence, no liver transplants from living donors). But that does not offer much guidance when it is not a matter of one life being used to save another but of comparing goods and evils other than those of directly taking life, e.g., the selling of one kidney in order to feed one's children, or simply as a source of additional discretionary income.

The worst conflicts then are likely to be those where, without taking the life of another, we can save someone's life by doing something we find doubtful at best or repugnant at worst. With those conflicts we are not likely to find what the lawyers would call a "bright line" or the rest of us a line undeniably valid and potent. None has yet appeared. It is helpful, to be sure, to be able to speak of what is inherently degrading or to note and respect some of our deepest repugnances. But even if we can achieve some rough agreement about that, that is not likely to help us with the hard cases, or those where our repugnances come into conflict, or where it seems inherently degrading both to act and not to act.

I want to sketch a possible third way of dealing with the problem at issue here, one that is not exclusively dependent on consequentialism or on feelings of what is repugnant or intrinsically degrading. Neither convention offers a sufficiently strong basis to offer serious, sustained resistance to the likely ongoing efforts to transcend limits, taboos, and traditional barriers in the forward march of biomedicine. My suggested approach will, however, make partial use of both those conventional approaches, but add some additional elements as well.

Let me first set the stage for my suggested approach. I take it for granted, even if I can not fully prove it, that human beings can go too far in their medical manipulations and thus do serious harm to themselves. I no less take it for granted that human beings can degrade and demean themselves. Unfortunately, we may not know untili after the fact rather than before that we have crossed a line we should not have crossed. And I can guess that it will happen again. Why do I say there will be ongoing efforts to transcend biomedical limits and barriers? The first reason is the cultural and moral power of medicine itself. That power draws on a number of almost irresistible elements: its promise to save and improve human life and to conquer illness and disease—a particularly potent force when what has aptly been called the "rescue principle" is at stake, that is, the direct saving of life; its promise to increase human choice and autonomy, a potent societal value; the gathering force of the disability rights movement, making a life with disability increasingly acceptable and protectable—and making a medicine that allows people to function in the face of disability all the more attractive and acceptable; and the high value given to scientific and medical progress, placing enormous burdens of disproof on those who would stand in its way.

I deliberately refrain here from attempting any kind of moral analysis or judgment of what I call the "irresistible elements." That would take me too far afield in a short paper. I only want to note their cultural power and, in particular, their power to muscle their way past taboos and efforts to draw lines. Not only do those elements tend to bias any examination of the consequences of progress in the direction of going forward (it being easier to project hoped-for benefits than to prove the certainty of harms). They also run roughshod over our repugnances, mainly by invoking one repugnance to overcome another (e.g., the kind of repugnance felt by Kass at allowing a child to die if a transplant would be available), or run afoul of pluralistic differences in feelings of repugnance (not all people feel repugnance at the idea of organ transplants or liken them to a form of cannibalism).

What I think needs to be fully appreciated, in short, is how much the forces that would move beyond limits and traditional taboos have going for them in our culture—and how little, by contrast, efforts to draw fixed lines have. Something else needs appreciating as well. If lines are to be drawn, and some advances considered now and forever out of bounds, two needs seem preeminent. One of them is that there be available moral principles and perspectives that make feasible the drawing of lines—that is, they must have a reasonably perspicuous and plausible rationale; and, no less importantly, they must have a strong emotional appeal, touching people's feelings as much as their minds—their violation would have to strike most people as unseemly, unfitting, and wholly objectionable.

Taken together, what is needed therefore are principles and perspectives themselves powerful enough to withstand the force of the "irresistible elements" I have described, and to do so in a way that is both rationally and emotionally appealing. A large order indeed. It is all the larger, moreover, because it is difficult to imagine finding principles that will not themselves need continuing interpretation as new medical possibilities appear. Even with relatively clear principles available with which to work, public policy can expect continuing struggles with each new advance.

I will offer here some principles that might push us in a helpful direction:

1. *Emotional repugnance should be taken seriously.* Instead of assuming that emotional reactions and repugnances should be replaced by reason alone—as is common in a policy ideology that prides itself on rationality— their source and force should always be given a full and careful airing. Why do we feel repugnance? What does it tell us about out hidden values and assumptions, and about our unconscious or only partially conscious standards of evaluation? What does it say about the kind of social tutoring that has instilled such repugnance? The rejection to date of any policy that would allow a market in organs rests on a deep repugnance to putting the body and its parts into the commercial arena. At the heart of such repugnance is doubtless a cluster of insights and intuitions: for instance, that the sale of body parts would itself reflect a social pathology that forced some people into such sales; or that the integrity of the body should not be violated save for altruistic reasons, any other reasons being endlessly open to corruption. Only by taking the repugnance as a point of departure have we been able to understand that there is good sense behind it, that the repugnance is no mere capricious anachronism.

2. *Consequences count and need to be construed as broadly as possible.* It is obvious that any public policy proposal must withstand a consequentialist scrutiny: what is likely to happen if the policy is adopted, to whom is it likely to happen, and what kind of direct and indirect effects are likely or

possible? The difficulty of implementing this principle, however, is that it will often be just about impossible to understand the long-term consequences of a medical advance or just what that advance will mean when combined with other advances. That is why it is usually so much easier to specify benefits than harms, and to specify short-term gains more than long-term liabilities.

Here I can only offer what may seem the purest, not to mention most reactionary, pipe dream: we should increasingly, in weighing consequences, assume the worst outcomes and put the burden on the optimists to overcome that assumption. I believe we have reached a point in medical progress where we can begin to assume that, unless proved otherwise, the consequences of medical advances are as likely to be harmful as beneficial—and that is precisely because we have made so much progress already, making future progress not less likely but more problematical in its beneficial outcome. Either the cost of the progress will be insupportably high, or the results will be ambiguous in their long-term value. This is surely likely to be the case in efforts to cope with the chronic and degenerative diseases of aging.

This principle will not, to be sure, directly tell us where to draw a line beyond which we should not go. But it will help us to dampen the enthusiasm for crossing all lines in the name of medical advancement that is now the reigning value and which so easily pushes aside our repugnances and hesitations. If the kind of initial enthusiasm that now greets almost any news of a medical "breakthrough" was counterbalanced by an instinctive wariness, a truculent or at least a firm "show me" quality, the struggle to set limits would be more manageable.

An analogy comes to mind. Forty or fifty years ago the prospect of a new manufacturing plant in a town brought forth great rejoicing: jobs, money, and a stronger tax base. That is no longer the likely reaction. Now that prospect will engender doubt, uneasiness, and the demand that it pass a stringent set of environmental impact standards; and few taxpayers will automatically believe any longer that their tax burden will soon be reduced. A comparable reaction to promises of medical advancements would be no less salubrious.

3. *The preservation of life merely for the sake of prolongation ought not be the highest goal of medicine.* As Leon Kass and others have reminded us, the preservation of life ought not to be the highest goal of medicine. It should have as a primary goal the avoidance of premature death, the healing of illness, the care of the sick, and the avoidance of untimely deaths that could easily be averted. But human beings are of their nature mortal creatures, destined to die. Life can, under the best of circumstances, only be prolonged for a time, not indefinitely. It is, instead, the preservation of good

health within a reasonably long lifespan that is a feasible and morally appropriate goal of medicine.

If the "rule of rescue" is to be overcome, and if a repugnance against a failure to provide any treatment that could prolong life is to be kept in reasonable check, then it is important that this principle be kept before the public eye. What medicine should strive for is to achieve as good a balance between length and quality of life as possible. That aim would put the value of preserving life in a sensible perspective, a recognition that it is good health, and the ability to function well, which ought to be the underlying rationale of the medical enterprise—and surely a reasonable goal in the formulation of public policy.

4. *The general health of the community as a whole should be the primary goal of health policy, not individual medical benefit.* The individualism of the American health care system, signaled by its emphasis on high-technology medicine primarily of benefit to individuals, is a potent force in pushing over boundary lines. But a health care system that put the overall health of the public first—and implemented that priority in its spending programs—*might* make it easier to stop progress from going in hazardous directions. It would at least have two important implications: that the rule of rescue could not so easily be invoked (for lack of high priority), and that individual needs would, in general, take second place to public needs.

There seems little doubt that, if the American system was more oriented toward public health and primary care, there would be less money for those technological "spectaculars" that seek relief for individuals. This would include organ transplants, the rescue of low-birthweight babies, and increasingly radical surgical procedures with elderly patients. All of these technological feats benefit individuals, but at a high cost and an almost infinitesimal gain to overall public mortality and morbidity outcomes.

Those are my four principles. Now a reader may well wonder whether they would in fact really be helpful in telling us which lines we should not cross. They would not, at least if the aim is to have principles that provide clear and distinct criteria for telling us what *ought* to be repugnant, and what *ought* to be understood as intrinsically harmful or degrading. The rejection of the direct killing of an innocent person to save the life of another (or many others) provides a traditional and still supremely valid principle of moral judgment. And the direct violation of the body of a person even if the benefits were great and it would not cause death is still another traditional, still valid principle (signaled by court refusals to force a sibling or parent to become an unwilling bone marrow donor even when a life is at stake). No less valid is the principle that we can not ignore the decisions of competent patients about the medical care they are, or are not, to receive.

But the hard cases in the years ahead are not likely to reduce so readily to those principles. Most troublesome in the future are likely to be those instances of small, incremental changes, not on their face obviously radical.

The purpose of my principles (meant to supplement, not replace, those just mentioned) is to implement a different strategy. It is to try to avoid in the first place those circumstances, and those public policies, that would most likely push us toward lines we would be sorry to have crossed once we had done so. We should try to avoid getting caught in those situations in the first place, aiming to significantly reduce, even if we can not altogether eliminate, temptations to press too far in the relief of suffering or the achievement of new benefits. Would these principles meet the tests I specified, that of rationality and of emotional force? The first two—the importance of our feelings and the necessity to take account of consequences—would meet them, but not necessarily at present the last two. The saving of life and the primacy of individual over common good are now well entrenched in public policy and popular sentiment. I can only say, in that case, that a major effort at public education and eventual change are therefore necessary. Precisely the indulgence of those values has made it hard to have a sensible allocation system, a reasonable set of goals for the health care system, and the possibility of restraint at the abyss of those forms of putative progress that would distort or harm our human nature.

In the end there is unlikely to be any effective way of setting boundaries for medical interventions without having medicine set within a cultural context that makes such a goal possible. I am drawn to Kass's language of what is seemly and proper precisely because it is the language of cultural shape and boundaries. But it also presupposes the possibility of some basic consensus, of a recognition that civic education must focus on the heart and feelings no less than the mind, and a willingness to live with less than full rational clarity. There will be no restraints unless medicine is part of a way of life that understands the need for restraints, particularly those that ask individuals on occasion to put aside their desires and preferences for the sake of the common good—and understanding the common good as requiring a special caution when it comes to overturning its biases and repugnances against bodily manipulation and intervention.

What I propose is, admittedly, a highly conservative approach. But only by working in that direction is there likely to be any possibility of counteracting those "irresistible elements" described above that at present work to transcend all limits. No one would have guessed, two or three decades ago, that communities could resist the blandishments of those who promised an economic cornucopia if new factories could be built. But many communities have learned to do so, by the simple device of a well-engrained skepticism about the benefits of progress. It is time for medicine to benefit from a similar skepticism, one that requires people to think about their goals, to ask hard questions, and to create a way of life that does not always seek to cross every frontier.

References

Callahan, Sidney. 1991. *In Good Conscience: Reason and Emotion in Moral Decision-making.* San Francisco: Harper/San Francisco.

Chadwick, Ruth F. 1989. "The Market for Bodily Parts: Kant and Duties to Oneself." *Journal of Applied Philosophy* 6(2):129–139.

Kass, Leon R. 1992. "Organs for Sale? Propriety, Property, and the Price of Progress." *The Public Interest* 107(Spring):65–86.

II

End-of-Life Decision Making:
Issues of Power and Policy

Introduction

Andrea L. Bonnicksen

Richard Selzer, a physician and essayist, writes of his dilemma with a patient who is in pain and dying but for whom the only way to end the pain is to give so much morphine and it would end the patient's life. The wife and mother and the patient himself agree on what must be done. "Do it," says the mother. "Do it now." Selzer administers morphine, but death does not occur (Selzer 1982:70–74).

Uneasy, he leaves the room and passes the mother on the way. "He didn't die," says Selzer. "He won't . . . or can't. He isn't ready yet." Selzer remembers the mother's answer:

" 'He is ready,' the old woman says. 'You ain't.' "

Administering a fatal dose of narcotics to ease dying is not an unknown practice in medicine, but historically it has been practiced as Selzer describes it: furtively and quietly by intuition and indirection.

While many observers agree that doctors have given lethal doses of narcotics they cannot account for the frequency or circumstance. Given the oblique presence of physician-assisted dying in the United States as a practice known only anecdotally, it is ironic that the act has received a label and entered the political lexicon as a matter upon which to be voted. An initiative to legalize physician-assisted dying appeared on the Washington state ballot in 1991, even before many articles on the merits of it as an allowed and regulated practice appeared in the professional literature and popular media. In years past, the practice of allowing "euthanasia" was debated for its morality. Today, the more neutral "physician-assisted dying" is debated as a public policy matter with proposed specific regulatory features.

In today's incarnation, assisted dying arose as a political and ethical issue following a series of maverick acts, including one doctor's unsigned essay about deliberately giving a lethal injection to a dying patient ("It's Over, Debbie" 1988), another doctor's signed essay about knowingly prescribing pills for a drug overdose (Quill 1991), a journalist's personal account of how she gathered drugs for her dying mother's planned overdose (Rollin 1985), a pathologist's invention and use of devices enabling suicide (Wilkerson 1992), and a self-help book on medical suicide written by a man who had helped his wife end her life when her cancer reached an advanced stage (Humphry 1991). Each event raised questions about the morality of persons ending their lives with the direct or indirect support of physicians, when they were terminally ill or suffering in a way that seemingly could not be controlled.

The presence of physician-assisted dying as a political issue on state ballots reflects its status as an act undergirded by power. Power themes weave through Selzer's story, for example. "Do it," says the mother, demanding, seemingly with power, that Selzer act. Selzer will not give the final dose, however, and shifts power to the patient who, he concludes, "isn't ready yet." The old woman, now powerless, throws the initiative back to the doctor. Her son is ready, she accuses, but "you ain't." The family demands, the doctor refuses, a stalemate results.

Assisted dying's odd life course from infrequent, ad hoc practice to sudden legislative issue is not unlike the way death and dying visit most families. Daily life goes on until a medical crisis confronts the family with the reality of mortality. In past decades this might have been met with reactions ranging from sadness and anger to eventual acceptance. Today, however, when about 75 percent of deaths in this country "are somehow timed or negotiated" (Malcolm this volume), the stages of dying are complicated by multiple medical decisions. Fatalism or acceptance has little place in contemporary death in medical centers. Decisions about end-of-life technologies are demanded and alternative courses of action are weighed.

In his essay in this part, Andrew H. Malcolm, an author and former reporter for the *New York Times*, writes of the way mortality unpredictably enters personal lives. For Malcolm mortality surfaced when his aging father remarked that he would rather not wake up the next day. Malcolm realized then with some surprise that the medical machines that kept his father's body going did "nothing to improve his lot." Later, his mother was hospitalized, unable to make decisions for herself. Someone had to those decisions about her end-of-life treatment and Malcolm was the one to do it. His essay shows how modern dying often compels decisions by those reluctant to assume the burden. His book, *Someday,* a widely read memoir about his mother and her death, helped give voice to the ubiquity of death and the special emotional dilemmas it raises in today's medical setting where life can be prolonged but not necessarily enhanced.

Malcolm's experience dealt with stopping medical treatments that merely staved off an inevitable death. Legislators have dealt with the forgoing or withdrawal of life-extending technologies since the 1970s when, partly in response to the Karen Ann Quinlan case, states enacted living will laws empowering individuals to write directives meant to guide end-of-life medical care if they should lose mental competence. Other state laws have enabled individuals to appoint friends or family members as proxy decision makers in the event they lost cognitive ability to make their own medical decisions. The usual presumption is that most individuals who sign advance directives (living wills or transfer of durable powers of attorney for health care) do so to ensure that heroic but futile treatments will not be used to prolong their lives.

In 1991 the federal government approved the concept of advance directives when Congress passed the Patient Self-Determination Act (PSDA). Under the terms of this law, patients entering hospitals, nursing homes, or other health care facilities are given the opportunity to sign an advance directive to give medical personnel a general idea of the patients' wishes regarding end-of-life treatment. Advance directives deal with the forgoing or withdrawing of advanced technologies. They enable patients to request full treatment or to avoid life-prolonging measures by not starting them in the first place or by withdrawing them if the prognosis is bleak. They do not facilitate aid-in-dying.

Elizabeth L. McCloskey's essay traces the legislative history of the PSDA. An assistant to U.S. Senator John Danforth (R-Mo.), a co-sponsor of the bill, McCloskey recalls going to work on the first day of her job to find a notes from the senator asking her to get a sense of the current thinking about end-of-life decision making. Her early inquiries eventually became part of a broad effort among physicians, professional associations, commentators, and lawmakers to build a policy that recognizes patient self-determination. According to McCloskey, "the final product offers federal weight behind the notion of patient participation in health care decision making."

The PSDA meets this goal in a skeletal manner by setting up an administrative structure to ease the way for patients who want to sign advance directives about their health care. It imposes no burden on patients who do not want to such a directive. While in theory the act celebrates autonomy, in practice as a federal directive it could, notes McCloskey, lead to "compulsory and perfunctory" compliance and rigid and habitual decision making that does not advance the true wishes of individual patients. Ritualistic use of advance directives, in which the mere presence of a signature sends messages about desired care, may empower health care workers more than intended if no effort is made to find out the fuller wishes of the patient. Robert F. Weir, chair of the Center for Bioethics at the University of Iowa, discusses how to keep autonomy alive as the PSDA predictably leads to more signed advance directives.

In an essay that implicitly endorses patient authority, Weir advocates for what he calls a "morally persuasive advance directive." This advance directive keeps qualitative questions alive and enables physicians to appreciate a person's full individuality in end-of-life decision making. Legislation is insidious if health care workers are guided only by what is written down, which is generally only a signature. Individuals must, notes Weir, let others know their values so that physicians and family members can respect as fully as possible their preferences, if and when they become incompetent patients, regarding the use of end-of-life technologies.

Patients who fill out values surveys or leave pictures and other reminders of their identities when cognizant protect their autonomous choices, Weir suggests. Advance directives work best when doctors are "persuaded" about a person's interests and preferences rather than left to guess at them merely by knowing that the person had signed a formal document. Public policy structures choices; morally persuasive advance directives enrich those choices and promote autonomy in the process.

Advance directives enable people to have a voice in the withholding or withdrawal of life-extending treatments. The issue of assisted dying differs in two significant ways. First, it involves mentally competent patients. Second, it is a step beyond the withholding or withdrawing of extraordinary care; it allows a deliberate act to bring a timed death. As visualized by its proponents, assisted dying is a medical procedure done at the enduring request of a terminally ill patient. Individuals are not committing suicide inasmuch as they are dying anyway. Physicians are therefore not "killing" patients, because the latter have requested the help in the face of unbearable suffering. The doctor's assistance varies in degree and type and can include, among others: 1) giving advice about how to take a lethal drug overdose; 2) giving advice *and* prescribing pills; 3) giving advice, prescribing pills, *and* being present to ensure that death occurs; and 4) administering a fatal overdose intravenously upon request.

Current terminology varies and that fact reflects the topic's complexity. Among the terms used are *physician-assisted suicide, assisted dying, aid-in-dying, physician-assisted dying,* and *voluntary euthanasia.* The first three methods are closer to assisted suicide because the patient is the one to take the pills, while the last is closer to physician-assisted dying or euthanasia in that the physician performs the act at the patient's behest.

Physician-assisted dying was first seriously defined as a public policy in November 1991 when the citizens of Washington state voted on Initiative 119. Discussed in volume II of this series, Initiative 119 would have enabled physician-assisted dying to take place if the patient was competent, if he or she clearly desired aid-in-dying, and if two physicians agreed in writing that the patient's condition was terminal. The initiative defined terminal illness as a condition deemed in writing by two physicians to be "incurable or irreversible" and, in the reasonable judgment of the physicians, that it would "result in death within six months." Terminal illness also included an irreversible coma or persistent vegetative state in which the patient had "no reasonable probability of recovery." The initiative failed by a 54–46 margin.

Critics of the Washington initiative contended, among other things, that it was not sufficiently restrictive. A year later residents in California voted on Proposition 161, the so-called Death with Dignity Act. Similar in tone to the Washington initiative but more detailed, it set forth the right of mentally competent but terminally ill adults to request aid in securing a timed end to life in a "painless, humane and dignified manner."

In the California proposition a physician could legally help a patient die if, among other things, two physicians, including the attending doctor, certified in writing that the patient's condition was terminal; the patient's request was "enduring" and made on more than one occasion; and the directive was witnessed by two unrelated people. Provisions were made for the patient to revoke the directive. The proposition stated that aid-in-dying was not suicide, and it absolved health care workers from liability if they followed the stated provisions. It also defined new crimes to cover the misuse of these provisions. For example, it would be a felony to pressure someone to sign a directive requesting aid-in-dying.

California's Proposition 161 failed by the same margin as Washington's Initiative 119: 54–46 percent. Other state measures have also been proposed, such as Michigan House Bill 5415 (1991), which shared with and added to some of the earlier provisions. Among other things, the Michigan bill proposed defining the method of aid-in-dying as "the intravenous injection of a substance causing painless and swift termination of life." It also would allow the practice to take place if the patient had either six months or less to live or suffered from pain so severe that eliminating it would cause the patient to lose awareness, and if the attending physician and one other physician have determined that the patient met detailed criteria set forth in the bill. The directive had to be signed at least two months before the death could take place and the patient had to have expressed the wish at least two times within seven days of the death. The bill would set up counseling procedures and it would define crimes relating to the abuse of physician-assisted suicide.

This bill, however, did not become law; in fact, the Michigan legislature did just the opposite in late 1992 when it passed a bill making assisting in a suicide a felony, at least temporarily while a state commission studied the matter (Wilkerson 1992). This stopgap law was enacted to give legislators time to craft a response to assisted dying while at the same time giving prosecutors a tool for stopping the activities of Dr. Jack Kevorkian, a pathologist who enabled the deaths of a number of people through machines he especially invented for the purpose.

Aid-in-dying measures are designed to give people control over their own deaths in limited circumstances. Ideally, one's death will be a "good" death, with pain managed, dignity preserved, and family present. In some cases, however, a good death is elusive, pain cannot be managed, and technological interventions thwart a person's efforts to maintain his or her dignity. The latter can be regarded as a medical failure, and physicians should listen seriously, some argue, to a patient who seeks to control the timing of death (Brody 1992).

The failures of Initiative 119 and Proposition 161 speak of the seriousness of physician-assisted dying and the speed with which it entered the policy arena as a matter to be decided upon. In the meantime, the debate over assisted death has expanded with proposals discussing the merits of physician-assisted dying that do not demand immediate policy decisions. The essay by Timothy E. Quill, Christine K. Cassel, and Diane E. Meier in this part approves physician-assisted suicide, providing clinical criteria are identified and followed. The authors condone physician-assisted suicide (they do not direct their comments to euthanasia) only if the doctor makes the means available but the patient performs the act that leads to death. They underscore the medical nature of the dying process in which a "meaningful doctor-patient relationship" is present, comfort care has been exhausted, and the patient repeatedly requests help in dying. To them, physician-assisted suicide balances power between the doctor and patient if preconditions are met and, in the end, the physician's judgment can circumvent the patient's autonomy.

Where Quill, Cassel, and Meier focus on physician-assisted suicide, the next author, David C. Thomasma, Director of the Medical Humanities Program at Loyola University, directs his comments to euthanasia. His essay questions the assumptions of power, goodness, and restraint in such criteria as proposed by Quill and collleagues. Thomasma questions not just the goodness of aid-in-dying, but also the assumption that it empowers terminally ill patients. His reach is sweeping enough, however, to be read as urging caution for physician-assisted suicide as well.

Thomasma notes that euthanasia has "always been associated with power," but that the nature of this power is ambiguous. Euthanasia is associated with patient empowerment in today's discussions but in other eras, notably the Nazi years before and during World War II, euthanasia was used by governments to deny individual life and autonomy. Tracing the coldness with which medical ideologues have terminated lives seen as "valueless," Thomasma warns of how easily practices that supposedly empower patients can meld into practices that crush them, especially in economic hard times. Thomasma is sympathetic to the fears of patients about dying in a technological era, however, and he proposes guidelines for comfort care for the dying as an alternative to legalized assisted dying. What may appear to be empowerment is not that at all, Thomasma argues, and he ends with the recommendation that we "cultivate a healthy respect for the role of evil in the human heart."

Carlos F. Gomez, a physician at the University of Virginia and the author of a book on euthanasia in the Netherlands, cautions in his essay that a practice that appears to promote a patient's autonomy may in fact turn into "unilateral decision-making on the part of physicians." He uses the Netherlands as his referent, where judicial interpretations are read as condoning euthanasia and where the practice occurs in the medical setting, although the frequency of voluntary and involuntary euthanasia is disputed. He traces the history of physician-assisted dying in the Netherlands and argues that governmental oversight does not necessarily prevent a serious abuse of the practice.

As to the issue of aid-in-dying in the United States, Gomez is worried not about "those of us who vote, and lobby, and write, and engage, and manipulate the political system to our advantage," but instead about "the marginalized, the stigmatized, the discouraged, the disenfranchised" who may be vulnerable to overzealous use of legalized aid-in-dying. He, too, suggests that aid-in-dying is a misdirected proposal and that the process of dying can be eased in alternative ways—by improving pain therapy, by recognizing families' perceptions of the demoralizing aspects of some deaths, and by placing a patient's "comfort, health, and well-being before our parochial obsession with the marvels of our technical wizardry."

Robert J. Miller, a physician and founding member and first president of the Academy of Hospice Physicians, continues with the theme set by Thomasma and Gomez that less ethically troublesome alternatives than aid-in-dying are preferable when a "good death" appears elusive. The Academy of Hospice Physicians was founded in 1988 with a vision of physicians extending their doctoring to include total patient care for patients who are dying. He recommends that the physician act as an "educator, a scientist, a politician, and philosopher" rather than as a passive promoter of autonomy who leaves patients free to choose among medical alternatives. Although he does not use the word "empowerment," his message promotes the idea that the dying patient's interests can best be promoted by sharing power with compassionate physicians. The physician can help achieve "a death with dignity that means more than a calm, controlled acceptance of death, but one that helps . . . patients die in a way that transforms the dying process into a final opportunity for self-enhancement, growth, and a search for meaning."

Although the essays by Weir, Miller, Quill, Cassel, and Meier, and Gomez recommend different avenues for trying to arrive at a good death, they all promote a model of careful patient-doctor interaction that will respect patients' wishes, reduce fears, and promote comfort. Public policy is a second or third recourse here, not the first. In a more theoretical vein, the essay that follows by David Orentlicher, a physician and attorney with the American Medical Association, notes that policies legalizing physician-assisted suicide may not only be undesirable but impossible, or at least they create intractable political conflict.

Orentlicher argues that assisted dying as a policy option runs into a contradiction in American thought between the fundamental legal principles of inalienability and egalitarianism. Inalienability refers to rights "so fundamental that they cannot be bought, sold, or otherwise transferred from one person to another." The right to life is an inalienable right, and this right cannot be compromised by aided dying. Still, policy alternatives such as Proposition 161 are written to ensure that the right to life is respected.

Even if substantive and procedural criteria are written into proposals, argues Orentlicher, they will conflict with egalitarianism, or the "equal status of each person under the law." The criteria designed to respect the right to life create distinctions that may deny persons equal treatment. To meet the criterion of egalitarianism, one may have to forfeit distinctions between who can and who cannot have access to physician-assisted suicide and thereby permit it "for everyone or no one." He notes that if "the state permits physician-assisted dying only for patients who meet a specific level of terminal illness and suffering, then it will be making the kinds of distinctions among its citizens that are particularly troublesome: distinctions that are based on judgments about the values of people's lives." He suggests the best way out of the potential dilemma is to forbid physician-assisted suicide altogether.

A distinguishing feature of contemporary biomedical policy is the dismantling of borders between the medical and the nonmedical in society. At one time medical decision making took place in a "sanctuary" of sorts in which 1) medical decision making tended to be separate from decisions about other aspects of life, 2) lobbying and monitoring essentially took place within the medical sector with physicians overseeing their own, and

3) conflicts that did move outside the medical sphere went to the courts more often than the legislatures.

Today's medical model is more akin to medical pluralism than medical sanctuary. Medical decision making has lost its discreteness, change occurs as a result of sparring among both medical and nonmedical actors, and it is not unknown for legislatures strategically to be regarded as preemptive avenues of first resort. The abortion controversy was an early bellwether of this. Whereas Justice Blackmun, writing for the Supreme Court in *Roe v. Wade* (1973), regarded pregnancy termination as a medical matter between doctor and patient, abortion has been decried by those outside the medical profession who use state legislatures and courts as avenues of first resort to prevent what they regard as a moral rather than a medical matter.

If abortion challenged the medical sanctuary during the 1970s and 1980s, it is not unreasonable to expect physician-assisted dying to do likewise, although to a lesser extent, in the 1990s. Moreover, it is not unreasonable to expect a medical matter involving another constituency to challenge the medical-societal border even further. Acquired immune deficiency syndrome (AIDS) affects, at least at present in this country, mostly men in their early and middle years. Many of those who have AIDS or who carry the human immunodeficiency virus (HIV) that leads to AIDS define their status as a social trait hitting at the core of their identity and existence.

In an essay on AIDS and empowerment, James A. Serafini, a New York psychologist, argues that AIDS is political and that the medical response to it is also political. AIDS is a lethal disease infiltrating the gay community with the insidious capacity both to unify community members at a basic psychological level and to reduce their numbers. Serafini's anger at the disease is echoed in his anger at the medical establishment, which he asserts has "appropriated the power of individuals." Medicine is "imperial" and the tactics of many in the gay community are meant to challenge this political structure.

Serafini urges a revamped structure of patient empowerment. He notes that the current system protects but does not promote autonomy. Informed consent documents and review boards "mediate against gross harm being done" but they do not enhance the patient's power: "They offer some safeguard against gross abuse, but the space between gross abuse and the enhancement of decision-making ability is vast." Members of ACT UP, a political lobbying and action group of which he is a part, "want the gap closed." He urges a shakeup of "science as usual" in matters of drug testing and he calls for enough information to be made available to people testing positive for HIV to be "advocates for their own health." Information is the key to "educational empowerment."

The essays in this part begin with the isolated voice of a journalist facing unwanted decisions at the end of the life of one beloved relative, and they end with the voice of a psychologist calling for broad, ideologically based changes in the medical research structure. In between are essays weighing alternative paths to ensure humane and compassionate end-of-life decision making both at the individual level among doctor, family, and patient, and at the policy level, where strangers have the capacity to condone, restrict, and permit activities that form choices at or near the end of life.

Recent struggles in medicine have revolved around the patient's role in decision making that force us to ask, "What should be the ideal physician-patient relationship?" (Emanuel and Emanuel 1992:2221). Similarly, matters relating to end-of-life decisions anticipate struggles revolving around the government's role in medical decision making that will challenge citizens to ask, "What should be the ideal relationship between private medical authority and public legislative action?" That the matter coalesces around death and dying—with its odd mixture of intimacy and ubiquity—foretells keen public interest; multiple voices and directions; and, if Proposition 161 and Initiative 119 are indications, the direct involvement of large numbers of citizens. Medical pluralism presents an ambitious task.

References

Anonymous. 1988. "It's Over, Debbie." *Journal of the American Medical Association* 259:272.

Brody, Howard. 1992. "Assisted Death—A Compassionate Response to a Medical Failure?" *New England Journal of Medicine* 327(19):1384–1388.

Emanuel, Ezekiel J., and Linda L. Emanuel. 1992. "Four Models of the Physician-Patient Relationship." *Journal of the American Medical Association* 267(16):2221–2226.

Humphry, Derek. 1991. *Final Exit: The Practicalities of Self-Deliverance and Assisted Suicide for the Dying.* Secaucus, N.J.: Carol Publishing Group.

Patient Self-Determination Act. 1991. Sections 4206 and 4751 of the Omnibus Budget Reconciliation Act of 1990. P.L. 101–508.

Quill, Timothy E. 1991. "A Case of Individualized Decision Making." *New England Journal of Medicine* 324(10):691–694.

Rollin, Betty. 1985. *Last Wish.* New York: Warner.

Selzer, Richard. 1982. *Letters to a Young Doctor.* New York: Simon and Schuster.

Wilkerson, Isabel. 1992. "Michigan Moves to Ban Doctors' Aiding in Suicides." *New York Times* (November 25):A7.

10

On the Road to Someday: A Personal Journey

Andrew H. Malcolm

Late one afternoon a few years ago, I walked into the bedroom of my chronically ill father. He was suffering from numerous serious though not necessarily terminal maladies, not the least of which was emphysema. Increasingly, he was tethering himself to his bed and that long, thin clear-plastic tube that flushed fresh air up his nose and eased the breathing of his cigarette-scarred lungs. He had irreparable hernias which hurt and badly strained his back. It was much easier for him just to lay down. He had, in that wonderful phrasing of George Burns, fallen in love with his bed.

There is something in us all that hates that inevitable role reversal when we become parents to our parents. The duties can range from silently fetching their forgotten purse or sweater from the restaurant table, the way we retrieve the forgotten toys of our children from the clutter of dirty dishes, to even cleaning, bathing, and tucking our parents in their own beds at nap and nighttime. Many accept these duties quietly and, well, dutifully. But I want to say clearly that for me, although natural and perhaps just, it was disgusting. My parents were my parents. I was their son. And even when I'd reached middle age with my own set of children, I didn't want that old, familiar, and comfortable relationship to change.

For most of my annual visit to their meticulously arranged apartment, my father had been acting like a pouty five-year-old trying to attract attention to his owies.

Yes, he was very ill. Yes, it was very painful. No, it would never get better. Throughout an interminable eighteen-month struggle against my mother's broken hip and lung cancer, my father had been a resolute rock, brooking no pessimism, no nay-saying, not even a discouraging word. Every day came her debilitating radiation treatments, her nervous nausea, her "sunburn," the well-meaning but mechanistic hospital technicians who nodded with familiarity as they saw this next old lady disrobe to reveal the indelible target painted on her skin for the medical machines.

In many ways, the draining experience becomes the visible treatment personified by possibly compassionate technicians and not the lethal disease eating away invisibly. Strangely, in our society so replete with wonderful technology, the fears often focus on that process, not the medical problem. Each year, for instance, fifteen percent of patients on kidney dialysis, watching their blood drained, cleansed, and pumped back in by amazing machines, voluntarily stop their treatments, imposing their own death sentence in a short time. Doesn't that make anyone else pause and think?

In his determination to beat my mother's cancer, my father made that draining routine into an event. He required her to dress up for each hospital session. So did he. While she underwent treatment, he chatted up the technicians like the conscientious plant manager he had been. He knew the workers in the cafeteria, too, and tried out his Spanish daily. He had "our table" carefully arranged when my mother emerged from radiation. There was her coffee, toast, and napkin, possibly a flower, and there was his coffee and corn muffin (maybe two). Only after she had begun to eat something would my father reveal that day's surprise destination for lunch, some new place he had scouted. After a pleasant drive he would deliver my mother to their bedroom for her nap and while she snoozed, he planned the next day's outing.

But now the cancer had been beaten, the hip healed, his son was visiting, and my father, the son of a tough one-room school marm and a farmer as dry and unrelenting as the Canadian prairies, had turned into a simpering sick man. My father was also an only child, who grew up with demanding farmyard and academic duties, broke the ice on the washbasin each winter's morning, hauled rocks and milk in horse-drawn sleighs and earned his bachelors and masters in three years because family money was running out. He generally fulfilled his stern parents' expectations to succeed, to quietly lift the family one more step up the ladder of achievement that was the unspoken assignment of immigrants in those days. Yet there he was, my childhood idol of strength and wisdom, unable to get into bed by himself, unable to sit for any period without fidgeting, unable to carry on an intelligent conversation without moaning again about his maladies.

I felt for him so strongly that I couldn't not look at him. So I stopped listening instead. The marvelous machines, medicines, and doctors could keep his body going but they could do nothing to improve his lot. Neither could I, save to extend the kind of caring ear and attitude that he had displayed during my long recovery from being a teenager. Time after time, he would eat very little for dinner, then voraciously consume junk food shortly after. He would skip his pills and exercises. He would ostentatiously absent himself from family gatherings to lay down, suggesting as he departed that everyone follow him into the bedroom to continue the discussion there, where he could rule as a supine sovereign.

My father had passed on that steely Scottish sense of sometimes frightening determination to his only child. He obviously needed a good talking to. Yet there I was procrastinating like a high school freshman facing his algebra homework, forced to choose between equations filled with x's and watching television, knowing the right choice, but making the wrong one anyway. For days I delayed confronting him.

Finally, at the end of my last afternoon there, I sat down on the opposite bed. I cleared my throat. And I said we had to have a talk. He had several loving people around him, ministering to his physical needs, doing his bidding, I said, but he wasn't keeping his part of the unsigned bargain. We seemed to be caring more about his health than he was. And he needed to shape up.

He listened very carefully to my reasoned pleading. He agreed with me. He said he knew how difficult it must have been for me to broach this subject. And then he said that most days he went to bed hoping he would not wake up.

I sat there in stunned silence. All words escaped me, the professional writer. I had my own family and a fairly long career that had involved foreign assignments and war zones, but here I was confronted with the absolutely unexpected, someone very dear to me saying that he did not want to live any longer. I had assumed, like most healthy Americans assume out of a desire for comfortable thinking and to avoid ever contemplating the "d" word, that everyone wanted to live as long as possible, as long as nature or God would allow. And then when it was time for the end, "It" would come with an inexorable finality and suddenness that required no thought or decision on anyone's part. I didn't know (and, honestly, never sought to learn) how often the end can come now at any number of places on a long, slow physical decline. But here was my own father, who taught me about always doing the best you can, about being able to overcome any obstacle, about conscientiously caring for other living creatures in my trust, here was my father, who delivered the warm baby bottle of midnight milk in my infancy, now saying his life was unbearable and he wished to die.

Five days later, in that lonely dimness of predawn in the bed he had come to see as his salvation from pain, my dad got his wish. "Cardiac failure," said the death certificate, which was signed by a doctor who did not examine the misshapen old body.

That night, as my aching head and numb mind laid down to sleep in that same bed after an endless day of funeral preparations, I went to place my glasses on the bedside table. But it was full. I replaced my glasses and peered closely. There, by the bedside, my father had placed a thumbnail-sized snapshot of his only son as a smiling, crewcut kid of twelve.

I was haunted by the entire experience. I still am. Dad's death was but part of it. Several months after the funeral I was in an airplane flying over Kansas on an assignment for the *New York Times* when I read a small article in a newspaper. It concerned an elderly man in Texas whose wife had been stricken with Alzheimer's disease years before. The husband visited her religiously every day, even though after a half-century of marriage, she no longer knew him. She spent much of the day screaming. The woman had contracted pneumonia in a nursing home, suddenly fallen into shock, and was near death. Ignoring the husband's wishes just to make her comfortable, a team of medical specialists with sophisticated machines and drug therapies had worked long, dedicated hours over the woman and brought her body, though not her mind, back into some semblance of balance. It was a real victory for humankind over the forces of darkness, something no doubt worth celebrating for a moment in the staff lounge.

The newspaper story said that the previous day the elderly man had walked into the hospital room for his morning visit. He had pulled out a pistol. He had shot his wife in the heart. And then he had shot himself in the heart, too.

Some weeks later I telephoned a spokesman for that Texas hospital. I said I wanted to talk about the elderly man who had killed his stricken wife.

And the hospital spokesman said to me, "Which one?"

That was a chilling moment, professionally and personally. I had thought, in that self-imposed emotional isolation that accompanies the death of a loved one, that my father was the only one who ever wanted out of a life of endless suffering, immune, for now, to medical technology's miracles. I thought I was the only one to feel guilt and to carry that secret in his heart. I am a professional storyteller. I sensed a powerful story to tell here, just one, of course, but one that I hadn't seen written anywhere in the popular media.

So with my editor's blessing I set out to do what became a two-part series on elderly suicides. They had climbed to twice the rate of young people in those days, although an untold number went undetected because, as in my father's case, the person was older, ill, and death was no surprise. What would announcing "suicide" accomplish? Dad's doctor wondered wearily to me.

Those two stories were it. I was to move on to others in a career that has produced several thousand. But wait. The mail began to arrive. Yes, yes, they wrote, the same thing happened in *my* family. Thank God you wrote this, they said, we thought we were the only ones in a quandary. You can't just write about the problem of elderly suicides, one state's deputy attorney general said, you must tell us where the solutions are being worked out.

Good point. That was nearly a decade ago. I have written many other stories on many other themes since then. And I have written scores of articles about many aspects of death in modern America and the ironic consequences of an advancing scientific culture that allows doctors and families, not God, to decide when death comes.

When, went the major theme, do we stop doing all the impressive technical things that we can do to keep a biological body working? When does all this equipment and skill prolong a life? When are we prolonging a death? And how do you tell the difference in an inattentive society that doesn't want to acknowledge the inevitability of death, let alone set rules to govern it? When, as one priest friend put it, do we stop trying to glue the autumn leaves back on? Who decides? And how?

Technology is advancing so rapidly, always presenting patients and families with new decisions, that society's slow-moving rulemakers can't keep up, even if they were inclined to interrupt their chronic squabbling over political turf issues. Thirty years ago no one needed to decide when to use or remove respirators; they didn't exist. About fifteen years ago no one needed to decide when to use or withhold stomach feeding tubes because the tubes and the chemical slurries did not exist. And many wonder if state legislatures, divided by powerful interest groups, are indeed the best place to debate such delicate personal issues as individual quality-of-life and end-of-life decisions.

Still the public controversies continue, fueled by a growing list of famous legal cases with names like Quinlan, Brophy, and Cruzan, and also by such infamous fatal diseases as AIDS. Quietly, hospitals and families have met in private to iron out their own ad hoc policies case by case. Usually, the doctors and families do not discuss the cases publicly afterward. So each family enters those antiseptic visiting rooms thinking it is the first to face such decisions.

I suppose it should not be surprising in a society that cannot yet agree when life begins that we have yet to reach a consensus on when life can end. It is a complex, painful decision whose priorities can change by the hour for the individuals involved. Sometimes it seems that the gods and the labs have delivered the most marvelous machines and methods to support failing bodies—lights that analyze blood through the skin, wires that clean out clogged arteries, radiation and sound waves that root out lethal anomalies, programmable respirators that read the strength of diseased lungs and push in only enough oxygen to complete the set breath, right down to sighs every few minutes. But it seems that left out of the packages are any instructions in English on when *not* to use them.

That requires a careful social consensus that may prove impossible to forge in a diverse democracy that often seems perversely intent on only one-half of the discussion equation, the talking half. Largely forgotten in the eagerness to be heard is the ability to hear the other side. Complex, painful social decisions have proven stubbornly difficult for this society to address because of all the other real and imagined distractions. Instead, we devote live TV time to learning the results of the epochal Elvis stamp contest.

Democratic societies are wonderfully rich in their freedoms. Unfortunately, democracy also includes the freedom to remain blissfully ignorant of many responsibilities that accompany such freedoms. We plan meticulously for marriage, careers, divorces, and babies, sometimes down to the precise moment of conception. We also plan carefully for taxes, the other inevitability. Munching popcorn, we watch the most graphic scenes of violence and death, real and fictitious, on our televisions.

But with American families now so widely scattered across a continent and aging retirees concentrated in the South, when it comes to talking about real death up close, we can always find some way to dodge deliberate discussions and embrace euphemisms, even with "Reach-Out America" rates. People don't die in America; they "pass away." Or, better yet, we say, "I lost my mother," as if somehow, someday some celestial security guard will come around the corner with our wandering mother in tow.

If, comfortable in her own mortality, a grandmother at the family dinner table says, "When I'm gone . . . " she is immediately cut off by a chorus from her offspring. "Oh, Grams," they say, "you're going to outlive us all." The subject is changed. The offspring have avoided confronting the elder's death and, by extension, their own. And the offspring's offspring, sitting there watching closely from behind their mountains of mashed potatoes, get the unspoken message quite clearly: death in America is right up there with sex as a conversational no-no.

As one result, despite the presumably well-known inevitability of everyone's demise, barely one-third of the population leaves a will concerning their property when they die. And despite nearly a generation of awareness since the pioneering Karen Ann Quinlan case first showed the public at large how much medical science can—and cannot—do, only an estimated ten to fifteen percent of Americans have living wills stipulating what kind of end-of-life medical care they desire. Even fewer have named proxy decision makers in the event of physical incapacitation.

Far easier to drift along in the warm belief that all progress is wonderful. That has been the widespread assumption for a century or two. We enjoy the advantages of, say, improving automobiles that can in twenty minutes move an entire family across a distance it took their grandparents two days to cover by wagon. Forgotten is the fact that more Americans have been killed by their countrymen in cars than have been killed by all the adversaries in all the wars in all the country's history.

We have applied the same myopia to medical progress. I set out, following that Texas murder-suicide, to write about the personal impact of medical technology and society's inability or unwillingness to wrestle with the accompanying moral and ethical dilemmas. It was a fascinating few years of learning. Many readers wrote to suggest stories or simply to relate their own family's anguish. Some sent poems they had written at hospital bedsides. These reactions were by no means scientific and I waited, surprisingly in vain, for the unsigned diatribes accusing me of being pro-death.

One lengthy page-one story examined the destruction of one young mother's body by ALS, or Lou Gehrig's disease, and the accompanying destruction of her entire family by the long drawn-out trauma resulting from family and medical indecisions about terminating her care. With the aid of a special printing device, the paralyzed patient kept a daily diary. And I interviewed all the medical participants and family members. So here we had, in one bed, the story of dedicated professionals doing their utmost to preserve a human body's functions while the intelligent person within that body cried out for a release that could only come with death.

Another story dealt with the emergence of hospital ethics committees, institutional efforts to establish a systematic process to hear and help deliberate delicate cases. In the early 1980s perhaps two percent of the nation's hospitals had such committees. Ten years later the American Hospital Association estimated that two-thirds did. There was no right or wrong in these lengthy discussions, simply a good-faith effort to find the truth that seemed right for this patient, this family, and this institution at this time, given the glaring absence of a wider social consensus. Some individuals, such as the Michigan doctor who devised the so-called suicide machine to ease the passing of dying patients, without implicating the doctor, sought to move society faster.

What seemed to be developing, judging by polls showing upward of 80 percent supporting doctor-assisted suicide in the event of a terminal illness, was a massive fear among elderly about losing control of their life (and their death). The concern, also revealed in my mail, was that once placed onto the modern conveyor belt of medical technology, impatient patients would be treated by well-trained, well-meaning, but nonetheless intrusive technicians. This quest into nontraditional corners for new medicines, alternative treatments, and even "suicide machines" reminded me of similar frustrations over the country's political and economic gridlocks that fueled that frantic search for political alternatives in 1992.

Another story dealt with the deaths of two women—one on a highway, the other from a stroke—and it followed all the arrangements and negotiations that led, within hours, to ten pieces of those bodies traveling all across the continent into the ravaged bodies of strangers awaiting salvation from such tragedy. From inside the ambulance to inside the operating rooms, it was an inspirational journey of sharing and sorrow, of joy and grief, and of a technology and expertise that quietly expands by the minute.

Another story dealt with one elderly man entering the hospital for back pain, the discovery of widespread, inoperable bone cancer and the delicate negotiations about his death filled with a sympathetic doctor's athletic euphemisms about "fourth down" and the "final gun." The man and his soon-to-be widow decided to forgo aggressive treatment. They sat together for several days, holding hands as the calcium content of his blood neared lethal levels. And when, in the wee hours of a Sunday morning, the alarms went off signaling cardiac arrest, the nurses and the new widow did nothing. The death certificate read: "Cardiopulmonary failure."

As a professional reporter, I tried to be extremely sensitive to the personal nature of these tales. I was always deeply grateful for the subjects' courage in permitting a stranger to witness their most personal and trying times. And, frankly, I was amazed that all sides in these discussions and disputes were so willing to talk. "No one has the answers," said one hospital attorney. And I know journalists cannot tell people what to think. Our role is to suggest what people think about.

The American Hospital Association in its brief for the Cruzan case, the first right-to-die dispute to reach the U.S. Supreme Court, estimated that 75 percent of all deaths in America today are somehow timed or negotiated, like the man with inoperable bone cancer. That means that virtually everyone at some time will be involved with such a decision for themselves or a relative. One obvious suggestion is for individuals to assume the responsibility for providing directions on their desired medical care. This requires society to lighten up a bit about something that is inevitable so that families can discuss the alternatives more openly and clearly. A growing number of high schools began requiring courses on death and dying as one way to increase awareness. The least these steps might accomplish is to avoid leaving surviviors to spend the rest of their lives wondering and doubting if they did the correct thing in withdrawing a respirator or the like without guidance. Without such considerations built on moral and ethical grounds I fear that, given today's fiscal realities, the decisions may someday come to be made on a more coldhearted financial basis. You have the right to want to live as long as you can, but do I have the obligation to pay for it?

Here I was trying to tell these stories with as much power and sensitivity as possible to a stubbornly inattentive public. I was personally moved, but I was also detached, like a police officer at yet another fatal traffic accident.

I never thought I would have to live it, too. What began as a professional search for stories suddenly became after several years a riveting personal sadness. From a long distance by telephone came the familiar voice of my mother's doctor. "Andrew," he said, "I'm afraid we have a serious problem with your mother."

Thus began my own journey through the emotional swamp of end-of-life decisions whose detailed discussions had been postponed too long. As the legally named proxy decision maker for my mother, I would see the other side of these secretive affairs. I had tried to feel my mother out before, telling her my views on extraordinary medical care in the face of relentless realities. She had seemed to respond. "Your father was lucky," she said. "He went quickly." Another day she said, "I don't want to stay past my time." Which at that moment prompted me to sigh with relief. At last some direction. Later, I realized exactly who was going to be left to interpret when her time was or wasn't—her only child.

Still, I felt I had a sense of her wishes. Then, one day alone in her apartment, she developed a sudden shortness of breath. By phone she summoned not one but two ambulances. If she wasn't sure when her time was, how could I be?

But then, several months after that ambulance call, there she was unconscious in her dark hospital room in the stainless steel bed with the railings, a frail skeleton of wrinkled skin and age spots, wearing flimsy hospital pajamas and a diaper, with sixteen tubes and wires running into and out of her seventy-five-year-old body. The pneumonia nearly killed her. Over several days her organs went into shock. Some indicators were stable, others in slight decline. Meanwhile, the respirator whooshed on obediently at a rhythm and pressure set by compassionate technicians who had never exchanged one word with her. Her right forefinger glowed like E.T.'s as another medical advance read her blood gases that told us her lungs were not working well. The heart labored on. I fell into that numbing routine of ICU hospital vigils and felt I deserved it—to the hospital early in the morning, wait for hours, grab a quick lunch, back to the room, wait all afternoon, eat a late dinner, back to her room, then back to my room and the TV with the loose knob. I never did get a comprehensible response from her.

The doctor was not hopeful. Mom would never recover even the limited mobility and quality of life she'd had two weeks before in the nursing home. Our best hope could be that after some months of pulmonary therapy, her lungs might develop sufficient efficiency for her to regain consciousness. Hopefully, in the meantime, no other organs would begin to fade. And even then, a good-sized spot of cancer had reappeared on one lung. So within a year she would almost certainly be back in the ICU.

Without saying a word, the doctor asked me what I thought. He, of course, knew of my previous conversations with Mom. And like most doctors, he knew that these decisions often involve more education by doctors of family members about the medical realities than medical care for the patients.

I postponed any decision. I ate dinner alone. I returned to my motel room. I threw up. I tossed and turned all night. I did not sleep. At 7 A.M., the doctor phoned, as agreed. "I'm at the hospital," he said. I went there. No change in Mom.

"Geez, doctor," I said holding back a flood of feelings, "I'd love to have my mother back. But I wonder about the point to all this."

When I was a little boy, I was often too full of questions. My father always had a patient answer for me. I didn't always understand the answer, especially, I realize now, when it involved death. But his answers certainly shaped my values. Why, for instance, my pet cat killed a bird? Dad said it had to do with something called "instinked." Or when a speeding vehicle hit my first dog, crippling and soon killing him.

"It's very sad," my father said. "And it's very painful. But you'll survive."

"No, I won't."

"And I'll survive."

"You? What do you have to do with this?"

"I loved Buddy, too. I was there when we met him, don't you remember?"

"Well, I don't want to survive."

"You can do whatever you have to do. Always remember that."

"It's too late."

"You have your whole life ahead of you."

"Without Buddy!"

"Everything dies sometime, son. Dogs, cats, trees, people, plants."

"I don't care about plants."

"Sometimes it's just sooner than we'd like."

Pause.

"But it hurts so much."

"Yes, I know. I hurt, too. That means you really love him. And he loved you very much. He had a good life with us. But you wouldn't want him crawling around here, always in pain, all crippled."

"Yes, I would. I'd take care of him. Forever."

"No, you wouldn't do that to him. Make him suffer. That's not my Andy. That would be selfish. That wouldn't be kind to him. That wouldn't be loving. And that wouldn't be the real Buddy, would it? He always wanted to be free, not tethered to pain or anything. Remember the chewed leash that first night? And every spring when he'd run away?"

"But he always came back."

"This was his home. You were here. You'll always have his memory."

"But I don't want a memory. I want him."

"Well, we don't always get what we want in life. And memories aren't so bad to have, Andy. Better than nothing."

"But I'll miss him, Dad."

"Of course, you will. And I will, too. But life goes on."

"I don't care."

"It has to."

"I don't care."

"Well, you better start caring. You've got a lot to do in life."

"What? Like what?"

"I don't know. That's the mystery. It's exciting. Don't you want to know what you were meant to do?"

Pause.

"No, I don't. And I don't care."

"Maybe you don't right now. Give it time. You will someday."

Someday. Someday. It was always someday. And now standing in that funny-smelling hospital hallway, I knew in my gut what was about to happen, although my head still played hide-and-seek. "It's so hard to know what's right," I told the doctor.

He nodded.

"She can't have any pain or choking."

"She'll be mildly sedated."

A deep breath. Oh, God, here we go. A swallowed sob. "I want to let her go."

Silence. No thunder. No lightning. No bells. No police. No nothing. The doctor's hand went to my shoulder and squeezed. That's it? No one to read me my rights?

They removed the respirator tube then. I stood there holding her hand, stroking her cheek, talking at her. At first her heartbeat jumped to 140 as the old body tried to adjust to the new workload. Then, slowly the pulse declined. For hours it held steady. Gee, maybe she was going to make it. Maybe her eyes would open. "Oh, Andy!" she'd exclaim. "You came!" And we'd hug and go home together again.

I was chatting with the nurse late in the afternoon. I saw the nurse's eyes dart over my shoulder to the monitors. "It won't be long," she said. I whirled. The pulse was forty-four. "How do you know?" I asked. I turned back for an explanation. But she was gone to the phone.

I looked at Mom. Mouth still open. Same little gasps. Forty. Oh, God, I thought, she's dying on me. Thirty-six. For a while that afternoon I had been afraid it wouldn't happen. Now I was afraid it would. Wait. Stop. Mom, don't go! I'm sorry about the fights. Is this what you wanted? Oh, God, give her peace. And me, too, maybe. Please.

The doctor arrived. He checked her pulse. Thirty-four. "She's ready, Andrew."

Oh, my. Fine. Well, hey, what about me? Wait, Mom. I'm not so sure. I . . .

Nine hours and five minutes after I authorized removal of the respirator, my mother expired in a windowless private hospital room with the television on. We were both alone together then. I felt terrifyingly small.

Another someday had come.

11

Limits and Possibilities: The Patient Self-Determination Act

Elizabeth L. McCloskey

No right is held more sacred or is more carefully guarded by the common law than the right of every individual to the possession and control of his own person, free from all restraints or interference by others, unless by clear and unquestionable authority of law.
   —U.S. Congress OTA 1987:92, citing U.S. Supreme Court

Nearly a century after the United States Supreme Court first recognized a person's right to self-determination in *Union Pacific Railway v. Botisford* in 1891, Congress passed the Patient Self-Determination Act. The Patient Self-Determination Act, enacted in November of 1990 as sections 4206 and 4751 of the Omnibus Budget Reconciliation Act of 1990 (OBRA '90), is the first federal law to confront squarely the ethical domain of medical decision making through advance directives. The story of this law is one of limits and possibilitites. The limits of medicine; the possibility of exercising control over one's medical decisions. The limits of the legislative process and the law; the possibility of those bound by the law to seize its spirit. The limits of life itself; the possibility of fashioning a good life.

The Patient Self-Determination Act

The provisions of OBRA '90, which are commonly referred to as the original title, the Patient Self-Determination Act (PSDA), are simple and straightforward. Health care institutions that accept Medicare and Medicaid patients are now required to inform all adult patients about their right to accept or refuse medical treatment, including their right to do so through an advance directive. Obligated institutions, which are hospitals, nursing homes, home health agencies, hospices, and health maintenance organizations, must also document in each patient's medical record whether or not the patient has an advance directive, and inform the patient about that particular institution's policies with respect to implementing advance directives. Providers must not discriminate against patients based on whether or not they have an advance directive, and must comply with the wishes of patients to the extent that state law allows. Finally, institutions must educate their staffs, and the public, about advance directives. In addition, states must develop a description of their laws with respect to advance directives (or patient self-determination, more broadly) for use by health care providers. The secretary of Health and Human Services, at the federal level, must mount a public education campaign and must provide technical assistance to the states as the states develop descriptive informational statements of their laws.

Medicine's Shortfalls

It has long been recognized in common law that physicians cannot treat patients against their will. The principle of self-determination was articulated in the context of medical decision making in 1914 in *Schloendorff v. Society of New York Hospital*, where Judge Cardozo wrote, "Every human being of adult years and sound mind has a right to determine what shall be done with his own body" (U.S. Congress OTA 1987:92).

Of course, decisions with respect to one's body—a person's right to self-determination—are traditionally weighed against countervailing state interests, such as the preservation of human life, the protection of third parties, the prevention of suicide, and the protection of the ethical integrity of the medical profession (Meisel 1989:96). The explosion of medical technology over the past twenty to thirty years has brought the issue of the relationship between these principles more sharply into focus, while at the same time challenging its clarity.

With increasingly more procedures and machinery available to respond to medical conditions that in the past would have been considered hopeless, the question of what shall be done with one's own body emerges with some regularity. Seventy years ago most people died at home, in the company of family and friends. A physician's role was as much as a comforter as a healer. Lewis Thomas, the noted author and physician, recalled his father's early experiences and views as a doctor in the 1920s:

> The general drift of his conversation was intended to make clear to me, early on, the aspect of medicine that troubled him most of all

through his professional life; there were so many people needing help, and so little that he could do for any of them. It was necessary for him to be available, to make all these calls at their homes, but I was not to have the idea that he could do anything much to change the course of their illnesses. It was important to my father that I understand this; it was a central feature of the profession. (Gordon 1992:50)

That recognition of the inherent limits of being a physician no longer defines the medical profession. Modern technology in the past several decades has created a medical climate in which it is almost always possible to prolong life through resuscitation, antibiotics, chemotherapy, transplants, dialysis, artificial hydration and nutrition, and other means. Now up to 75 percent of people spend their last days in a hospital or medical center (NCHS 1991:308). It is estimated that 70 percent of all Americans will have to make a decision some day regarding whether to continue to use life support systems to keep a family member alive (Times Mirror Center 1990:1).

Not only have medical advances made the question of what one wants done to one's body more relevant, but expanding medical options have also made it possible to maintain one's life beyond the point at which one maintains any decision-making ability whatsoever, whether due to a permanently unconscious state or other condition, leaving it more difficult to ascertain what it is a person wants done to her body. While death has never been a completely private matter, these phenomena have brought death, and the decisions surrounding it, irreversibly into the public domain.

Karen Ann Quinlan's well-known face testifies to the increasingly public nature of death. Many in today's generation grew up with her image—her long hair, neatly parted down the middle. She symbolized the changing parameters of life and death, and signaled the increasingly difficult questions that we as a society must confront regarding the limits of medicine.

The facts of the Quinlan case are familiar (*In the Matter of Karen Quinlan* 1976). Karen Ann Quinlan stopped breathing at the age of twenty-one. She was brought to an emergency room in an unconscious state, and when she was stabilized a feeding tube was inserted and a respirator attached. She had lapsed into a coma and was diagnosed as being in a persistent vegetative state. Her father sought removal of the respirator; her physicians as well as the local prosecutor and the state attorney general opposed the request; and the question was ultimately brought before the New Jersey Supreme Court, which granted the father's request for guardianship over his daughter and, with this status, to make medical decisions on her behalf. This decision was the first of its kind in which authority to stop medical treatment for an incapacitated person was given, even though the likely consequence was death. Although Karen Quinlan survived the removal of the respirator for nine more years, her case set a precedent that has been followed by many state courts. Approval to cease medical treatment, even when the outcome will almost certainly be death, has been allowed in case after case. Yet at issue in many of these cases has not been the validity of the principle of self-determination, but how to protect the state's interest in a third party by ensuring certainty regarding a patient's own views.

The need to ensure certainty about an incapacitated patient's views has led to the development of advance directive statutes. Almost all states authorize a person to leave word in advance about one's views of life-sustaining treatment to take effect when one is terminally ill and unable to speak for oneself, or in some states, when one becomes permanently unconscious. In 1976, the same year that the Quinlan case was decided, the state of California enacted the first significant state statute recognizing a person's "right to die." The California law, known as the Natural Death Act, authorized individuals to execute directives with which to allow the withholding or withdrawal of life-sustaining procedures in a terminal condition. Other states followed California by enacting "living will" statutes, as well as "durable power of attorney" statutes that allow individuals to designate a chosen person to make medical decisions on their behalf in the event of incapacitation.

The most painful court cases have emerged when a family member believes she knows the choices her incapacitated loved one would have made, but for lack of any clear, legally authorized directive, those wishes are denied. The case of Dan Delio illustrates (*Delio v. Westchester County Medical Center* 1987). In 1986 Dan Delio underwent minor surgery to repair a rectal fistula. A mistake by the anesthesiologist rendered Mr. Delio permanently unconscious, in a persistent vegetative state. His life was sustained through the use of artificial nutrition and hydration. He and his wife had previously had extensive conversations regarding persistent vegetative states and Mr. Delio had clearly expressed his desire to Dr. Delio not to be kept alive, "not even for one day," through medical intervention in that state. Yet because he had not formally appointed Dr. Delio with his durable power of attorney, the medical facility denied her request to stop treatment. It was not until a year later, when the New York State Appellate Court ruled in the Delios' favor, that medical treatment was stopped. Dr. Delio testified to the dramatically public nature of death when she spoke before the U.S. Senate Finance Committee:

The loss of my husband was tragic enough yet then I was then forced to plead publicly to strangers for his death. You cannot imagine the psychological trauma involved in pleading for the death of the person you love most in this entire world. (S. Hrg. 101–1168, 1990:17)

The Limits of Laws

The public nature of this personal anguish, and the seeming inadequacy of the various state laws to address this problem, led to the eventual move toward federal legislation. In the late 1980s, as stories such as the Delios' and others became more familiar, a gap in public policy was revealed. Although most states by 1989 had codified the right to refuse or accept medical treatment, and authorized means to extend that right beyond competency, many people were unaware of these laws and of how to protect their right to decide should they lose the capacity to speak for themselves. Furthermore, health care providers were not playing a large role in bringing these mechanisms to patients' attention. A 1986 Gallup poll revealed that at that time only 9 percent of the population had executed an advance directive (Steiber 1987:72). A later Harvard study indicated that, although 95 percent of people would like to plan in advance for medical decisions, many had not done so, citing a lack of physician initiative as the most common reason (Emanuel et al. 1990:738A). In addition, a survey of hospitals conducted before enactment of the PSDA found that only 4 percent of hospitals routinely ask patients whether they have an advance directive that they would like to make a part of their medical record (Van McCrary and Botkin 1989:2411). Had Dan Delio been told upon admission for his routine operation that he had a right to execute an advance directive, and had he been asked if he had executed any such directive, perhaps he could have appointed his wife as a proxy, thereby avoiding the year-long court battle that ensued.

The story of Nancy Cruzan and her family also poignantly highlighted the need for education about advance directives (*Cruzan v. Director, Missouri Department of Health* 1990). At the age of twenty-six, Nancy Cruzan suffered severe head injuries from a near-fatal car accident. Having stopped breathing for at least fifteen minutes before help arrived, Nancy Cruzan's brain injuries were irreversible and she was left in a persistent vegetative state. After several years of being kept alive through artificial nutrition and hydration with no improvement whatsoever, her family sought to terminate medical treatment and allow her to die. Their request was denied and was ultimately appealed to the U.S. Supreme Court.

Although the state of Missouri had not yet enacted living will legislation at the time of her accident in 1981, had she left clear and convincing evidence of her wishes, according to the Supreme Court decision, the state would have been obligated to allow treatment to be stopped.

A Federal Role?

Senator John C. Danforth (R-Mo.) was struck by the gap between people's wishes and the implementation of those wishes. He understood that for many people their worst nightmare would be to spend their last days in an intensive care unit, unconscious, hooked up to medical machines. As an Episcopal priest who spends time visiting the sick and elderly in their homes, he has had many conversations with people about just that subject. These personal encounters led Senator Danforth to pose hard ethical questions. On the first day I came to work for Senator Danforth in the fall of 1989, the following note was waiting for me at my desk:

> Liz—Here is something you can start on when I am in Wyoming. Maybe you could begin pulling together some thoughts and material. Perhaps someone at YDS (Yale Divinity School) could give you some help. However, please don't attribute any conclusions to me as I have none.
>
> What are the ethics of extending the length of life?
>
> We cannot artificially end life (thou shalt not kill), but how about artificially extending life? Is that always good, sometimes good?
>
> Is it good to extend the life of a senile ninety-year-old who wears diapers? How about "neonatal care" for a baby who would otherwise die?
>
> What's the difference in these two cases, or should we have a difference?
>
> In ethics, is keeping people alive the highest good? Should our priority be to keep people breathing?
>
> Is it "playing God" to make distinctions on the basis of quality of life? Do we have a lesser degree of care to the comatose patient than to someone else?
>
> The usual way to approach these questions is by economics: How much should we spend on health care? I'd like to think about a different approach. What is our duty to keep people alive? What does basic religious ethics say about this? —Jack (Danforth 1989)

Clearly aware that our priority should not be to "keep people alive" when they are dying and want no further medical intervention, aware of the need for advance directives, and concerned that use of these helpful documents was minimal, Senator Danforth sought to construct public policy that was responsive, responsible, and reasonably attainable. What could be done to further enable patients to exercise their rightful decision-making role? What could be done to fashion a federal law that at its root recognized the limited power of medicine?

The surest approach would probably have been to enact a federal law that would preempt state law and make uniform the right to execute an advance directive. Codifying a model directive law at the national level though, however valid a principle, would not have met the practical test of achievability at that time due to the variations in state laws, the commitment of the anti-abortion groups to block a national law, and the relative newness of the issue as a national concern. What emerged from Danforth's push to grant federal recognition to patient self- determination drew substantially from the recommendations of a panel of twelve physicians who published a seminal article on the topic of hopelessly ill patients (Wanzer et al. 1989:845). Although the approach chosen by Senator Danforth is limited, given the competing interests involved in the legislative process, it is quite a step forward and has laid the groundwork for more sweeping consideration of advance directives at the federal level.

The Legislative Process

Politics will, to the end of history, be an area where conscience and power meet, where the ethical and coercive factors of human life will interpenetrate and work out their tentative and uneasy compromises. (Niebuhr 1960:4)

The legislative history of the Patient Self-Determination Act provides a small sample of Reinhold Niebuhr's operative principle. Consideration of conflicting interests in the drafting of the PSDA could lead only to a modest effort to capture the idea of patient self-determination and human dignity. Even given the narrow approach of the original legislation, modifications after its introduction were necessary to ensure its passage. Health care providers, for instance, asserted that they wanted to play some role in promoting patient participation in decision making, but they resisted federal requirements that would lead to greater administrative burdens. Through their national association, the American Medical Association (AMA), physicians lobbied to be excluded from any legislative requirement to inform patients about advance directives. Despite the fact that physicians are generally regarded as a critical component in the patient decision-making process, there are no requirements imposed on them to educate patients about advance directives. This exclusion, to some, represents a major flaw in the Act (Obade 1990:321). The AMA has managed to limit regulatory action affecting its practice to reimbursement policy, rather than compliance with various federal conditions to which institutional providers, hospitals, nursing homes, and others that accept Medicare and Medicaid patients are subject.

The American Hospital Association (AHA) was also involved in shaping the legislation by seeking to ensure that while hospitals may be required to comply with new provisions, those requirements would not be the "conditions of participation" that are closely and strictly regulated by the agency overseeing Medicare and Medicaid, the Health Care Financing Adminstration (HCFA). In prepared testimony before the Senate Finance Committee on July 20, 1990, a representative from the AHA said,

> While the AHA strongly supports the goals of the Patient Self-Determination Act and believes that the legislation will acccomplish those goals, we do not support its tie to the Medicare Conditions of Participation. The requirements for participation in the Medicare program are meant to provide Medicare beneficiaries with access to high-quality health care. Providers should not be at risk of termination from the Medicare program due to a requirement not related to fundamental delivery of care. (S. Hrg. 101–1168, 1990:123)

Although other witnesses argued that understanding and respecting the wishes of patients goes to the heart of quality health care, the enacted provisions did not take the form of "conditions of participation." Instead, the requirements are technically "agreements with providers" that will be monitored, but not with the vigor that they otherwise would be if the bigger stick were wielded.

The hospitals also initially withheld support from the legislation due to the singular burden on health care institutions to educate patients about the law in the state, without any mandated assistance from the state. Arguing that such a requirement placed medical institutions in the awkward position of providing legal advice, the AHA successfully ensured that a state agency, acting through itself or a private entity, would develop informational documents for use by Medicare and Medicaid providers.

Nursing home associations were other groups of health care providers that influenced the form of the bill. As originally drafted, the legislation would have required providers to "periodicially review" the wishes of patients to ensure that advance-directive documents represented the most current views of patients. Nursing homes sought the deletion of a continual review process, arguing that monitoring of such a requirement would be onerous.

Still another interest that led to modifications of the legislative proposal was that of the "pro-life" groups, such as the National Right to Life and the United States Catholic Conference, which sought to limit its scope. The bill as introduced would have required states without any formal advance-directive laws to enact them; it would have required health care institutions to recognize validly executed advance directives from other states as validly executed in the state where the patient is being treated. Despite the fact that the lack of uniformity of state laws and the lack of easy portability of advance directives have become growing concerns, both these provisions were dropped as a means of easing the potentially fatal opposition of the pro-life groups. Their lobbyists viewed any mandated change in state law as the first step toward nationalizing advance directives through federal standards. Having been successful at getting restrictive advance directives laws passed in some states, these groups were not anxious to see a federal law potentially preempt those hard-won efforts.

The original legislation included a study to be conducted by the secretary of Health and Human Services to determine whether the act had been effective in achieving greater understanding and utilization of advance directives. A companion House of Representatives bill also contained a study provision, but the research was to be undertaken by the Institute of Medicine of the National Academy of Science, which the pro-life groups perceived as inclined toward termination of medical treatment, and thus not to be trusted to conduct an unbiased study. When one of the House sponsors of this provision, Representative Henry Waxman (D-Calif.), would not agree to the Senate version of the study during a House/Senate conference on the underlying legislation, the entire advance-directive section of the bill was in jeopardy. Thus, to avoid controversy and to ensure passage, the study provision was dropped completely.

Even with these modifications, some of which are arguably good policy, and others of which are meant to gain the support of critical factions, the final product offers federal weight behind the notion of patient participation in health care decision making. As enacted, the legislation contains basic and minimal requirements, as outlined earlier. Despite its limited aims, the passage of this legislation, with relatively little controversy, only a year after its introduction, is remarkable. Although the President's Commission for the Study of Ethical Problems in Medicine and Biomedical and Behavorial Research had, ten years earlier, hailed the development of state laws on advance directives, national policy had never previously touched this subject. The real test of its success, however, is whether it serves as an impetus for health care providers to use its minimal requirements as the basis for sound institutional policy.

The PSDA's Impact

> What good, for instance, would a law be if no one respected it, no one defended it, and no one tried responsibly to follow it? It would be nothing but a scrap of paper. (Havel 1992:18)

If the legislative process of the PSDA reveals the tension between the actual and the possible, so too does the letter of the law itself. Human dignity is the fundamental principle underlying the PSDA, but capturing such a principle in statutory language is nearly impossible. Mandating sensitivity seems an oxymoron. Requiring good conversations seems only to destroy them.

The argument was made, as the PSDA was pending in Congress, that a federal law could hinder, rather than help, the cause of patient participation in decision making. A concern was raised that if health care institutions were required to convey information to patients, compliance would become compulsory and perfunctory. Voluntary efforts, on the other hand, would ensure more effective patient education (Capron 1990:35). In addition, codification of advance directives at both the state level and the national level poses the risk of institutionalizing advance directives as the *only* means of allowing incapacitated patients' views to be respected (Wolf et al. 1991:1670). Certainly the intent of the PSDA was not to squelch ongoing educational efforts surrounding patient decision making nor to further entrench the troublesome notion that, without an advance directive, medical treatment should never be stopped for incompetent patients.

The challenge is to ensure that a law serve its purpose rather than violate it. Rather than being bound by a law's limitations, the trick is to exploit its possibilities. The danger regarding the PSDA has been that the law will stay flat, at most an annoying paperwork requirement, without attempts to capture its spirit by those to whom it applies. That result would render the law ineffective and, worse, irrelevant. Encouraging and promoting the involvement of those people affected by the law during its legislative process, however, has helped to avoid that potential pitfall. The basic democratic principle of a participatory government rings true in the context of the PSDA. It makes sense that when people are instrumental in crafting a law, they are eager to ensure its usefulness. Despite its modest objectives, the Patient Self-Determination Act is a law in which many ethicists, providers, consumers, and others have staked a claim. Thus, early indicators are that, instead of simply being a "scrap of paper," the PSDA has had life breathed into it by the many people throughout the country who are committed to making it work.

In California, the California Consortium on Patient Self- Determination, an association of providers, academics, state agencies, attorneys, and others, gathered over the course of several months to develop together an appropriate means of informing Californians about their advance-directive rights. The American Bar Association, also committed to ensuring the effectiveness of the act, has devoted major resources to assisting the states in developing consumer-friendly informational materials. A group of researchers, organized by Joanne Lynn, M.D., and some of her former colleagues at George Washington University, is contacting all the states, rating their informational materials, and providing them assistance in improving their documents.

Perhaps the most promising result has been the willingness of individual institutions, particularly hospitals, to seize the opportunities that the PSDA presents. Many institutions have dedicated their staff and resources not only to implement, but to improve upon, the requirements of the law. For example, St. John's Mercy Medical Center in St. Louis has developed impressive, accessible materials to help educate its patients about the usefulness of planning ahead for medical decisions. Other institutions have used the law as an impetus for extensive staff training. Studies currently under way are evaluating the response of such institutions.

Nothing in the legislative language of the bill could have guaranteed a positive response. But a law can point beyond itself to a larger principle, and it is that which the Patient Self-Determination Act may have done.

The Ultimate Limitation

Without the awareness of death, nothing like the "meaning of life" could exist, and human life would therefore have nothing human in it. (Havel 1998:240)

The real meaning of the PSDA lies in its recognition of the limits of medicine to triumph completely over death. National health policy, as it manifests itself in the Medicare and Medicaid titles of the Social Security Act, does not really represent a coherent and comprehensive approach to health care, and has not ever codified a recognition of limits. Medicare fiscal intermediaries and state Medicaid agencies are obligated to reimburse for all "medically necessary" care that is administered by a reimbursable provider. In almost every year since these programs have been enacted,

Congress has expanded the original benefits outlined in the law. As Medicare and Medicaid consume more and more of the federal budget—they are two of the fastest growing sectors of the domestic budget, next to the growth in the national debt—it looks *less* as if the nation recognizes the limits of medicine. Our public policy has mirrored the public faith in the miracle of medicine, the belief that medicine can ultimately conquer our immortality. Paul Ramsey recognized the flaw in this tendency twenty years ago in the *Patient as Person*, where he wrote:

> But not everything can be done in the provision of medical services that human ingenuity devises and money can buy, or men need, even if there were no other human claims and social needs calling for expenditure of the nation's resources. . . . When measured against the human need any nation, and mankind as a whole, possesses only what must be called sparse medical resources, and sparse social resources for meeting the other human needs as well. The blunt truth is that this is permanently the human condition. (Ramsey 1972:268–269)

We are making a mistake, Ramsey went on to argue,

> when death is regarded as an unmitigated disaster, and men hope to be saved from illness and death by scientific and medical technology in a measure that true religion never cared to promise. (Ramsey 1972:269)

The Patient Self-Determination Act marks a simple acceptance, at the national level, of the definitional limits of medicine. It may help lay the first stone in building fundamentally new public perceptions of issues relating to sickness, health, life, and death. It may help individuals, on a personal basis, to understand the limited nature of medicine. A shift in understanding of this magnitude is necessary if we are to reorganize our health care system in order to ensure a basic level of health care to all people and continue to invest in other national priorities such as education, the infrastructure, and our economy, which help sustain fruitful and meaningful lives. Without an understanding of medicine's limits, it may not be possible to structure a health care system that leaves room for other such commitments. And without any room to fulfill the commitments that enhance rather than simply sustain life, human existence runs the risk of losing its richness and texture.

It is difficult for lawmakers to make this kind of observation. Former Governor Richard Lamm of Colorado lost political standing, and a reelection bid, in the late 1980s when he pointed out that simply maintaining life should not be our dominant goal. Many argued in response, however, that policymakers should not be in the business of making distinctions between "quality of life" and life itself. As more people are faced with decisions about terminating medical treatment for themselves or a loved one, and as more people, particularly in the middle class, feel the squeeze of health care costs generally, it will become more possible to speak about how to accept medicine's limits in our own lives and how to rationally order our health care priorities in the aggregate.

Walker Percy, an admirer of the scientific method and scientific progress, made an observation that rings true today in the health care context. It is paradoxical, he noted, that the more science transforms the world and benefits humanity, the less is said about "what it is like to be born as an individual, to live and to die" in that world (Jones 1987:42).

The Patient Self-Determination Act helps direct people to those questions, to spark discussion—both in and out of a medical context—about what it means to be born, to live and die as a human being. Only when we allow these philosophical yet highly practical issues to enter the health care debate can we hope to fashion a health care system, and a world, that makes sense.

References

California Health and Safety Code. 1989. 65–7185–7195 (West Supp.).

Capron, Alexander Morgan. 1990. "The Patient Self-Determination Act: Not Now." *Hastings Center Report* 20(5):35–36.

Cruzan v. Director, Missouri Department of Health. 1990. 497 U.S. 261, 110 S.Ct. 2841.

Danforth, John C. 1989. Personal communication.

Delio v. Westchester County Medical Center. 1987. 129 A.D.2d 516 N.Y.S. 2d 677.

Emanuel, L. L., M. J. Barry, J. D. Stoeckle, and E. J. Emanuel. 1990. "A Detailed Advance Care Directive; Practicality And Durability." *Clinical Research* 38:738A.

Gordon, John Steele. 1992. "How America's Health Care Fell Ill." *American Heritage* 43(3):49–65.

Havel, Vaclav. 1988. *Letters to Olga.* Translated by Paul Wilson. New York: Knopf.

Havel, Vaclav. 1992. *Summer Meditations.* Translated by Paul Wilson. New York: Knopf.

Jones, Malcolm. 1987. "Moralist of the South." *New York Times* (March 22):42.

Meisel, Alan. 1989. *The Right to Die.* New York: John Wiley and Sons.

National Center for Health Statisitcs. 1991. *Vital Statistics of the United States, 1988.* Hyattsville, Md.: Public Health Service. II(A):308.

Niebuhr, Reinhold. 1960. *Moral Man and Immoral Society: A Study in Ethics and Politics.* New York: Scribner's.

Obade, Claire C. 1990. "The Patient Self-Determination Act: Right Church, Wrong Pew." *Journal of Clinical Ethics* 1(4):320–322.

Office of Technology Assessment, U.S. Congress. 1987. *Life-Sustaining Technologies and the Elderly.* OTA-BA-306. Washington, D.C.: U.S. Government Printing Office.

Omnibus Budget Reconcilation Act. 1990. Pub. L. No. 101–508:4206, 4751.

President's Commission for the Study of Ethical Problems in Medicine and Bio-medical and Behavorial Research. 1983. *Deciding to Forgo Life-Sustaining Treat-ment: A Report on the Ethical, Medical, and Legal Issues in Treatment Decisions.* Washington, D.C.: U.S. Government Printing Office.

In re Quinlan. 1976. 70 N.J. 10, 355 A.2d 647, rev'g 137 N.J. Super 227, 348 A.2d 801 (1975), cert. denied, 429 U.S. 922 (1976).

Ramsey, Paul. 1972. *The Patient as Person: Explorations in Medical Ethics.* New Haven: Yale University Press.

S.Hrg. 101–1168. 1990. *Living Wills.* Hearing Before the Subcommittee on Medicine and Long-Term Care of the Committe on Finance, United States Senate, 101st Cong., 2d sess., on S.1766. Washington, D.C.: U.S. Government Printing Office.

Steiber, Steven R. 1987. "Right to Die: Public Balks at Deciding for Others." *Hospitals* (March 5):72.

Times Mirror Center for the People and the Press. 1990. *Reflections of the Times: The Right to Die.* Washington, D.C.

Van McCrary, S., and Jeffrey Botkin. 1989. "Hospital Policy on Advance Directives: Do Institutions Ask Patients About Living Wills?" *Journal of the American Medical Association* 262:2411–2412.

Wanzer, Sidney H., Daniel Federman, S. James Adelstein, Christine K. Cassel, et al. 1989. "The Physician's Responsibility Toward Hopelessly Ill Patients: A Second Look." *New England Journal of Medicine* 320(13):844–849.

Wolf, Susan M., Philip Boyle, Daniel Callahan, Joseph J. Fins et al. 1991. "Sources of Concern about the Patient Self-Determination Act." *New England Journal of Medicine* 325(33):1666–1671.

12

Advance Directives as Instruments of Moral Persuasion

Robert F. Weir

We live in an age of advance directives in health care, at least in a formal and legal sense. If this development counts as good news, as I think it does in many ways, our gratitude can be directed at a number of individuals, families, and organizations that have collectively transformed the way many people in the United States think about treatment-related decisions at the end of life.

For example, we are in debt, morally speaking, to Nancy Cruzan's family and the families of many other nonautonomous patients over the past two decades who endured lengthy court battles in order to have affirmed the legal right of patients to refuse life-sustaining treatment, even when the patients can no longer make their preferences known. We are in debt to the professionals and volunteers at Concern for Dying and the Society for the Right to Die, two organizations now collectively called Choice in Dying, for their work in educating state legislators around the country to the importance of right-to-die legislation. We are in debt to state legislators themselves, many of whom exhibited political courage in passing right-to-die legislation in the face of emotional and often hostile "pro-life" opposition. We are in debt to Senators John Danforth and Daniel Moynihan, and their colleagues in Congress who formulated and passed the Patient Self-Determination Act (PSDA) in 1990, thus giving hospitals, nursing homes, and other health care institutions a federal mandate (as of December 1991) to provide patients with information about advance directives (Patient Self-Determination Act 1990).

The results of these efforts are striking. The legal right of adult patients to refuse life-sustaining treatment, whether the decision is made by an autonomous patient or the surrogate of a nonautonomous patient, has been affirmed in dozens of legal cases (Meisel 1989). The residents of the District of Columbia and forty-seven states (exceptions are Massachusetts, Michigan, and New York) now have laws, usually called "natural death" acts or "living will" laws, that provide them with the legal option of signing a statutory advance directive that can communicate personal preferences regarding life-sustaining treatment (Hackler, Moseley, and Vawter 1989; King 1991). The residents of the District of Columbia and forty-eight states (exceptions are Alabama and Alaska) now have durable-power-of-attorney (DPA) legislation that provides them the opportunity of designating a legally sanctioned surrogate who can, should the need arise, make decisions on their behalf regarding the initiation, continuation, or abatement of life-sustaining treatment (Choice in Dying 1992). In addition, a national survey by the *Boston Globe* in November 1991, found that 24 percent of adult Americans now have advance directives of some sort (Choice in Dying 1992). With the continuing influence of the PSDA, which went into effect after this survey, the number of signed, "active" advance directives should dramatically increase (Emanuel 1991; Johnson 1991).

One might think that from the perspective of an advocate of advance directives, right-to-die legislation, and the PSDA, all would be right with this evolving state of affairs. Such is not the case, however, at least with this advocate of these important developments. My concern is that the moral foundation underlying the original purpose of advance directives in health care is in danger of being eroded by the excessive emphasis that many people place on advance directives as legal instruments. Worse yet, this emphasis on advance directives as legal instruments, along with the routinized manner in which the PSDA is implemented in many hospitals, threatens to undermine and obscure the importance of the personalized preferences that many patients have and may want to communicate to their physicians about their health care.

I want to make the case for understanding and using advance directives in health care as instruments of moral persuasion, in addition to whatever status they may have as legal instruments in various jurisdictions. To make the case I will discuss several types of advance directives, present some standard criticisms of advance directives, indicate some problems concerning advance directives as legal instruments, and provide several reasons for considering advance directives as important instruments of moral persuasion.

Types of Advance Directives

In terms of their *legal* status, advance directives are of two types. Some advance directives, the ones enacted into law by legislators in all fifty states and the District of Columbia, are "statutory directives": they have an undeniable legal status in a given jurisdiction based on the wording of the specific legislative statute that brought them into being. Whether they are directives connected with "living will" laws or with some kind of DPA statute, these directives have the force of state law behind them. Given the rapid development of these directives in recent years, many people tend to think that these legal instruments are the only kind of advance directives available to individuals who want to communicate in advance their preferences regarding future medical care.

There are, however, other advance directives that are "nonstatutory" in nature. They are not legal instruments, did not come into existence because of the passage of a state law, and do not contain in their wording any threat of legal action against physicians who refuse to follow the preferences and requests expressed in them. They are not without legal weight, as demonstrated by several court decisions that interpreted such documents as important pieces of evidence regarding a patient's decision to refuse life-sustaining treatment (*Lurie v. Samaritan Health Service* 1984; *John F. Kennedy Memorial Hospital v. Bludworth* 1984; *In re Conroy* 1985; *Saunders v. State* 1985). Yet their primary status is that of *morally persuasive documents*: the persons who formulate and/or sign such documents do so because they want these documents to *speak for them* when they can no longer speak for themselves in a conventional manner. Through such documents they anticipate being able to influence physicians, relatives, and any other participants in the decision-making process to carry out their expressed preferences—without legal threats.

In terms of their *substantive* purpose, advance directives are of two different types. Some advance directives, commonly called "instruction directives" or "treatment directives," are intended to accomplish three interrelated purposes: provide information about a person's preferences regarding the use of medical treatment in the event of critical or terminal illness, give a rationale for these preferences, and persuade physicians and relatives to act according to these stated preferences in the event the signer of the directive subsequently loses the capacity to communicate the preferences in person. Since the first advance directive for health care was developed in the 1930s, numerous people in our society have developed and/or signed an advance directive for precisely these purposes: to stipulate what kinds of medical treatment they want or do not want, to indicate their reasons for those treatment choices, and to *persuade others* to abide by their wishes (Weir 1989).

Other advance directives, usually called "proxy directives," have a different purpose. Rather than containing information and requests concerning medical treatment, these advance directives are intended to designate another person (or persons) to make health care decisions on the behalf of the document's signer should that individual later become nonautonomous or legally incompetent. This kind of advance directive enables the signer to specify the person, plus an alternate or two, who is to be entrusted with decisions that quite probably will be life-or-death decisions made years later in an intensive care unit or other high-technology clinical setting.

A proxy directive may delegate responsibility to the proxy or surrogate in a fairly broad manner, or specify that the surrogate will have the right and the responsibility on the behalf of the document's signer to consent to medical treatment, refuse medical treatment, expend or withhold funds for medical treatment and services, change physicians, and/or change institutional settings. Whether the surrogate's mandate is general or specific, a proxy directive also is aimed at persuasion: to persuade an attending physician in the future, should the need arise, to consult with the patient's chosen surrogate, listen to the surrogate's interpretation of the now-nonautonomous patient's previous preferences, and cooperate with the surrogate's decision regarding the continuation or abatement of life-sustaining treatment.

The current generation of advance directives, both statutory and nonstatutory, consists largely of composite directives intended to accomplish the multiple goals of the instruction and proxy directives. Individuals who develop and/or sign composite directives follow a dual strategy in trying to influence decisions made about their medical care in any future circumstances of critical or terminal illness involving personal incapacity on their part. By providing written (or taped) information and instructions regarding medical treatment wanted or not wanted under certain future clinical circumstances, an individual can possibly influence decisions made at that time about medical treatment even if the designated surrogate is unavoidably absent. By designating a trusted relative or friend who should be capable of interpreting the patient's value system and treatment preferences at that future time of illness, an individual can possibly influence the decisions to treat or to abate treatment even if the exact wording of the advance directive is vague, open to criticism or conflicting interpretations, or not specific to the medical technology applicable to the case.

Standard Criticisms of Advance Directives

In spite of their current popularity, advance directives are the subject of substantial and repeated criticism. Some of the criticisms are directed at all advance directives, some are directed only at nonstatutory directives, some are directed only at instruction directives, and some are directed more at problems related to the implementation rather than to the substantive content of the documents. In abbreviated form, the criticisms are as follows:

1. Advance directives, especially instruction directives, are often written in such vague language that they are basically useless in clinical settings. For example, references to "extraordinary means," "heroic measures," and "imminent death" are not of great help in making decisions about abating life-sustaining treatment. A related problem is that the vague wording of many directives, both statutory and nonstatutory, simply does not fit or provide guidance for the clinical situation that subsequently comes to exist.

2. By contrast, some advance directives are too detailed. In particular, the medical directive (Emanuel and Emanuel 1989) is sometimes criticized on two grounds: its detailed case scenarios and list of technological possibilities can be intimidating to those without medical training, and the highly specific preferences contained in it may effectively preclude a physician subsequently caring for the patient from having sufficient discretionary flexibility (Pelligrino 1992).

3. Instruction directives, especially those that are developed and signed years in advance, do not anticipate changes that are likely to occur over the intervening years. As a consequence, signers of such documents fail to allow for the changes that may come to them, their interests, and their preferences by the time they are critically or terminally ill (Buchanan and Brock 1989). In a similar fashion, they fail to anticipate or allow for therapeutic options that might emerge by the time they are ill or injured. Of particular concern is the possibility that their previously declared preferences may come to be in direct conflict with their subsequent best interests, as those interests are assessed by physicians, relatives, and others involved in their medical case (Eisendrath and Jonsen 1983; Brock 1991; Robertson 1991).

4. Standard instruction directives also permit signers of the documents to indicate preferences about treatments by simply listing technological interventions wanted or not wanted, without any indication of the benefits that might come from the actual use of these technologies in certain clinical situations. For someone to indicate in advance "whether he or she would

want dialysis, a ventilator, or feeding tubes, without knowing what using these procedures would yield, is incomprehensible" (Lynn 1991:102).

5. Advance directives that are instructional only, with no selection of a surrogate who might help interpret and support the patient's stated preferences, are problematic because they tend to place the patient's family (and close friends) "outside the loop." Such written documents, standing in isolation from the patient's relatives and friends, can later lead to conflict between the attending physician and family and may (especially if the document is nonstatutory in nature) simply be dismissed by the physician as "a worthless piece of paper." For some critics, this minimization of the family's role is a reason for not having an instruction directive, especially if one prefers, in the event that personal autonomy is lost, to trust subsequent decisions to members of a loving family (Lynn 1991).

6. Instruction directives can be used to request or demand extreme measures, without providing an attending physician with the rationale behind the stipulated choices. Such choices can go either way, by demanding treatment that the physician regards as futile in the given medical circumstances or by refusing treatment that the physician regards as beneficial to the patient. If the signer of the document subsequently loses cognitive function and is in a critical or terminal condition, the inflexible wording of the document can cause unnecessary psychological and moral problems for the physician.

7. Proxy directives, whether statutory or nonstatutory, can be problematic in several ways. Some individuals may sign proxy directives in an irresponsible manner, simply trying thereby to avoid the difficult task of thinking seriously about the decisions that will become necessary in the event of critical or terminal illness. Other persons may sign proxy directives without providing their surrogates with sufficient information so that they can later make informed choices on the behalf of a now-nonautonomous patient. Still other persons may sign proxy directives without giving sufficient thought to the character of the chosen surrogate or the possible conflicts that might arise in the future, thus allowing for circumstances that might lead the surrogate to make less than trustworthy decisions for the patient.

Problems with Advance Directives as Legal Instruments

Nevertheless, advance directives are, on balance, a valuable addition to the health care scene in this country, in spite of the limitations and weaknesses they can have. Similarly, the development of statutory advance directives is, on balance, a positive development for patients, their families, and their physicians. All parties involved in medical cases are better off when they know what the relevant state law says about patients' rights, the legal obligations of physicians, and the legal circumstances in which life-sustaining treatment may be initiated, continued, decelerated, or stopped.

The availability of statutory advance directives in all states and the District of Columbia is, however, a mixed blessing. On the one hand, living in a legal jurisdiction that has advance directive connected with a "living will" law and/or a DPA statute means that patients in that jurisdiction can, in theory, more easily exercise their legal right to refuse medical treatments they do not want, even if they later lose the cognitive ability to communicate their treatment preferences to an attending physician at the time of critical or terminal illness. On the other hand, some patients in some hospitals (perhaps many patients in many hospitals) may not actually have their autonomous decision making about life-sustaining treatments enhanced at all, depending on the kind of information about advance directives that has been distributed by state medical, legal, and hospital organizations, how hospital administrations in a given jurisdiction have responded to the PSDA, how hospital attorneys and other hospital staff interpret advance directives, the kind of information about advance directives that has been given to patients, how much physicians know about various kinds of advance directives, and how open individual physicians are to working with patients and surrogates to carry out the preferences expressed in a patient's advance directive.

At the very least, some patients and their surrogates will not benefit from living in a jurisdiction that has statutory advance directives as possible options for its citizens. At worst, a number of informed patients, physicians, and surrogates of patients may conclude, especially when advance directives are interpreted as legal instruments only, that living in an age of statutory advance directives can actually be more restrictive of patient (and physician) choice than expansive of choice. To understand that possible conclusion, consider the following problems that arise when advance directives are interpreted as legal instruments only.

1. Statutory advance directives, especially directives that are instructional in nature, are problematic in many states because they are restricted to certain categories of citizens who "qualify" for their use. In some states, such statute-backed directives gain the force of law only when patients are certified in some manner (e.g., the opinion of two physicians) to be "terminally ill." In some states, terminally ill patients are excluded from using the legislature-formulated directive if they are pregnant. In a number of states, even terminally ill patients who are not pregnant do not qualify to sign the statutory advance directive if they want to refuse, among other kinds of life-sustaining treatment, the technological provision of nutrition and hydra-

tion. In most states, patients who are terminally ill and not pregnant still do not qualify to sign a statutory advance directive if they are legal minors.

The result is that as persons increasingly become concerned about the excesses of high-technology medicine and want to take steps to indicate their preferences about the possible use of various medical technologies to sustain their lives, they sometimes discover that they cannot sign a statutory directive because they do not qualify to do so under the provisions of their state law. Depending on what they know or are told about advance directives (e.g., on admission to a hospital), they may wrongly conclude that they have no other alternative for effectively persuading their physician(s) about their treatment preferences.

2. Statutory advance directives are problematic in some states because the statutes themselves are inconsistent with each other. As the end product of intense lobbying by interest groups, compromises made with "pro-life" and physician groups, and multiple revisions in wording, one piece of right-to-die legislation can be at serious variance with other right-to-die legislation in the same state. For example, a "living will" statute may preclude patients from refusing technological feedings while a DPA statute permits persons in the same state to appoint surrogates who will, should the need arise, have the legal authority to refuse all forms of life-sustaining treatment on the patient's behalf.

Judicial interpretations of the state statutes in refusal-of-treatment court cases sometimes further complicate the meaning of the law as it applies to clinical cases. As Fenella Rouse observes: "A national assessment of existing state statutes and companion case law results in a bewildering, complicated patchwork. Not only is the law in neighboring states often radically different, but some states have internally inconsistent legislation or case law that interprets apparently clear legislative language to mean the opposite of what, on its face, it says" (Rouse 1990:356).

3. Statutory advance directives are problematic because most of them are not portable. They are written, as is other state law, for the citizens of individual states with no intention on the part of the legislators that the laws will have a reciprocal status with comparable laws in other states. Even if such reciprocity were desired, the varying content of legislation and, less often, case law would create serious practical problems. Some of the specific differences pertain to the definition of "terminally ill," the pregnant status of patients, the legal status of technological feeding, the identification and role of surrogates, the legal responsibilities of physicians, and whether a state even has natural-death-act legislation or DPA legislation.

The practical result is significant. A citizen in one state (e.g., Illinois) could have signed a "living will" directive and a directive designating a surrogate who would be empowered—in Illinois—to act on the patient's behalf. However, if that individual should become hospitalized in neighboring Iowa, Indiana, Missouri, or any other state as a result of an acute illness or serious accident, the previously stated preferences that would have had legal force in Illinois will have no such effect in the state where the patient is hospitalized. The previously signed documents might be given legal status as evidence should a court hearing take place in the other state, but surely would not be regarded in the hospital context as having the force of state law.

4. The directive portion of many statutory advance directives is problematic because of the limitations imposed by the language in the directive. Especially with statutory directives that are instructional in nature, citizens are often limited to the exact wording of the legislature-formulated directive or, at best, language similar to the wording of the state-sponsored directive. In some states (e.g., Indiana) citizens are limited to indicating their agreement with one of several directives by checking an appropriate box. Only a few state statutes permit citizens latitude in personalizing their statutory instruction directive, with New Jersey offering the most comprehensive options to its citizens through advance directives formulated by a legislative commission (New Jersey Commission 1991).

Brochures recently developed by the American Medical Association (AMA) specifically address this problem. In the brochure on advance directives prepared for patients, the AMA states: "If you do not like the limitations of your state's model form, you should consider using an alternative form" (AMA 1992a:7). The brochure prepared for physicians indicates that patients are not limited to the language or style of the statutory directive in the jurisdiction: "An advance directive *of any kind* would represent clear evidence of the patient's wishes" (AMA 1992b:4; emphasis added).

5. Some state health care and legal associations, hospital administrators, and offices of hospital legal counsel mislead patients and their surrogates by suggesting that statutory advance directives are the only advance directives available. By adhering to the letter of the law, they interpret the PSDA to mean that health care institutions are legally obligated to provide information only about advance directives enacted by state law (Wolf 1991). The fact that patients and their surrogates might benefit from knowing about other, nonstatutory advance directives does not seem to matter. Thus, patients in some states are given information brochures formulated by medical, hospital, and legal associations in the state that do not mention, even in passing, that nonstatutory advance directives are also available as options—as is the option of drafting their own personalized forms.

6. The emphasis on statutory advance directives, to the exclusion of nonstatutory directives, contributes to the legalistic and litigious nature of con-

temporary medicine. By emphasizing the role of advance directives as legal instruments only, attorneys and hospital administrators continue the recent trend of using legal documents to define and limit the relationship between physicians and their patients. On the part of physicians, this emphasis on legal documentation feeds the point of view that says, "if it isn't written down, it didn't happen." On the part of patients, the exclusionary emphasis by some attorneys and hospital administrators on advance directives as legal instruments means that patients are encouraged to think of the physician-patient relationship primarily in legal terms: physicians won't do "the right thing" unless forced by threat of law to do so.

7. If carried to the extreme, the emphasis on "writing it down" in legally enforceable documents could, in some states, get to the point of having content-based standards of acceptability for advance directives. Courts in New York (*In re Westchester County Medical Center* 1988) and Missouri (*Cruzan v. Harmon* 1989) have already required a "clear and convincing" standard of evidence for abating treatment that is technology-specific in cases involving nonautonomous patients (Weir and Gostin 1990; Rouse 1991). Thus, for example, if a permanently unconscious patient's life is being sustained by means of gastrostomy tube feedings, her previously expressed wishes not to be "kept alive like a vegetable" may not be recognized, at least in these two states, unless she had specifically mentioned tube feedings in an advance directive or verifiable conversations with relatives or friends.

It is at least possible that some physicians, hospital administrators, and hospital attorneys, motivated by a fear of litigation, could conclude that the same, unconscionably high standard of evidence applies to advance directives. If the physician of a nonautonomous patient (e.g., a patient in a persistent vegetative state) did not possess, and the patient's surrogate could not produce, an advance directive from the previously autonomous patient that specifically addressed the type of technology that was sustaining the patient's life, the physician might decide that there was insufficient, legally protective evidence of the patient's wishes to permit the termination of treatment. Simply put, an advance directive that did not contain technology-specific, "clear and convincing" evidence of the patient's preferences would not, for legal or quasi-legal reasons, be an acceptable indication of the patient's treatment choices during critical or terminal illness.

Good Reasons for Having an Advance Directive

Given the problematic aspects of advance directives, why should any of us sign an advance directive for health care? Are there good reasons, other than legal considerations, for having an advance directive? I think so. Consider the following advantages that composite advance directives can provide as instruments of moral persuasion—even if they are not backed up by a state statute.

1. Advance directives, depending on their formulation, can provide significant information about an individual's value system. A variant of advance directives, known as a values history form, provides explicit, detailed information about the signer's values that may have an impact on how he or she thinks about disabling conditions, pain and other suffering, longevity, and the use of medical technology to sustain life (Lambert, Gibson, and Nathanson 1990; Doukas and McCullough 1991). Some standard advance directives, such as those provided by the Catholic Health Association and the American Protestant Health Association, give a reasonably clear indication of how the signer's religious beliefs and value system have an impact on choices about life-sustaining treatment (Catholic Health Association; American Protestant Health Association). Other standard forms, such as the generic form distributed by Choice in Dying, provide less information about the signer's general value system, but supply helpful information regarding the value choices the signer has made about terminal illness, palliative care, being maintained in a prolonged state of unconsciousness, and the use of medical technology (including technological feeding) to sustain life when there is no reasonable prospect of recovery (Choice in Dying 1992).

One of the AMA brochures mentioned earlier provides another alternative. The brochure on advance directives prepared for patients includes a simple form on personal treatment goals that patients can complete and attach to a DPA directive, thereby indicating to their surrogate(s) the level of cognitive and physical functioning they would want subsequent to treatment and the importance they would place on the financial cost of the treatment (American Medical Association 1992a).

This information about an individual's value system can be beneficial in two ways prior to a patient's critical or terminal illness, as well as at later moments of difficult decision making by some combination of patient, surrogate, physician, and medical team. One benefit goes to the individual who formulates and/or signs an advance directive. Even the relatively simple act of signing a standard advance directive requires an individual to think seriously about the meaning of life, the activities and relationships that give value to one's personal life, the importance one places on avoiding prolonged unconsciousness or severe pain, and the person(s) one is willing to entrust with the power to make a life-or-death decision should that become necessary. This benefit is increased for individuals who take the time and make the effort to formulate personalized advance directives, for in so doing they take on the significant task of *explaining who they are* (quite possibly to an unknown future physician or medical team) in an effort to *persuade others to respect their preferences* regarding life-sustaining treatment.

The other benefit goes to the individual's physician (if there is an ongoing relationship with a primary care or personal physician), the individual's designated surrogate(s), and possibly to other relatives and close friends. Any prudent individual who formulates and signs an advance directive is probably going to have the foresight of making several copies of the signed document and distributing them to persons who, because of role or relationship, are thought likely to be present in the event of a future illness or accident that might render the individual unable to consent, refuse treatment, or otherwise communicate personal preferences regarding treatment options. A personal physician who receives a copy of the document has the opportunity, perhaps years in advance, of discussing the document with the patient, getting a better understanding of the patient's values, and gaining information about the patient that might prove helpful later in formulating a care plan or responding to a medical emergency involving this patient. In a similar manner, designated surrogates receiving a copy of the document will be better prepared for a future role they hope never to have.

2. Advance directives can be helpful in promoting the autonomous choices made by patients. Such documents are reminders to physicians, relatives, and close friends of patients that the illness, pain, suffering, chance for restored health, continued existence, and possible death of the patient that physicians and other parties to a case deliberate about are, after all, hardly objective factors to the patient involved. Rather, such matters are of intense personal interest and concern, and one way of effectively documenting that interest and concern is to express in advance and in writing (or on tape) one's personal preferences about possible medical options in as clear, decisive, and persuasive manner as possible.

In addition, an advance directive that is personalized can indicate the weight the signer places on his or her autonomous choices. It is possible, for example, that an individual who signs an advance directive will try to communicate through that document that his or her choices are to be regarded as absolute: "I *never* want to be stuck on machines." Another person may indicate a variation of importance that should be placed on his or her autonomous choices, with the weight differing depending on the type of medical condition, the nature of the disability involved, the nature and severity of suffering experienced, or the kind of medical treatment that would be necessary to sustain life.

Moreover, an advance directive can, if personalized, serve as a reminder of *who the autonomous agent is* who is communicating preferences and, when read in retrospect, *who the now-nonautonomous patient was* when he or she was sufficiently concerned about future medical care to try to indicate choices about treatments wanted or not wanted later in life. The most helpful advance directives in this regard are documents that clearly reflect both the signer's value system and choices about possible treatments that are geared to specific clinical situations. An additional feature of an advance directive that is especially helpful in geriatric cases is the inclusion of one or more pictures of the patient during the youth and prime of life, thus providing a reminder to a physician (and the patient's surrogate) of a life that was characterized by years of autonomous choices.

3. Advance directives, both statutory and nonstatutory in nature, can alleviate psychological and moral problems that might otherwise be encountered by the patient, the patient's surrogate, and the patient's physician. Individuals who formulate and/or sign advance directives gain considerable psychological benefit by alleviating their fears about overtreatment, their anxiety about "ending up like Nancy Cruzan," and their concerns about being the focal point of an unduly protracted hospitalization that could bring tremendous suffering and financial ruin to their families (Areen 1991).

The chosen surrogate(s), family members, and friends of a person who signs an advance directive also stand to benefit from this kind of advance planning for critical or terminal illness, especially if the person's choices about treatments and surrogates are openly discussed with family and friends as well as documented in writing. More specifically, persons who are emotionally attached to the signer of an advance directive have the opportunity, in advance, of knowing the individual's preferences regarding life-sustaining treatment, understanding the individual's rationale for those preferences (a rationale that might later apply to other treatment choices not anticipated by the individual), and having a much clearer view of what the individual thinks about other matters that might become important in future decisions by surrogates (e.g., the expected role of surrogates, the economic aspects of prolonged critical care). An additional benefit for surrogates, family members, and close friends that might be realized in the future is the avoidance, because of patient's advance planning, of the agonized doubts and uncertainty that now characterize the comments made by many families who have prolonged vigils near ICUs and other clinical settings, comments like "I don't know what he (or she) would want us to do."

The patient's physician(s) also stand to benefit, in at least two ways. Not only does the patient's personal physician benefit by understanding the patient better now, but that physician and any other physicians who may be responsible for the patient's care in the future will also benefit by having conflict with other medical colleagues and the patient's family reduced over the medical management of a critical illness or a life-threatening condition. The physician(s) in the future will know, at least in general terms, what the patient's views were regarding some medical conditions and some life-sustaining treatments and, possibly more important, what the patient's perspective was on the ethical and legal matter of abating life-sustaining treatment. Armed with that documented knowledge, the physician(s) need not refrain from carrying out the patient's earlier wishes because of an excessive fear of being sued by the patient's surviving family.

4. Advance directives, even if not backed up by state law, are likely to bring about important conversations between physicians and their patients that would otherwise not take place. Few other events in a physician-patient relationship are as certain to instigate a discussion about treatment options and patient preferences as is the delivery of a signed advance directive to a patient's physician(s), especially if the directive is personally delivered by the patient or the patient's surrogate. Even an uninformed physician who receives such a document is likely to be inquisitive about the document—and to be influenced, to some degree, by its content.

Physicians who are better informed about patients' rights, advance directives, and the PSDA will welcome advance directives from patients. Moreover, they will take the occasion as an opportunity to discuss with individual patients the content of their directives, their reasons for having a directive, the clinical settings in which the directive is most likely to be used, and possibly some common clinical circumstances or treatment options that are not addressed in the document. In short, a responsible physician will try, through conversation, to be clear about the patient's values and preferences just in case circumstances arise, subsequent to illness or accident, in which the patient can no longer communicate those values and preferences in person. If possible and practical, a follow-up discussion with the patient about treatment preferences will also include the person(s) chosen to be the patient's surrogate(s).

5. Advance directives can, if nonstatutory in nature, be effective in jurisdictions other than the place of residence. In contrast to the limited geographical area in which statutory forms have legal standing, nonstatutory directives can have moral influence far from home. Of course the degree of moral influence will be lessened if, rather than being interpreted by a physician who has known the patient for years, a patient's earlier preferences about treatments and surrogates are subsequently interpreted by a physician or medical team who never knew the patient prior to the illness or accident that destroyed the patient's decision-making capacity.

If, however, the physician or medical team subsequently providing care for the patient is in another state, they should have no moral or legal reason immediately to reject the patient's advance directive as being inapplicable, as they might well do with a statutory directive from another state. Likewise, they should have no reason to seek legal advice about the directive, unless they are unduly anxious about the possibility of litigation. Rather, *if they are persuaded* by the patient's stated preferences, if they think the directive sufficiently fits the clinical situation that exists, and if they believe the patient's surrogate to be trustworthy (should a surrogate appear at the hospital), they will have good reasons for carrying out the patient's wishes even if the patient's home is two thousand miles away.

The implications are clear for all of us. The *moral weight* of an advance directive is related to, but not dependent on, the document's legal status. A statutory advance directive has legal standing in a particular jurisdiction, but may not be morally persuasive to the physician(s) in a case occurring in that jurisdiction. By contrast, a nonstatutory advance directive can be morally persuasive to the physician(s) and other parties to a case, even if the document does not meet the statutory requirements of the jurisdiction in which the case takes place.

In terms of the future, is it possible to maximize the chances that an advance directive will be morally persuasive when it is needed? I think so, especially if signers of advance directives take the following steps. First, individuals wanting to persuade physicians and other parties to a possible future case involving them should communicate instructions about treatment choices by a) formulating a personalized composite directive or b) signing a standard composite directive that most nearly reflects the value system and preferences of the signer. The standard form can be either statutory or nonstatutory in nature.

The wording of the instructional portion of the directive should, as much as possible, anticipate future clinical circumstances and the technologies that could be used to sustain life in those circumstances. The wording should provide a close "fit" between the signer's preferences about treatment options and the clinical reality that might come to exist, with the signer indicating the results that he or she would want treatment to accomplish and the reasons he or she has for refusing some kinds of treatment in the anticipated circumstances.

Second, persons signing a composite advance directive should designate a trusted relative or friend as a surrogate in the event personal autonomy is lost, select an alternate surrogate or two, and make sure that all of them understand the circumstances in which various kinds of life-sustaining treatment are to be initiated, continued, or abated. If the primary surrogate selected is a friend rather than a relative, the chances of the signer's wishes being carried out will be increased by providing the rationale in the directive for the friend's selection.

Third, the signer of a composite advance directive should, if the directive is nonstatutory in nature, also execute the appropriate statutory form in the place of residence for designating a surrogate. By supplementing a nonstatutory directive with a statutory DPA form, the signer will provide the person(s) selected as surrogate(s) with unquestionable legal standing to represent the patient's views, should that become necessary.

Fourth, the signer of a composite advance directive should initiate appropriate conversations about treatment-related decisions with a physician who might be responsible for managing a plan of care in the event the signer subsequently becomes critically or terminally ill. In this manner the signer of the document can increase the chances that the directive will, at a time of need, be regarded by the physician (and other physicians) as an important indicator of the patient's long-held views, rather than merely being a written form presented on admission to a hospital (or to a physician by the patient's surrogate at a time of medical crisis).

Finally, anyone signing an advance directive should communicate that fact to family members and close friends not selected as the surrogate(s). Better yet, to minimize the chances of family conflicts and maximize the chances that persons important to the patient will be persuaded by the patient's treatment preferences, relatives and close friends should be given copies of the document. In this manner, they will be given months or years to "come around" to accepting a patient's moral and legal right to refuse unwanted medical treatment, a matter of moral persuasion that could become important to all parties to a case in the event that anticipated, possible clinical circumstances become real.

References

American Medical Association. 1992a. *Advance Medical Directives for Patients*. Chicago: American Medical Association.

American Medical Association. 1992b. *Advance Medical Directives for Physicians*. Chicago: American Medical Association.

American Protestant Health Association. n.d. "Instructions for My Care in the Event of Terminal Illness."

Areen, Judith. 1991. "Advance Directives Under State Law and Judicial Decisions." *Law, Medicine and Health Care* 19:91–100.

Brock, Dan. 1991. "Trumping Advance Directives." *Hastings Center Report* 21:S5–S6.

Buchanan, Allen, and Dan Brock. 1989. *Deciding for Others*. Cambridge: Cambridge University Press.

Catholic Health Association. n.d. "Christian Affirmation of Life."

Choice in Dying. 1992. "Advance Directive: Living Will and Health Care Proxy."

Choice in Dying. 1992. *Choice in Dying News* 1:1–8.

Cruzan v. Harmon. 1989. 760 SW2d 408, *cert granted* (Mo.).

Doukas, David, and Laurence McCullough. 1991. "The Values History: The Evaluation of Patient's Values and Advance Directives." *Journal of Family Practice* 32:145–153.

Eisendrath, Stuart, and Albert R. Jonsen. 1983. "The Living Will: Help or Hindrance?" *Journal of the American Medical Association* 249:2054–2058.

Emanuel, Linda. 1991. "PSDA in the Clinic." *Hastings Center Report* 21:S6–S7.

Emanuel, Linda L., and Ezekiel Emanuel. 1989. "The Medical Directive: A New Comprehensive Advance Care Document." *Journal of the American Medical Association* 261:3288–3293.

Hackler, Chris, Ray Moseley, and Dorothy Vawter, eds. 1989. *Advance Directives in Medicine*. New York: Praeger.

In re Conroy. 1985. 98 N.J. 321, 486 A.2d 1209.

In re Westchester County Medical Center (O'Connor). 1988. 72 NY2d 517, 534 NYS2d 886, 531 NE2d 607, amended 1988.

Johnson, Sandra. 1991. "PSDA in the Nursing Home." *Hastings Center Report* 21:S3–S4.

John F. Kennedy Memorial Hospital, Inc. v. Bludworth (Landy). 1984. 452 So.2d 921 (Fla.).

King, Nancy M. P. 1991. *Making Sense of Advance Directives*. Dordrecht: Kluwer Academic Publishers.

Lambert, Pam, Joan McIver Gibson, and Paul Nathanson. 1990. "The Values History: An Innovation in Surrogate Medical Decision-Making." *Law, Medicine and Health Care* 18:202–212.

Lurie v. Samaritan Health Service. 1984. No. C510198 (Ariz. Super. Ct. Mariopa Co., March 24).

Lynn, Joanne. 1991. "Why I Don't Have a Living Will." *Law, Medicine and Health Care* 18:101–104.

Meisel, Alan. 1989. *The Right to Die*. New York: John Wiley and Sons.

New Jersey Commission on Legal and Ethical Problems in the Delivery of Health Care. 1991. *Advance Directives for Health Care*. Trenton: State of New Jersey.

Patient Self-Determination Act: Omnibus Budget Reconciliation Act of 1990. 1990:4206, 4751. Pub. Law 101–508.

Pellegrino, Edmund D. 1992. "Ethics." *Journal of the American Medical Association* 268:354–355.

Robertson, John A. 1991. "Second Thoughts on Living Wills." *Hastings Center Report* 21:6–9.

Rouse, Fenella. 1990. "Advance Directives: Where Are We Heading after Cruzan?" *Law, Medicine and Health Care* 18:353–359.

Rouse, Fenella. 1991. "The Role of State Legislatures After Cruzan: What Can—and Should—State Legislatures Do?" *Law, Medicine and Health Care* 19:83–90.

Saunders v. State. 1985. 129 Misc.2d 45, 492 N.Y.S.2d 510.

Weir, Robert F. 1989. *Abating Treatment with Critically Ill Patients*. New York: Oxford University Press.

Weir, Robert F., and Larry Gostin. 1990. "Decisions to Abate Life-Sustaining Treatment for Nonautonomous Patients." *Journal of the American Medical Association* 264:1846–1853.

Wolf, Susan M. 1991. "Honoring Broader Directives." *Hastings Center Report* 21:S5–S6.

13

Proposed Clinical Criteria for Physician-Assisted Suicide

Timothy E. Quill, Christine K. Cassel, and Diane E. Meier

One of medicine's most important purposes is to allow hopelessly ill people to die with as much comfort, control, and dignity as possible. The philosophy and techniques of comfort care provide a humane alternative to more traditional, curative medical approaches in helping patients achieve this end (Wanzer et al. 1984, 1989; Council on Ethical and Judicial Affairs 1992; Rhymes 1990; Broadfield 1988; Wallston et al. 1988). Yet there remain instances in which incurably ill patients suffer intolerably before death despite comprehensive efforts to provide comfort. Some of these patients would rather die than continue to live under the conditions imposed by their illness, and a few request assistance from their physicians.

The patients who ask us to face such predicaments do not fall into simple diagnostic categories. Until recently, their problems have been relatively unacknowledged and unexplored by the medical profession, so little is objectively known about the spectrum and prevalence of such requests or about the range of physicians' responses (National Hemlock Society 1988; Center for Health Ethics and Policy 1988; Heilig 1988; Overmyer 1991). Yet each request can be compelling. Consider the following patients: a former athlete, weighing eighty pounds (36 kg) after an eight-year struggle with the acquired immunodeficiency syndrome (AIDS), who is losing his sight and his memory and is terrified of AIDS dementia; a mother of seven children, continually exhausted and bedbound at home with a gaping, foul-smelling, open wound in her abdomen, who can no longer eat and who no longer wants to fight ovarian cancer; a fiercely independent retired factory worker, quadriplegic from amyotrophic lateral sclerosis (ALS), who no longer wants to linger in a helpless, dependent state waiting and hoping for death; a writer with extensive bone metastases from lung cancer that has not responded to chemotherapy or radiation, who cannot accept the daily choice he must make between sedation and severe pain; and a physician colleague, dying of respiratory failure from progressive pulmonary fibrosis, who does not want to be maintained on a ventilator but is equally terrified of suffocation. Like the story of "Diane," which has been told in more detail (Quill 1991), here are personal stories of courage and grief for each of these patients that force us to take very seriously their request for a physician's assistance in dying.

Our purpose is to propose clinical criteria that would allow physicians to respond to requests for assisted suicide from their competent, incurably ill patients. We support the legalization of such suicide, but not of active euthanasia. We believe this position permits the best balance between a humane response to the requests of patients like those described above and the need to protect other vulnerable people. We strongly advocate intensive, unrestrained care intended to provide comfort for all incurably ill persons (Wanzer et al. 1984, 1989; Council on Ethical and Judicial Affairs 1992; Rhymes 1990; Broadfield 1988; Wallston et al. 1988). When properly applied, such comfort care should result in a tolerable death, with symptoms relatively well controlled, for most patients. Physician-assisted suicide should never be contemplated as a substitute for comprehensive comfort care or for working with patients to resolve the physical, personal, and social challenges posed by the process of dying (Meier and Cassel 1983). Yet it is not idiosyncratic, selfish, or indicative of a psychiatric disorder for people with an incurable illness to want some control over how they die. The idea of a noble, dignified death, with a meaning that is deeply personal and unique, is exalted in great literature, poetry, art, and music (Aries 1982). When an incurably ill patient asks for help in achieving such a death, we believe physicians have an obligation to explore the request fully and, under specified circumstances, carefully to consider making an exception to the prohibition against assisting with a suicide.

Physician-Assisted Suicide

For a physician, assisting with suicide entails making a means of suicide (such as a prescription for barbiturates) available to a patient who is otherwise physically capable of suicide and who subsequently acts on his or her own. Physician-assisted suicide is distinguished from voluntary euthanasia, in which the physician not only makes the means available but, at the patient's request, also serves as the actual agent of death. Whereas active euthanasia is illegal throughout the United States, only thirty-six states have laws explicitly prohibiting assisted suicide (Newman 1991; Glantz 1987/88). In every situation in which a physician has compassionately helped a terminally ill person to commit suicide, criminal charges have been dismissed or a verdict of not guilty has been brought (Newman 1991; Glantz 1987/88; L. Gostin, personal communication). Although the prospect of a successful prosecution may be remote, the risk of an expensive, publicized professional and legal inquiry would be prohibitive for most physicians and would certainly keep the practice covert among most of those who participate.

It is not known how widespread physician-assisted suicide currently is in the United States, or how frequently patients' requests are turned down by physicians. Approximately 6,000 deaths per day in the United States are said to be in some way planned or indirectly assisted (Malcolm 1990), probably through the "double effect" of pain-relieving medications that may at the same time hasten death (Council on Ethical and Judicial Affairs 1992; Meier and Cassel 1983) or the discontinuation of or failure to start potentially life-prolonging treatments. From 3 to 37 percent of physicians responding to anonymous surveys reported secretly taking active steps to hasten a patient's death, but these survey data were flawed by low response rates and poor design (National Hemlock Society 1988; Center forHealth Ethics and Policy 1988; Heilig 1988; Overmyer 1991). Every public-opinion survey taken over the past forty years has shown support by a majority of Americans for the idea of physician-assisted death for the terminally ill (Malcolm 1990; Gest 1990; Hemlock Society 1990, 1991). Referenda with loosely defined safeguards that would have legalized both voluntary euthanasia and assisted suicide were narrowly defeated in Washington state in 1991 (Misbin 1991) and in California, and similar initiatives are under consideration in Florida, New Hampshire, and Oregon.

A Policy Proposal

Although physician-assisted suicide and voluntary euthanasia both involve the active facilitation of a wished-for death, there are several important distinctions between them (Weir 1992). In assisted suicide, the final act is solely the patient's, and the risk of subtle coercion from doctors, family members, institutions, or other social forces is greatly reduced (Glover 1977). The balance of power between doctor and patient is more nearly equal in physician-assisted suicide than in euthanasia. The physician is counselor and witness and makes the means available, but ultimately the patient must be the one to act or not. In voluntary euthanasia, the physician both provides the means and carries out the final act, with greatly amplified power over the patient and an increased risk of error, coercion, or abuse.

In view of these distinctions, we conclude that legalization of physician-assisted suicide, but not of voluntary euthanasia, is the policy best able to respond to patients' needs and to protect vulnerable people. From this perspective, physician-assisted suicide forms part of the continuum of options for comfort care, beginning with the forgoing of life-sustaining therapy, including more aggressive symptom-relieving measures, and permitting physician-assisted suicide only if all other alternatives have failed and all criteria have been met. Active voluntary euthanasia is excluded from this continuum because of the risk of abuse it presents. We recognize that this exclusion is made at a cost to competent, incurably ill patients who cannot swallow or move and who therefore cannot be helped to die by assisted suicide. Such persons, who meet agreed-on criteria in other respects, must not be abandoned to their suffering; a combination of decisions to forgo life-sustaining treatments (including food and fluids) with aggressive comfort measures (such as analgesics and sedatives) could be offered, along with a commitment to search for creative alternatives. We acknowledge that this solution is less than ideal, but we also recognize that in the United States access to medical care is currently too inequitable, and many doctor-patient relationships too impersonal, for us to tolerate the risks of permitting active voluntary euthanasia. We must monitor any change in public policy in this domain to evaluate both its benefits and its burdens.

We propose the following clinical guidelines to contribute to serious discussion about physician-assisted suicide. Although we favor a reconsideration of the legal and professional prohibitions in the case of patients who meet carefully defined criteria, we do not wish to promote an easy or impersonal process (Jecker 1991). If we are to consider allowing incurably ill patients more control over their deaths, it must be an expression of our compassion and concern about their ultimate fate after all other alternatives have been exhausted. Such patients should not be held hostage to our reluctance or inability to forge policies in this difficult area.

Proposed Clinical Criteria for Physician-Assisted Suicide

Because assisted suicide is extraordinary and irreversible treatment, the patient's primary physician must ensure that the following conditions are clearly satisfied before proceeding. First, the patient must have a condition that is incurable and associated with severe, unrelenting suffering. The patient must understand the condition, the prognosis, and the types of comfort care available as alternatives. Although most patients making this request will be near death, we acknowledge the inexactness of such prognostications (Poses et al. 1989; Schonwetter et al. 1990) and do not want to exclude arbitrarily persons with incurable, but not imminently terminal, progressive illnesses, such as amyotrophic lateral sclerosis or multiple sclerosis. When there is considerable uncertainty about the patient's medical condition or prognosis, a second opinion or opinions should be sought and the uncertainty clarified as much as possible before a final decision about the patient's request is made.

Second, the physician must ensure that the patient's suffering and the request are not the result of inadequate comfort care. All reasonable comfort-oriented measures must at least have been considered, and preferably have been tried, before the means of a physician-assisted suicide are provided. Physician-assisted suicide must never be used to circumvent the struggle to provide comprehensive care or find acceptable alternatives. The physician's prospective willingness to provide assisted suicide is a legitimate and important subject to discuss if the patient raises the question, since many patients will probably find the possibility of an escape from suffering more important than the reality.

Third, the patient must clearly and repeatedly, of his or her own free will and initiative, request to die rather than continue suffering. The physician should understand thoroughly what continued life means to the patient and why death appears preferable. A physician's too-ready acceptance of a patient's request could be perceived as encouragement to commit suicide, yet it is important not to force the patient to "beg" for assistance. Understanding the patient's desire to die and being certain that the request is serious are critical steps in evaluating the patient's rationality and ensuring that all alternative means of relieving suffering have been adequately explored. Any sign of ambivalence or uncertainty on the part of the patient should abort the process, because a clear, convincing, and continuous desire for an end of suffering through death is a strict requirement to proceed. Request for assisted suicide made in an advance directive or by a health care surrogate should not be carried out.

Fourth, the physician must be sure that the patient's judgment is not distorted. The patient must be capable of understanding the decision and its implications. The presence of depression is relevant if it is distorting rational decision making and is reversible in a way that would substantially alter the situation. Expert psychiatric evaluation should be sought when the primary physician is inexperienced in the diagnosis and treatment of depression, or when there is uncertainty about the rationality of the request or the presence of a reversible mental disorder the treatment of which would substantially change the patient's perception of his or her condition (Conwell and Caine 1991).

Fifth, physician-assisted suicide should be carried out only in the context of a meaningful doctor-patient relationship. Ideally, the physician should have witnessed the patient's previous illness and suffering. There may not always be a preexisting relationship, but the physician must get to know the patient personally in order to understand fully the reasons for the request. The physician must understand why the patient considers death to be the best of a limited number of very unfortunate options. The primary physician must personally confirm that each of the criteria has been met. The patient should have no doubt that the physician is committed to finding alternative solutions if at any moment the patient's mind changes. Rather than create a new subspecialty focused on death (Benrubi 1992), assistance in suicide should be given by the same physician who has been struggling with the patient to provide comfort care, and who will stand by the patient and provide care until the time of death, no matter what path is taken (Jecker 1991).

No physician should be forced to assist a patient in suicide if it violates the physician's fundamental values, although the patient's personal physician should think seriously before turning down such a request. Should a transfer of care be necessary, the personal physician should help the patient find another, more receptive primary physician.

Sixth, consultation with another experienced physician is required to ensure that the patient's request is voluntary and rational, the diagnosis and prognosis accurate, and the exploration of comfort-oriented alternatives thorough. The consulting physician should review the supporting materials and should interview and examine the patient.

Finally, clear documentation to support each condition is required. A system must be developed for reporting, reviewing, and studying such deaths and clearly distinguishing them from other forms of suicide. The patient, the primary physician, and the consultant must each sign a consent form. A physician-assisted suicide must neither invalidate insurance policies nor lead to an investigation by the medical examiner or an unwanted autopsy. The primary physician, the medical consultant, and the family must be assured that if the conditions agreed on are satisfied in good faith, they will be free from criminal prosecution for having assisted the patient to die.

Informing family members is strongly recommended, but whom to involve and inform should be left to the discretion and control of the patient. Similarly, spiritual counseling should be offered, depending on the patient's background and beliefs. Ideally, close family members should be an integral part of the decision-making process and should understand and support the patient's decision. If there is a major dispute between the family and the patient about how to proceed, it may require the involvement of a hospital ethics committee or even of the courts. It is to be hoped, however, that most of these painful decisions can be worked through directly by the patient, the family, and health care providers. Under no circumstances should the family's wishes and requests override those of a competent patient.

The Method

In physician-assisted suicide, a lethal amount of medication is usually prescribed that the patient then ingests. Since this process has been largely covert and unstudied, little is known about which methods are the most humane and effective. If there is a change in policy, there must be an open sharing of information within the profession, and a careful analysis of effectiveness. The methods selected should be reliable and should not add to the patient's suffering. We must also provide support and careful monitoring for the patients, physicians, and families affected, since the emotional and social effects are largely unknown but are undoubtedly far-reaching.

Assistance with suicide is one of the most profound and meaningful requests a patient can make of a physician. If the patient and the physician agree that there are not acceptable alternatives and that all the required conditions have been met, the lethal medication should ideally be taken in the physician's presence. Unless the patient specifically requests it, he or she should not be left alone at the time of death. In addition to the personal physician, other health care providers and family members should be encouraged to be present, as the patient wishes. It is of the utmost importance not to abandon the patient at this critical moment. The time before a controlled death can provide an opportunity for a rich and meaningful goodbye between family members, health care providers, and the patient. For this reason, we must be sure that any policies and laws enacted to allow assisted suicide do not require that the patient be left alone at the moment of death in order for the assisters to be safe from prosecution.

Balancing Risks and Benefits

There is an intensifying debate both within and outside the medical profession about the physician's appropriate role in assisting dying (Council on Ethical and Judicial Affairs 1992; Weir 1992; Cassel and Meier 1990;

Reichel and Dyck 1989; Angell 1988; Rachels 1975; Lachs 1976; van der Maas, et al. 1991; Singer and Siegler 1990; Orentlicher 1989; Wolf 1989; Gaylin et al. 1988; Vaux 1988; Gomez 1991; Brahams 1990; Leenen 1990). Although most agree that there are exceptional circumstances in which death is preferable to intolerable suffering, the case against both physician-assisted suicide and voluntary euthanasia is based mainly on the implications for public policy and the potential effect on the moral integrity of the medical profession (Singer and Siegler 1990; Orentlicher 1989; Wolf 1989; Gaylin et al. 1988; Vaux 1988; Gomez 1991; Brahams 1990; Leenen 1990). The "slippery slope" argument asserts that permissive policies would inevitably lead to subtle coercion of the powerless to choose death rather than become burdens to society or their families. Access to health care in the United States is extraordinarily variable, often impersonal, and subject to intense pressures for cost containment. It may be dangerous to license physicians to take life in this unstable environment. It is also suggested that comfort care, skillfully applied, could provide a tolerable and dignified death for most persons and that physicians would have less incentive to become more proficient at providing such care if the option of a quick, controlled death were too readily available. Finally, some believe that physician-assisted death, no matter how noble and pure its intentions, could destroy the identity of the medical profession and its central ethos, protecting the sanctity of life. The question before policymakers, physicians, and voters is whether criteria such as those we have outlined here safeguard patients adequately against these risks.

The risks and burdens of continuing with the current prohibitions have been less clearly articulated in the literature (Weir 1992; Cassel and Meier 1990; Reichel and Dyck 1989; Angell 1988; Rachels 1975; Lachs 1976; van der Maas et al. 1991). The most pressing problem is the potential abandonment of competent, incurably ill patients who yearn for death despite comprehensive comfort care. These patients may be disintegrating physically and emotionally, but death is not imminent. They have often fought heroic medical battles only to find themselves in this final condition. Those who have witnessed difficult deaths in hospice programs are not reassured by the glib assertion that we can always make death tolerable, and patients fear that physicians will abandon them if their course becomes difficult or overwhelming in the face of comfort care. In fact, there is no empirical evidence that all physical suffering associated with incurable illness can be effectively relieved. In addition, the most frightening aspect of death for many is not physical pain, but the prospect of losing control and independence and of dying in an undignified, unesthetic, absurd, and existentially unacceptable condition.

Physicians who respond to requests for assisted suicide from such patients do so at substantial professional and legal peril, often acting in secret without the benefit of consultation or support from colleagues. This covert practice discourages open and honest communication among physicians, their colleagues, and their dying patients. Decisions often depend more on the physician's values and willingness to take risks than on the compelling nature of the patient's request. There may be more risk of abuse and idiosyncratic decision making with such secret practices than with a more open, carefully defined practice. Finally, terminally ill patients who do choose to take their lives often die alone so as not to place their families or caregivers in legal jeopardy (Quill 1991).

Conclusion

Given current professional and legal prohibitions, physicians find themselves in a difficult position when they receive requests for assisted suicide from suffering patients who have exhausted the usefulness of measures for comfort care. To adhere to the letter of the law, they must turn down their patients' request even if they find them reasonable and personally acceptable. If they accede to their patients' requests, they must risk violating legal and professional standards, and therefore they act in isolation and in secret collaboration with their patients. We believe that there is more risk for vulnerable patients and for the integrity of the profession in such hidden practices, however well intended, than there would be in a more open process restricted to competent patients who met carefully defined criteria. The medical and legal professions must collaborate if we are to create public policy that fully acknowledges irreversible suffering and offers dying patients a broader range of options to explore with their physicians.

References

Angell, M. 1988. "Euthanasia." *New England Journal of Medicine* 319:1348–1350.

Aries, P. 1982. *The Hour of Our Death*. New York: Vintage.

Benrubi, G. I. 1992. "Euthanasia—the Need for Procedural Safeguards." *New England Journal of Medicine* 326:197–199.

Brahams, D. 1990. "Euthanasia in the Netherlands." *Lancet* 335:591–592.

Broadfield, L. 1988. "Evaluation of Palliative Care: Current Status and Future Directions." *Journal of Palliative Care* 4(3):21–28.

Cassel, C. K., and D. E. Meier. 1990. "Morals and Moralism in the Debate over Euthanasia and Assisted Suicide." *New England Journal of Medicine* 323:750–752.

Center for Health Ethics and Policy. 1988. *Withholding and Withdrawing Life-Sustaining Treatment: A Survey of Opinions and Experiences of Colorado Physicians*. Denver: University of Colorado Graduate School of Public Affairs.

Charlson, M. E. 1987. "Studies of Prognosis: Progress and Pitfall." *Journal of General Internal Medicine* 2:359–361.

Conwell, Y., and E. D. Caine. 1991. "Rational Suicide and the Right to Die—Reality and Myth." *New England Journal of Medicine* 325:1100–1103.

Council on Ethical and Judicial Affairs, American Medical Association. 1992. "Decisions Near the End of Life." *Journal of the American Medical Association* 267:2229–2233.

Gaylin W., L. R. Kass, E. D. Pellegrino, and M. Siegler. 1988. "Doctors Must Not Kill." *Journal of the American Medical Association* 259:2139–2140.

Gest, T., 1990. "Changing the Rules on Dying." *U.S. News and World Report* (July 9):22–24.

Glantz, L. H. 1987/88. "Withholding and Withdrawing Treatment: The Role of the Criminal Law." *Law, Medicine and Health Care* 15:231–241.

Glover, J. 1977. *Causing Death and Saving Lives.* New York: Penguin.

Gomez, C. F. 1991. *Regulating Death: Euthanasia and the Case of the Netherlands.* New York: Free Press.

Heilig, S. 1988. "The SFMS Euthanasia Survey: Results and Analyses." *San Francisco Medicine* (May):24–26.

Hemlock Society. 1990. "1990 Roper Poll on Physician Aid-in-Dying, Allowing Nancy Cruzan to Die, and Physicians Obeying the Living Will." New York: Roper Organization.

Hemlock Society. 1991. "1991 Roper Poll of the West Coast on Euthanasia." New York: Roper Organization.

Jecker, N. S. 1991. "Giving Death a Hand: When the Dying and the Doctor Stand in a Special Relationship." *Journal of the American Geriatric Society* 39:831–835.

Lachs, J. 1976. "Humane Treatment and the Treatment of Humans." *New England Journal of Medicine* 294:838–840.

Leenen, H. J. J. 1990. "Coma Patients in The Netherlands." *British Medical Journal* 300:69.

Malcolm, A. 1990. "Giving Death a Hand: Rending Issue." *New York Times* (June 14):A6.

Meier, E. E., and C. K. Cassel. 1983. "Euthanasia in Old Age: A Case Study and Ethical Analysis." *Journal of the American Geriatric Society* 31:294–298.

Misbin, R. I. 1991. "Physicians' Aid in Dying." *New England Journal of Medicine* 325:1307–1311.

National Hemlock Society. 1988. 1987 *Survey of California Physicians Regarding Voluntary Active Euthanasia for the Terminally Ill.* Los Angeles: Hemlock Society, February 17.

Newman, S. A. 1991. "Euthanasia: Orchestrating 'The Last Syllable of . . . Time.' " *University of Pittsburgh Law Review* 53:153–191.

Orentlicher, D. 1989. "Physician Participation in Assisted Suicide." *Journal of the American Medical Association* 262:1844–1845.

Overmyer, M. 1991. "National Survey: Physicians' Views on the Right to Die." *Physicians Manage* 31(7):40–45.

Poses, R. M., C. Bekes, F. J. Copare, and W. E. Scott. 1989. "The Answer to 'What are My Chances, Doctor?' Depends on Whom is Asked: Prognostic Disagreement and Inaccuracy for Critically Ill Patients." *Critical Care Medicine* 17:827–833.

Quill, T. E. 1991. "Death and Dignity—A Case of Individualized Decision Making." *New England Journal of Medicine* 324:691–694.

Rachels, J. 1975. "Active and Passive Euthanasia." *New England Journal of Medicine* 292:78–80.

Reichel, W., and A. J. Dyck. 1989. "Euthanasia: A Contemporary Moral Quandary." *Lancet* 2:1321–1323.

Rhymes, J. 1990. "Hospice Care in America." *Journal of the American Medical Association* 264:369–372.

Schonwetter, R. S., T. A. Teasdale, P. Storey, and R. J. Luchi. 1990. "Estimation of Survival Time in Terminal Cancer Patients: An Impedance to Hospice Admissions?" *Hospice Journal* 6:65–79.

Singer, P. A., and M. Siegler. 1990. "Euthanasia—a Critique." *New England Journal of Medicine* 322:1881–1883.

van der Maas, P. J., J. J. M. van Delden, L. Pijnenborg et al. 1991. "Euthanasia and Other Medical Decisions Concerning the End of Life." *Lancet* 338:669–674.

Vaux, K. L. 1988. "Debbie's Dying: Mercy Killing and the Good Death." *Journal of the American Medical Association* 259:2140–2141.

Wallston, K. A., C. Burger, R. A. Smith et al. 1988. "Comparing the Quality of Death for Hospice and Non-Hospice Cancer Patients." *Medical Care* 26:177–182.

Wanzer, S. H., S. J. Adelstein, R. E. Cranford et al. 1984. "The Physician's Responsibility toward Hopelessly Ill Patients." *New England Journal of Medicine* 310:955–959.

Wanzer, S. H., D. D. Federman, S. J. Adelstein et al. 1989. "The Physician's Responsibility toward Hopelessly Ill Patients: A Second Look." *New England Journal of Medicine* 320:844–849.

Weir, R. F. 1992. "The Morality of Physician-Assisted Suicide." *Law, Medicine and Health Care* 20:116–126.

Wolf, S. M. 1989. "Holding the Line on Euthanasia." *Hastings Center Report* 19(1) (Suppl.):13–15.

14

California Proposition 161: Physician-Assisted Death—Terminal Condition—Initiative Statute

❖

This initiative measure is submitted to the people in accordance with the provisions of Article II, Section 8 of the Constitution.

This initiative measure adds a title to the Civil Code, and amends a section of the Penal Code.

SEC. 1. Title 10.5 (commencing with Section 2525) is added to Part 4 of Division 3 of the Civil Code, to read:

Title 10.5. Death with Dignity Act

2525. Title

This title shall be known and may be cited as the Death With Dignity Act.

2525.1. Declaration of Purpose

The people of California declare:

Current state laws do not adequately protect the rights of terminally ill patients. The purpose of this Act is to provide mentally competent terminally ill adults the legal right to voluntarily request and receive physician aid–in–dying. This Act protects physicians who voluntarily comply with the request and provides strong safeguards against abuse. The Act requires the signing of a witnessed revocable Directive in advance and then requires a terminally ill patient to communicate his or her request directly to the treating physician.

Self–determination is the most basic of freedoms. The right to choose to eliminate pain and suffering, and to die with dignity at the time and place of our own choosing when we are terminally ill is an integral part of our right to control our own destinies. That right is hereby established in law, but limited to ensure that the rights of others are not affected. The right should include the ability to make a conscious and informed choice to enlist the assistance of the medical profession in making death as painless, humane, and dignified as possible.

Modern medical technology has made possible the artificial prolongation of human life beyond natural limits. This prolongation of life for persons with terminal conditions may cause loss of patient dignity and unnecessary pain and suffering, for both the patient and the family, while providing nothing medically necessary or beneficial to the patient.

In recognition of the dignity which patients have a right to expect, the State of California recognizes the right of mentally competent terminally ill adults to make a voluntary revocable written Directive instructing their physician to administer aid–in–dying to end their life in a painless, humane, and dignified manner.

The Act is voluntary. Accordingly, no one shall be required to take advantage of this legal right or to participate if they are religiously, morally, or ethically opposed.

2525.2. Definitions

The following definitions shall govern the construction of this title:

(a) "Attending physician" means the physician selected by, or assigned to, the patient who has primary responsibility for the treatment and care of the patient.

(b) "Directive" means a revocable written document voluntarily executed by the declarant in accordance with the requirements of Section 2525.3 in substantially the form set forth in Section 2525.24.

(c) "Declarant" means a person who executes a Directive, in accordance with this title.

(d) "Life–sustaining procedure" means any medical procedure or intervention which utilizes mechanical or other artificial means to sustain, restore, or supplant a vital function, including nourishment and hydration which, when applied to a qualified patient, would serve only to prolong artificially the moment of death. "Life–sustaining procedure" shall not include the administration of medication or the performance of any medical procedure deemed necessary to alleviate pain or reverse any condition.

(e) "Physician" means a physician and surgeon licensed by the Medical Board of California.

(f) "Health care provider" and "health care professional" mean a person or facility or employee of a health care facility licensed, certified, or otherwise authorized by the law of this state to administer health care in the ordinary course of business or practice of a profession.

(g) "Community care facility" means a community care facility as defined in Section 1502 of the Health and Safety Code.

(h) "Qualified patient" means a mentally competent adult patient who has voluntarily executed a currently valid revocable Directive as defined in this section, who has been diagnosed and certified in writing by two physicians to be afflicted with a terminal condition, and who has expressed an enduring request for aid–in–dying. One of said physicians shall be the attending physician as defined in subdivision (a). Both physicians shall have personally examined the patient.

(i) "Enduring request" means a request for aid–in–dying, expressed on more than one occasion.

(j) "Terminal condition" means an incurable or irreversible condition which will, in the opinion of two certifying physicians exercising reasonable medical judgment, result in death within six months or less. One of said physicians shall be the attending physician as defined in subdivision (a).

(k) "Aid–in–dying" means a medical procedure that will terminate the life of the qualified patient in a painless, humane, and dignified manner whether administered by the physician at the patient's choice or direction or whether the physician provides means to the patient for self–administration.

2525.3. Witnessed Directive

A mentally competent adult individual may at any time voluntarily execute a revocable Directive governing the administration of aid–in–dying. The Directive shall be signed by the declarant and witnessed by two adults who at the time of witnessing, meet the following requirements:

(a) Are not related to the declarant by blood or marriage, or adoption.

(b) Are not entitled to any portion of the estate of the declarant upon his or her death under any will of the declarant or codicil thereto then existing, or, at the time of the Directive, by operation of law then existing.

(c) Have no creditor's claim against the declarant, or anticipate making such claim against any portion of the estate of the declarant upon his or her death.

(d) Are not the attending physician, an employee of the attending physician, a health care provider, or an employee of a health care provider.

(e) Are not the operator of a community care facility or an employee of a community care facility.

The Directive shall be substantially in the form contained in Section 2525.24.

2525.4. Skilled Nursing Facilities

A Directive shall have no force or effect if the declarant is a patient in a skilled nursing facility as defined in subdivision (c) of Section 1250 of the Health and Safety Code and intermediate care facility or community care facility at the time the Directive is executed unless one of the two witnesses to the Directive is a Patient Advocate or Ombudsman designated by the Department of Aging for this purpose pursuant to any other applicable provision of law. The Patient Advocate or Ombudsman shall have the same qualifications as a witness under Section 2525.3.

The intent of this paragraph is to recognize that some patients in skilled nursing facilities may be so insulated from a voluntary decision–making role, by virtue of the custodial nature of their care, as to require special assurance that they are capable of willingly and voluntarily executing a Directive.

2525.5. Revocation

A Directive may be revoked at any time by the declarant, without regard to his or her mental state or competency, by any of the following methods:

(a) By being canceled, defaced, obliterated, burned, torn, or otherwise destroyed by or at the direction of the declarant with the intent to revoke the Directive.

(b) By a written revocation of the declarant expressing his or her intent to revoke the Directive, signed and dated by the declarant. If the declarant is in a health care facility and under the care and management of a physician, the physician shall record in the patient's medical record the time and date when he or she received notification of the written revocation.

(c) By a verbal expression by the declarant of his or her intent to revoke the Directive. The revocation shall become effective only upon communication to the attending physician by the declarant. The attending physician shall confirm with the patient that he or she wishes to revoke, and shall record in the patient's medical record the time, date, and place of the revocation.

There shall be no criminal, civil, or administrative liability on the part of any health care provider for following a Directive that has been revoked unless that person has actual knowledge of the revocation.

2525.6. Term of Directive

A Directive shall be effective unless and until revoked in the manner prescribed in Section 2525.5. This title shall not prevent a declarant from reexecuting a Directive at any time in accordance with Section 2525.3, including reexecution subsequent to a diagnosis of a terminal condition.

2525.7. Administration of Aid-in-Dying

When, and only when, a qualified patient determines that the time for physician aid–in–dying has arrived and has made an enduring request, the patient will communicate that determination directly to the attending physician who will administer aid–in–dying in accordance with this Act.

2525.8. No Compulsion

Nothing herein requires a physician to administer aid–in–dying, or a licensed health care professional, such as a nurse, to participate in administering aid–in–dying under the direction of a physician, if he or she is religiously, morally, or ethically opposed. Neither shall privately owned hospitals be required to permit the administration of physician aid–in–dying in their facilities if they are religiously, morally, or ethically opposed.

2525.9. Protection of Health Care Professionals

No physician, health care facility, or employee of a health care facility who, acting in accordance with the requirements of this title, administers aid–in–dying to a qualified patient shall be subject to civil, criminal, or administrative liability therefore. No licensed health care professional, such as a nurse, acting under the direction of a physician, who participates in the administration of aid–in–dying to a qualified patient in accordance with this title shall be subject to any civil, criminal, or administrative liability. No physician, or licensed health care professional acting under the direction of a physician, who acts in accordance with the provisions of this chapter, shall be guilty of any criminal act or of unprofessional conduct because he or she administers aid–in–dying.

2525.10. Transfer of Patient

No physician, or health care professional or health care provider acting under the direction of a physician, shall be criminally, civilly, or administratively liable for failing to effectuate the Directive of the qualified patient, unless there is willful failure to transfer the patient to any physician, health care professional, or health care provider upon request of the patient.

2525.11. Fees

Fees, if any, for administering aid–in–dying shall be fair and reasonable.

2525.12. Independent Physicians

The certifying physicians shall not be partners or shareholders in the same medical practice.

2525.13. Consultations

An attending physician who is requested to give aid–in–dying may request a psychiatric or psychological consultation if that physician has any concern about the patient's competence, with the consent of a qualified patient.

2525.14. Directive Compliance

Prior to administering aid–in–dying to a qualified patient, the attending physician shall take reasonable steps to determine that the Directive has been signed and witnessed, and all steps are in accord with the desires of the patient, expressed in the Directive and in their personal discussions. Absent knowledge to the contrary, a physician or other health care provider may presume the Directive complies with this title and is valid.

2525.15. Medical Standards

No physician shall be required to take any action contrary to reasonable medical standards in administering aid–in–dying.

2525.16. Not Suicide

Requesting and receiving aid–in–dying by a qualified patient in accordance with this title shall not, for any purpose, constitute a suicide.

2525.17. Insurance

(a) No insurer doing business in California shall refuse to insure, cancel, refuse to renew, reassess the risk of an insured, or raise premiums on the basis of whether or not the insured has considered or completed a Directive. No insurer may require or request the insured to disclose whether he or she has executed a Directive.

(b) The making of a Directive pursuant to Section 2525.3 shall not restrict, inhibit, or impair in any manner the sale, procurement, issuance or rates of any policy of life, health, or disability insurance, nor shall it affect in any way the terms of an existing policy of life, health, or disability insurance. No policy of life, health, or disability insurance shall be legally impaired or invalidated in any manner by the administration of aid–in–dying to an insured qualified patient, notwithstanding any term of the policy to the contrary.

(c) No physician, health care facility, or other health care provider, and no health care service plan, insurer issuing disability insurance, other insurer, self–insured employee welfare benefit plan, or nonprofit hospital service plan shall require any person to execute or prohibit any person from executing a Directive as a condition for being insured for, or receiving, health care services, nor refuse service because of the execution, the existence, or the revocation of a Directive.

(d) A person who, or a corporation, or other business which, requires or prohibits the execution of a Directive as a condition for being insured for, or receiving, health care services is guilty of a misdemeanor.

(e) No life insurer doing business in California may refuse to pay sums due upon the death of the insured whose death was assisted in accordance with this Act.

2525.18. Inducement

No patient may be pressured to make a decision to seek aid–in–dying because that patient is a financial, emotional, or other burden to his or her family, other persons, or the state. A person who coerces, pressures, or fraudulently induces another to execute a Directive under this title is guilty of a misdemeanor, or if death occurs as a result of said coercion, pressure, or fraud, is guilty of a felony.

2525.19. Tampering

Any person who willfully conceals, cancels, defaces, obliterates, or damages the Directive of another without the declarant's consent shall be guilty of a misdemeanor. Any person who falsifies or forges the Directive of another, or willfully conceals or withholds personal knowledge of a revocation as provided in Section 2525.5, with the intent to induce aid–in–dying procedures contrary to the wishes of the declarant, and thereby, because of such act, directly causes aid–in–dying to be administered, shall be subject to prosecution for unlawful homicide as provided in Chapter 1 (commencing with Section 187) of Title 8 of Part 1 of the Penal Code.

2525.20. Other Rights

This Act shall not impair or supersede any right or legal responsibility which any person may have regarding the withholding or withdrawal of life–sustaining procedures in any lawful manner.

2525.21. Reporting

Hospitals and other health care providers who carry out the Directive of a qualified patient shall keep a record of the number of these cases, and report annually to the State Department of Health Services the patient's age, type of illness, and the date the Directive was carried out. In all cases, the identity of the patient shall be strictly confidential and shall not be reported.

2525.22. Recording

The Directive, or a copy of the Directive, shall be made a part of a patient's medical record in each institution involved in the patient's medical care.

2525.23. Mercy Killing Disapproved

Nothing in this Act shall be construed to condone, authorize, or approve mercy killing.

2525.24. Form of Directive

In order for a Directive to be valid under this title, the Directive shall be in substantially the following form:

Voluntary Directive to Physicians

Notice to Patient:
This document will exist until it is revoked by you. This document revokes any prior Directive to administer aid–in–dying but does not revoke a durable power of attorney for health care or living will. You must follow the witnessing procedures described at the end of this form or the document will not be valid. You may wish to give your doctor a signed copy.

Instructions for Physician's Administration of a Medical Procedure to End My Life in a Painless, Humane, and Dignified Manner
This Directive is made this ____ day of _____ (month) _____ (year).
I, _____, being of sound mind, do voluntarily make known my desire that my life shall be ended with the aid of a physician in a painless, humane, and dignified manner when I have a terminal condition or illness, certified to be terminal by two physicians, and they determine that my death will occur within six months or less.
When the terminal diagnosis is made and confirmed, and this Directive is in effect, I may then ask my attending physician for aid–in–dying. I trust and hope that he or she will comply. If he or she refuses to comply,

which is his or her right, then I urge that he or she assist in locating a colleague who will comply.

Determining the time and place of my death shall be in my sole discretion. The manner of my death shall be determined jointly by my attending physician and myself.

This Directive shall remain valid until revoked by me. I may revoke this Directive at any time.

I recognize that a physician's judgment is not always certain, and that medical science continues to make progress in extending life, but in spite of these facts, I nevertheless wish aid–in–dying rather than letting my terminal condition take its natural course.

I will endeavor to inform my family of this Directive, and my intention to request the aid of my physician to help me to die when I am in a terminal condition, and take those opinions into consideration. But the final decision remains mine. I acknowledge that it is solely my responsibility to inform my family of my intentions.

I have given full consideration to and understand the full import of this Directive, and I am emotionally and mentally competent to make this Directive. I accept the moral and legal responsibility for receiving aid–in–dying.

This Directive will not be valid unless it is signed by two qualified witnesses who are present when you sign or acknowledge your signature. The witnesses must not be related to you by blood, marriage, or adoption; they must not be entitled to any part of your estate or at the time or execution of the Directive have no claim against any portion of your estate, nor anticipate making such claim against any portion of your estate; and they must not include: your attending physician, an employee of the attending physician; a health care provider; an employee of a health care provider; the operator of the community care facility or an employee of an operator of a community care facility.

If you have attached any additional pages to this form, you must sign and date each of the additional pages at the same time you date and sign this Directive.

Signed: _____

401. <<+ Suicide, aiding, advising or encouraging. +>> Every person who deliberately aids, or advises, or encourages another to commit suicide, is guilty of a felony. <<+ Death resulting from a request for aid–in–dying pursuant to Title 10.5 (commencing with Section 2525) of Division 3 or Part 4 of the Civil Code shall not constitute suicide, nor is a licensed physician who lawfully administers aid–in–dying or a health care provider or licensed health care professional acting under the direction of a physician,

liable under this section. Death resulting from aid–in–dying pursuant to a Directive in accordance with the Death With Dignity Act does not, for any purpose, constitute a homicide. +>>

SEC. 3. Amendment of Initiative

This Act may be amended only by a statute passed by a two–thirds vote of each house of the legislature and signed by the Governor.

15

Euthanasia as Power and Empowerment

David C. Thomasma

It may seem odd to link personal empowerment with efforts to legalize euthanasia. This is especially true when one considers the Nazi experience and the Holocaust, for these are the backdrop of any current discussion of euthanasia. Hence, my title combines the ways in which euthanasia has been a source of power over individuals exercised by the state, and the ways in which euthanasia is seen as a source of individual control over the dying process, the antithesis of state control. Because of the extremes on either side, the term *euthanasia*, originally meaning a "kind" or "mild" death, has acquired emotionally laden significance. For its opponents, euthanasia on the part of physicians or family members is equivalent to the evil perpetrated by the Nazis. For supporters, euthanasia is another of a family of rights due to individuals in modern society. Opponents and proponents could not be further apart.

Thus we have an irony. Euthanasia in recent times has come to represent all that is evil about state control over individual lives, and yet it is also seen as a rescuer from suffering and the burdens of dying in a technological society. This essay will examine the role of power and empowerment in the current debate over euthanasia in the United States. In part, then, this examination can aid in untangling the conflicting meanings of the term that occur in the current national debate and public policy disputes.

In this essay I will first sketch what can be learned from the Nazi experience; second, outline the factors that shape the current debate in the United States; then draw parallels between these and comparable factors in the Nazi experience about euthanasia and physician-assisted suicide, and draw some conclusions.

The Nazi Experience

Euthanasia has always been associated with power. For the most part, it has acquired a negative connotation, since the power with which it was associated most often in modern times was that of the state. Even though euthanasia had been discussed since the Middle Ages, and for about seventy years in German-speaking countries before the 1930s (Thomasma 1988), the Nazi experience has become a backdrop for the discussion of euthanasia. After the Second World War, the old connotation of euthanasia as mercy was displaced in the popular imagination by the nightmare revelations of a belligerent system of "health care" in which social hygiene, racial purity, and wartime triage reigned supreme. These new elements added to the discussion of euthanasia are the principal reasons its usage changed. No longer was it the tool of empowerment for individuals facing a certain and painful death, but the tool of a society willing to judge that some lives were "valueless"—lives of impure genetic heritage, infirmity, and ballast existence on the state—and lives not worth living. They had to be exterminated.

Nazi Germany was the first modern state to totally embrace the technological capacities of science and industry and turn them toward social goals. All modern states seek to do that today; the defect of the Nazis lay, not in this newfound ability to harness the media, science, medicine, popular culture, and industry to social goals, but in the social goals themselves (Lifton 1986; Roth 1984). In trying to understand what happened in Nazi Germany, incomprehensible though it may be, familiarity with these social goals is essential.

Social Hygiene

Peaking in the 1920s, a new scientific movement arose throughout the industrialized world that proposed that government should take much more control over the health of its citizens than it had heretofore. Germany was one of the first states to implement a national health plan. In fact, Weimar Republic medical care was the envy of the world. Within the context of this plan, and the social costs of providing health care, efforts were made at prevention of serious diseases. Some of the attention focused on altering behaviors that led to ill health, such as smoking. Dresden, for example, was the first city to issue a citywide ban on smoking in public places, as early as 1939 (Proctor 1992:28, n. 23). Some of the other state-sponsored activities included work on the relationship between sociobiology and crime, the ill effects of exposure to x-rays and asbestos, support for midwifery, urging high-fiber and low-fat diets, and even laws requiring every German bakery to produce whole-grain bread. Nazi physicians restricted the use of DDT and rationed tobacco for pregnant women since it would harm the fetus. But most attention was paid to prevention through the elimination of genetic "impurities," a point I will return to in the next section, for it is the best-known rationale for Nazi euthanasia policies.

Because of its emphasis on "social hygiene," and its incorporation of many of the newest "scientific" ideas on the interrelation between human behavior, social health, and technological innovations, the Nazi party was very popular among university graduates. In fact, the Nazis were not "foisted" upon an unwilling populace, as the popular myth would have it, but they rose to power with a large measure of popularity, much of which came from the intelligentsia and business. While over half of Germany's physicians joined the Nazi party by 1942, 8 percent had joined before the party ever even came to power (Proctor 1992:26). Hence, physicians in varying degrees not only cooperated with the party and its goals for the national health, they helped shape them.

While there is nothing inherently immoral about physicians joining a political party whose views about communism and the latest scientific and medical research about social health they may share, some physicians knew, of course, that by embracing these views they would be wresting power from the socialist and communist physicians, many of whom were Jewish. More than half of the physicians in Berlin were Jewish, many holding prominent positions in the profession. Certainly, most who joined the party did so in part out of self-interest. The real moral problem lay in the Nazi goal of social hygiene that overwhelmed the traditional medical duties and virtues of promoting the best interests of patients by putting the patient first. Although surely some physicians had qualms of conscience, most Nazi physicians thought they were promoting the goals of a better civil society. In fact, no one forced them to participate in the euthanasia project. Every action was voluntary in this regard. It seemed, instead, to be their duty as citizens and as professionals to encourage social hygiene.

The chief Nazi physician and medical ethicist, Rudolph Ramm, echoing an earlier statement of the previous century, could therefore write: "Only a good person can be a good physician" (Proctor 1992:17; Ramm 1942),a sentiment no one could disagree with. Yet these words echo through time in demonstrating how closely linked are our sense of moral duty and the social goals set by the society in which we live. If the latter are accepted uncritically, then we have failed in our moral duty. Not only is the "unexamined life not worth living," as Socrates said long ago, it is also dangerous. How could these intelligent and well-educated people have participated in programs that exercised life-and-death dominion over individual, vulnerable human lives?

Eugenics

Among the most dramatic of the new wave of developments after the turn of the century was the exploration of the role of genetics in producing poor health and mental retardation. The literature in the world medical journals was filled with insights about this major cause of disease. Not only did the literature contain scientific discoveries; it also contained proposals for reducing genetically based disease. Removing the "polluters" of the genetic purity of the human race was the first and foremost interest of those promoting social hygiene (Proctor 1988).

However, the Nazis were not the only ones to accept this line of thought. Sterilization of the retarded, it was widely believed, would be a major step toward "cleaning up" the human gene pool. In fact, it was practiced in the United States. Foster Kennedy, in an article in the *American Journal of Psychiatry* even advocated the killing of retarded children, "nature's mistakes," as he termed them (Kennedy 1942). German physicians worried constantly in their journals about how far ahead of them the United States was in eugenics. By the late 1920s some 15,000 individuals had been sterilized in the United States,

> most while incarcerated in prisons or homes for the mentally ill. German racial hygienists throughout the Weimar period expressed their envy of American achievements in this area, warning that unless the Germans made progress in this field, America would become the world's racial leader. (Proctor 1992:21)

The power of eugenics as a scientific discipline was coupled in Nazi Germany with an intolerance for other races.Germany came very late to the family of nations; there had never been a unified Germany until after World War I. Furthermore, postwar Germany arose within the context of a psychology of humiliating defeat. The same chauvinism that is often a part of the early stages of nationalism found a receptive audience in Germany regarding the peoples on its borders. Germany's democratic structure was not the vision of Germans themselves so much as the vision of the allied victors. The rush to define this new state, while long the goal of German-speaking people, easily latched onto genetic, or ethnic, purity as a condition of being truly "German." Parenthically, a point to be pressed further, too, is that even in America, the American Medical Association refused to admit black physicians. As Proctor points out, this permitted the Nazis to argue that they were not the only ones to protect racial "purity" in the professions and in society as a whole (Proctor 1992:23; "Keine Negeraerzte" 1939–40).

Therefore, social hygiene utilized eugenics in pursuit of its goals to destroy individual autonomy and create a mass society. In a state in search of its own national identity, an intolerant and dictatorial regime underlined its weakness in world affairs and ignored its defeat in the First World War by proclaiming its people in "scientific" terms as the "master race." The Nazis further consolidated their power by proclaiming themselves the last bastion against world communism. The fact that so many socialists and communists were Jewish conveniently tied social hygiene, capitalism, industriousness, and well-run social order with eugenics, a science that would eliminate "alien" and nonproductive strains from the national identity.

Wartime Triage

Perhaps the least-understood feature of Nazi Germany's euthanasia efforts was the explicit use of wartime triage as a rationale for eliminating "valueless life." If times were different, Nazi physicians argued, economics would not be a factor in the problem of social hygiene. But because of the high rate of inflation between the wars, and the necessity for providing beds for soldiers and others who were needed for the coming war effort, "unnecessary eaters," a major burden on the state, would have to be eliminated.

Proctor maintains that "the fundamental argument for forcible euthanasia was economic" (Proctor 1992:24). The use of this argument was a preemptive effort to free up beds and conserve resources for the coming war. Hitler's first directive that euthanasia be permitted for special cases of medical need occurred in 1939, coinciding with the invasion of Poland. It made euthanasia of the seriously and terminally ill more easily justifiable. Quickly, however, euthanasia turned into mercy killing (euthanasia without request). Proctor notes (1992:24) that the first mental patients were gassed in Posen, in Poland, on October 15, 1939, just forty-five days after the invasion by Germany. By 1941, euthanasia was part of the normal hospital routine in Germany. At one point psychiatrists actually worried that they would have no more patients; the field would simply become too small (Mueller-Hill 1988:42). The application of "mercy" to this population was based on an earlier justification. During World War I half of all German mental patients starved to death, according to one estimate, 45,000 in Prussia alone (Proctor 1992:24). These were the "useless eaters" who were simply too far down on the ration list to obtain food. Such an experience, coupled with the long campaign by the Nazis to stigmatize the handicapped and the mentally ill as having lives not worth living, led very quickly to the inauguration of the liquidation program.

Expendability of some human lives is a judgment regarding the balance between the quality of life of vulnerable individuals and the needs and wants of society itself. From a purely utilitarian standpoint, those who contribute nothing to society, and drain its resources, are expendable. Drs. Binding and Hoche, Nazi party euthanasia theorists, called such people "ballast existence." In their view, when economic times are prosperous, society does not ask questions about caring for expendable individuals. When times get difficult, however, then such "ballast existence" must be eliminated: "The question of whether the expense of maintaining these categories of ballast existence is in every aspect justifiable was not an urgent one in former times of prosperity. Today conditions are different and we have to consider it" (Binding and Hoche 1920 as quoted in Lauter and Meyer 1984). Note how easily the notion of triage conflates with the economic justification for mercy killing.

Factors Shaping the Debate

In contrast to the killings carried out on the vulnerable and socially undesirable in Nazi Germany, "euthanasia" today has an entirely different connotation. Some of the factors that shape the debate in the United States today are among the following.

Powerlessness

Euthanasia has come to stand for the ultimate patient's-rights metaphor, the "way out" of serious suffering for oneself and one's family. Strongly committed pro-lifers have clutched my arm after panel discussions and presentations, alarmed by the violence and anti-life forces in our society, and yet they make an exception for euthanasia, noting that in modern health care, there must be a way out for those who suffer. This feeling most probably stems from the feeling of powerlessness amid modern medical technology and the expensive health care system under whose care almost 80 percent of us will die.

Ignoring Wishes and Preferences

Many Americans take the path of what is called "passive," or indirect, euthanasia. Passive euthanasia accomplishes a "good" death by restraining the use of our technology. Sufficient fears exist, however, that doctors and hospitals will not honor one's wishes regarding technological care near the end of life that the National Patient Self-Determination Act was passed as law, effective December 1, 1991. Not everyone takes advantage of the provisions of this law, which requires health care institutions to notify patients of their rights to advance directives. Only about 10 percent of patients do so. When they do, the document is to be placed in the chart and the institution must notify the patient of how it intends to respond to these advance directives. Should an institution not agree, then the patient would know ahead of time what to expect, and could ask for a transfer elsewhere. However, it would be legally dangerous for an institution to directly override an advance directive. This usually only occurs when a family is divided about how or when to apply it.

There is some concern, for example, that doctors and institutions will ignore advance directives, especially if the patient becomes incompetent yet is stable, e.g., after a stroke. Should the advance directives include foregoing fluids and nutrition or a respirator, health care professionals worry about "standing by and letting someone die" who is not terminally ill. Since many patients and families have heard such stories or have seen the conflict between autonomy and paternalism, displayed through movies such as *Whose Life is It Anyway* or on talk shows or soap operas, there is pressure in our society to have, at least, some final "way out" of this dilemma, the right to die, the right to euthanasia.

For some, like former U.S. Surgeon General C. Everett Koop, withholding treatment from incompetent patients is a violation of the patient's constitutional right to life. This is a vitalist position that few physicians would employ at the bedside for competent patients (Loewy 1987). The opposite view is expressed, for example, by Joseph Fletcher, an early and strong proponent of the right to die. "Death control . . . is a matter of human dignity. Without it persons become puppets. To perceive this is to grasp the error lurking in the notion that life, as such, is the highest good" (Fletcher 1974).

Infantilization

One reason adults feel infantilized in today's health care institutions, and therefore at risk of losing control over their own dying process, is that modern health care has become so technological and specialized that it must be practiced in institutions. In this alien environment, individuals are told where to go, when to get up, when tests will be conducted, and how to behave. One's family is also subject to the rules of the institution. Furthermore, seriously ill patients are flat on their backs; should discussions occur they are always ones in which specialists "look down" on them, both literally and figuratively, thus disrupting normal forms of communication (Bergsma and Thomasma 1982).

Technologization of Care

Most Americans are sympathetic with people who must die a slow, lingering, painful death due to severe terminal illness. We can understand how, even when pain may be controlled, the suffering that accompanies dying must also be addressed. For this reason a good argument can be made that doctors should assist in dying, in bringing about a so-called good death, especially in the face of burgeoning medical technology (Cerne 1990). For the most part this can be accomplished by what is called passive euthanasia, by withholding or even withdrawing medical technology at the patient's request. Sometimes this may be accomplished in the absence of an explicit request, as suggested in the Appleton Consensus (Stanley 1989).

Most medical technology was invented for the purpose of prolonging life. When it is used indiscriminately, it unnecessarily prolongs the dying process. Withholding and withdrawing, then, are forms of taking responsibility for our technology ("The Care of the Dying" 1989). Keeping unnecessary technology out of the dying process at the request of the patient and family is a way of honoring the primacy of human life and human values over mere existence . In this regard Jonsen wonders just what exactly life support supports: "We talk about the maintenance of life; we don't often talk about the maintenance of personhood. It interests me little, indeed, not at all, to be alive as an organism. In such a state I have no interests. It is enormously interesting for me to be a person . . . it is the perpetuation of my personhood that interests me; indeed, it is probably my major and perhaps my sole real interest" (Jonsen 1988).

Care by Strangers

A further impetus for legalizing euthanasia is that most health care practiced in institutions is by strangers. The patient does not know the caregivers, as he or she might know their primary-care physician or nurse practitioner. Instead, a veritable army of new people approach the dying patient with their recommendations. Additionally, the caregivers do not know the patient nor the patient's values, given a patient's incapacity to convey them.

Normally, the patient's value hierarchy governs the medical interaction. In this hierarchy, the patient's ultimate values and life plans often influence and sometimes supersede the therapeutic plan of the caregivers. If a patient becomes incompetent this hierarchy of values (personal over medical) is reversed, and the lower values governed by medical care will tend to supersede the higher values the patient worked hard during his or her life to develop (Pellegrino and Thomasma 1989). In this scenario, there is a great danger that the patient's values will be ignored simply by not being known or conveyed. Should the patient become incompetent and not left any advance directives, care decisions usually turn on the physician's recommendations and the patient's family. The latter's discussion of what their loved one would want is often tempered by their own fears of not abandoning that person during his or her dying process, and by the overwhelming nature of life-prolonging health care technology.

The Dutch Experience

Some lessons can be taken from the Dutch experience with euthanasia. It can no longer be called an "experiment" since some physicians, like Pieter Admiraal, an anesthesiologist who works with terminal cancer patients, have been performing active, direct euthanasia since the mid-1960s. Against the backdrop of the Nazi experience, the Dutch have challenged all our preconceptions. This is especially true for the Dutch, since they suffered greatly under Nazi rule. They have always been known to Americans as "solid" people, not easily swayed by the newest fashion. "Extreme" is not a description of the Dutch that might immediately come to mind. So why have the Dutch embraced euthanasia so readily?

Surely the reasons reflect the general concerns mentioned already. In addition, for many Dutch people, senseless dying is just that, it makes no sense. The Dutch are a frugal people, too. In light of the costs of prolonged treatment for cancer or other devastating diseases, the proportion between treatment and outcome becomes very important. This is especially true within the context of a national health plan. Active, direct euthanasia is offered within the context of an extensive and intensive terminal treatment program. Physicians work directly with the patients and are known to them for extensive periods of time. Often euthanasia occurs in the home, under the direction of the family practitioner, most of whom have known the patients all their lives, and are familiar with the patient's values (Van der Wal 1992). In fact, in a mandatory report to the government prosecutor, a Dutch physician who anticipates performing active, direct euthanasia must spell out the patients' values as they lead to this request, how no other solution seems possible for the control of pain and suffering, and how an additional physician concurs that terminal illness is present and that nothing further can be done (Remmelink 1992).

This context of care differs markedly from the situation in the United States, one that I have characterized as occurring largely between strangers in an impersonal environment for the patient. Dutch physicians regularly visit their patients in their homes during the dying process. In fact, very few requests for euthanasia come from residents of nursing homes, as compared with the number coming from people cared for by their own general practitioners (Van der Wal 1992; Kimsma and van Leeuwen 1993). In fact, the Dutch experience is so different from the American that it would be more instructional to compare them by way of their differences.

First, terminal care is offered as part of a comprehensive national health plan, such that no person need be concerned that his or her care will "bankrupt" their heirs, or even the system itself. Free from worries about the personal costs of care, the Dutch can concentrate on their loved ones and their environment during the dying process. Unlike the United States, where about 80 percent of individuals die in institutions, and where up to 40 percent of the Medicare and Medicaid budget is spent during the last three months of life, the Dutch tend to die at home, surrounded by their loved ones. Third, their care is undertaken by their personal physician whom they have known over a lifetime, and who is or becomes quite familiar with their value system. There are no institutional urgencies involved when the Dutch ask to be euthanized, nor is their physician placed at risk economically and legally (assuming the right procedures are followed). Fourth, since the action of euthanasia is nonetheless still illegal, a rigorous system of checks and balances is required. The physician must feel strongly that every possible alternative has been tried and that the continuation of life would be meaningless from the perspective of the patient's own value system. Finally, as noted, euthanasia itself is offered only in the context of a very thorough terminal care program, not as a convenient escape from the necessities of offering such a terminal care program, as it might be seen to do in the United States.

Intentionality

In addition to the public policy discussion about legalizing active, direct euthanasia and physician-assisted suicide, the debate over the morality of such actions also continues. For the most part, ethicists and legal scholars have come to accept the notion that there is no morally significant difference between the decision to withhold or withdraw treatment in order to let a patient die and the decision to offer direct assistance in dying (Rachels 1975; Thomasma 1988). As recently as 1992 in the first trial of Dr. Jack Kevorkian over his assistance at the suicide of individuals who were not terminally ill, Judge Breck noted that there was no legal distinction between a doctor withdrawing life support and a doctor injecting a patient with lethal drugs: "In both cases, the physician is causing death to occur" ("Kevorkian Cleared of Murder Charge" 1992). In November 1992, Kevorkian assisted Catherine Andreyev, forty-six, in her suicide. Kevorkian noted about intention that "the aim of suicide is to end a life. . . . The aim of this is to terminate unbearable suffering. I've made progress because for one more human being, suffering is ended" ("Kevorkian Helps Another Woman" 1992).

It must be acknowledged, in the struggle to gain control of the dying process, that for some individuals death is a good thing. If so, then helping to bring about that death is also a good and moral act. The debate in the United States and elsewhere should center on the methodology used to bring about a good death, not on the morality of intending the death of another (Thomasma and Graber 1990).

Nonetheless, Western religious ethics does concentrate on intentionality. If one never intends the death of another, but instead the relief of suffering, even if the action taken results in death, such as giving a high enough dose of morphine to alleviate pain, then that person has not assumed dominion over the life of another human being. Thus, it is argued, the parents of Nancy Beth Cruzan never intended that she die when they withdrew her feeding. They would have rejoiced if she were miraculously to recover and be herself again. But death was foreseen as the most obvious result of such withdrawal nevertheless. To this way of thinking, intentionality matters a great deal, since it maintains "purity of heart." No one assumes godlike power over another person, but the end result, the relief of unbearable suffering, is the same.

Similarly, the distinction between active and passive euthanasia, or direct and indirect, does hinge on intentionality. If one intends the death of another, then there is no moral difference between active and passive euthanasia, as most ethicists have argued, and Judge Breck is correct in noting the lack of legal distinction as well. However, if one intends not death but the relief of suffering, then the distinction acquires validity. By withdrawing burdensome technologies, or death-delaying interventions, one relieves the sufferings and burdens of dying in a technological environment, "allowing nature to take its course." One does not bring the death about directly, though it may be foreseen and is not morally repulsive

(Gillon 1986). In other words, one does not determine the moment of death by direct intervention.

This philosophical concern about intentionality bears weight in the public policy arena as well. As Reinhard Priester has noted ("Kevorkian Helps Another Woman" 1992), Dr. Kevorkian's actions may be motivated by a crusade to legitimate his kind of actions by steadily eroding the public concern over physician-assisted suicide and euthanasia ("Kevorkian Helps Another Woman" 1992). If it happens often enough, people tend to get used to it. Public discussion about such a serious matter should take place throughout society before efforts are under way to get such actions legalized. Taking power over the dying process is both an intensely personal concern and a public policy concern. If it is not a legitimate act, then how can we ask our physicians for this kind of help at the end of our lives?

For proponents of autonomy, worries about intentionality seem to be a very fine point indeed. Their argument is that individuals have control over their own lives, and that unbearable suffering demands a response from physicians (Miller 1987). Some members of the Hemlock Society, a right-to-die advocacy group, disagree that physicians should control dangerous substances with which individuals might be able to kill themselves whenever they wished were they available without prescription. They maintain that the right to die is an individual's entitlement, and that any delays caused by the supposed need for advanced and thorough public discussion is a stalling tactic taken by conservatives to deny them their rights. Furthermore, it simply won't do to continue to provide the type of assistance as given by physicians such as Timothy Quill (1991), since, in order to avoid the legal ramifications of assisting in suicides in states where that is illegal, physicians tend to abandon their patients. The patients who do utilize physician-assisted suicide must do so in isolation, cut off from the presence of family and caregivers. The arguments in favor of gaining control over the dying process focus instead on the individual's need to be surrounded by loved ones and supporters as death approaches.

Although physician-assisted suicide and euthanasia may be morally distinct issues from the point of view of intention, from the point of view of empowerment over the dying process they are not. Three euthanasia-legitimation initiatives, first in California, then in Washington, and then again in California, have failed to gain acceptance by a majority of citizens voting, but only by a narrow margin (Kushner 1993). Regarding assisted suicide, Rosenblum and Forsythe reviewed current legislation and judicial opinions on the right to assisted suicide and concluded that state statutes suggest that "the prospects for the legalization of assisted suicide in the near future are very good," but later caution that in American law this right may begin to appear "through current judicial trends in the nontreatment of incompetent patients [rather] than through explicit legislative acceptance" (Rosenblum and Forsythe 1990). These authors, however, are very concerned about the possible trend toward what they regard as mistreatment of the vulnerable.

Historical Contrasts and Parallels with Today's Debate

No one could seriously argue that the United States today is in danger of becoming like Nazi Germany, and that therefore euthanasia should not be legalized. There may be other reasons for resisting euthansia's legalization, as we shall see, but we do not have the unique configuration of social goods, powerful state, accommodating professionals, and willing citizenry that was found in Germany between the wars. Hence, what happened in Nazi Germany is not really germane to the debate about euthanasia in the United States today.

This is a comforting thought, but not one without its own dangers. The greatest danger is to ignore all of the lessons learned from world history. Some of the factors shaping today's debate are very close to those that shaped the discussion in Nazi Germany that led to social programs eliminating the vulnerable and weak (Thomasma 1990). The movement toward legalizing euthanasia was widely discussed, as it is in the United States today. It was supposedly from the arguments of mercy that Hitler signed into law the permission for certain designated physicians to kill patients (*Gnadentod*, or "merciful death") judged "incurably sick by medical examination" (Proctor 1992:23). This order is not far from Dr. Kevorkian's suggestion that only certain trained physicians, called obitiarists, would be able to carry out euthanasia for those who request it (Kevorkian 1991).

As we have seen, however, Hitler's order soon was focused on the retarded and mentally ill. By 1941, 70,000 patients in mental institutions had been euthanized (Proctor 1992:23–26; 1988:179–189). For the Nazis this was just one step toward a greater social hygiene, which included the eventual elimination of Jews, gypsies, and socialists of all stripes. It takes a powerful state to unleash these destructive forces within the medical community itself. Yet so far our international and national discussion concentrates entirely on voluntary active euthanasia.

The power, rather than the empowerment, of euthanasia, stems from a social desire to provide an orderly and healthy society. Think of our current movement for environmental cleanliness and preservation. Greater and greater efforts will be made in the future toward underlining our "social responsibility" to monitor, control, and renew scarce resources.

How soon would we turn our attention from other costs to the high cost of caring for extremely elderly and debilitated persons? Already the discussion of euthanizing the demented elderly has begun in the United States (Thomasma 1992).

At first blush, what would appear to be the explicit downgrading of the intrinsic value of human life seems very foreign to our way of thinking. Most Americans would react with dismay, even horror, at such a statement. We also have the advantage of hindsight into the devastating consequences of such thinking. The stench of the death camps is a pall that still hangs over Western civilization.

Yet attitudes of superiority and of devaluing individual lives creep into our own thinking as well, for instance, while constructing what we consider to be rational allocation plans for health care. While we intend to minimize suffering and maximize the common good, large numbers of individuals face neglect. Perhaps the biggest worry about euthanasia today is the forthcoming crisis in health care that will be created by an increasingly elderly population. Those over eighty-five years of age in the next fifty years will increase fivefold, from three million to fifteen million citizens. Many of these people will be dependent on long-term nursing home care. Such care is the most expensive medical cost for the elderly. In all state budgets, Medicaid is the second largest budget item after education. People over eighty-five, in fact, take four times as much money to cover a hospitalization than those under eighty-five. There will be fewer individuals "in the middle," able to bear the burden of caring for the young and the elderly. The phenomenon of the elderly (seventy to eighty-five years of age) caring for the "old old" (those over eighty-five) has already begun.

Recall that the fundamental argument for forcible euthanasia is almost invariably economic. Once the official mechanism for active voluntary euthanasia is in place, habits of finding other areas for "mercy," coupled with hard economic times, could easily lead to involuntary euthanasia. This is yet another form of the traditional slippery slope argument, based on fears about the violence in American society and the natural human propensity to find technical solutions to difficult social problems, ones we can only imagine for the future, but ones that our children must face soon enough. If we set the wrong precedents in the present, why would we think the same sort of thinking that occurred in Nazi Germany would not arise again?

Proponents of direct euthanasia usually argue that fences can be built on the slope, legal requirements that would eschew even the most remote possibility of a society turning mercy into murder once more (Cassel and Meier 1990). The United States is a nation under the rule of law. If anything, we tend to appeal too readily to law to resolve disputes. It is one of our

strengths, that in a highly pluralistic culture, we are able to resolve fundamental disagreements by such an appeal.

Does the evidence so far support the view that concerns about misuse
and abuse can be met by establishing those "fences" in the law? While no
immediate conclusion can be drawn at this time, it is important for academic debate to include an awareness of the level of social violence in American society today, where individuals are killed simply because another
person wants their sports jacket, or small children are killed in projects on
their way to school. This violence not only manifests itself in the inner city.
It is a pandemic of our society. It infects us even when we are wary of it, it
barrages us in "coming attractions" in the movie theaters. Hence, the smile
of reason from the Enlightenment is, today, an anachronism. Humanism
itself, it seems to me, does not take sufficient account of the power of evil
in human society and in human hearts, an acknowledgement we must
make. It is the respect we must pay to all those who did lose their lives in
the Holocaust. Thus, it is not entirely inconceivable that the Nazi experience could be a preview of our own coming attractions.

The heart of a massive public discussion ought to include the question
about what sort of society we ought to be. Have we become so frighten-
ingly fractured that people feel the need to dispatch themselves early in a
chronic disease rather than trust others to care for them? Christine Cassel
has expressed her concern that elderly people, in light of the Cruzan decision, will want to commit suicide rather than subject themselves to possible violations of their values in nursing homes and hospitals after they
become senile (Cassel and Meier 1990); there is evidence of a growing
trend in elder suicide (Conwel, Rotenberg, and Caine 1990). Will people
increasingly feel threatened by high-technology hospitals where they are
stripped of their values at the same time they are stripped of their clothing
and put into the beds? Do we have to carry all sorts of lengthy legal documents on our person about our wishes regarding medical technology
should we become ill or get in an accident? On a trip, will we be warned by
relatives about our advance directives and living wills?

That being said, it is also important to recognize that a constant focus on
the voluntariness of euthanasia in all discussion and debate about euthanasia can assure avoidance of mercy killing. What the Nazis did was not
euthanasia, but murder, purely and simply, for the "good" of the state. If
quality-of-life judgments and social-utility judgments are constantly held
in check by our cultural and historical memory of the Holocaust, then we
will be well on the way toward providing a humane solution to the problem of suffering at the end of life.

Is American society ready for euthanasia, properly understood? The
answer is no. For the Dutch, euthanasia must remain an illegal activity so

that it can be closely monitored. More than that, though, euthanasia should never be made an accepted social practice. By legalizing it, one immediately alters perceptions, like the Germans who made it part of "routine" medical practice. Instead, by keeping it illegal, its use must be rather extensively justified in each instance, so that one would not be prosecuted (Kimsma and van Leeuwen 1993). Some physician-ethicists like Eric Cassel and Howard Brody do argue in favor of physician-assisted suicide, but only if such cases are first subject to individual review, and only if they are intended to relieve unmitigated suffering (Cassel 1992; Brody 1992). Others argue that physicians should never directly cause death, since this will lead to public mistrust of the profession at a time when it is already subject to criticism for its appropriation of power over individual lives.

Independent, then, from the question of whether euthanasia is a justifiable moral act, or might be justifiable in a limited number of instances at the borders of ethical behavior, the question of strategy and social policy must also be assessed. This assessment must include more attention to issues of power and empowerment, since these are almost always suggested in the debate, even in the titles of articles such as "Prisoners of Technology" (Angell 1990), "Dignity" (Brooks 1984), and "Futility" (Tomlinson and Brody 1990).

Conclusion

The syndicated cartoonist who creates "Mr. Boffo" has a strip where a man is about to jump off a building, with a person giving him advice. The caption is "Right Advice, Wrong Time Award." The advice the potential suicide has been given is: "Jump; count to ten, then pull the cord."

This cartoon illustrates the concerns we have about urging euthanasia too soon, and about neglecting other forms of caring for the dying. We move too quickly in our society toward an easy "technical" solution to difficult moral and personal problems. Our society is not yet ready for active, direct euthanasia because it lacks the patience to develop guidelines for adequate terminal care, in the context of which proponents of active, direct euthanasia acquire their most telling arguments. Outside of this context, what looks on the surface like empowerment through legalization of euthanasia might turn out to be a danger in the United States like it was in Nazi Germany, for instance, should we ever enter again into a depression or other severe economic crisis.

It is always a dangerous move to empower the state over individuals; this is more true today than it was fifty years ago, when the technology had not developed to the extent it that it has today. Furthermore, we should cultivate a healthy respect for the role of evil in the human heart and human affairs. While such a respect is often missing in humanistic and autonomy-based writings, it is, as we have seen, very germane to the question of promoting euthanasia.

References

Angell, M. 1990. "Prisoners of Technology—The Case of Nancy Cruzan (Editorial)," *New England Journal of Medicine* 322:1226–1228.

Bergsma, J., and D. C. Thomasma. 1982. *Healthcare: Its Psychosocial Dimensions*. Pittsburgh: Duquesne University Press.

Brody, H. 1992. *The Healer's Power*. New Haven: Yale University Press.

Brooks, S. A. 1984. "Dignity and Cost-Effectiveness—A Rejection of the Utilitarian Approach to Death." *Journal of Medical Ethics* 10:148–151.

"The Care of the Dying: A Symposium on the Case of Betty Wright." 1989. Law, Medicine and Health Care 17(3) (Fall):205–268.

Cassel, C., and D. E. Meier. 1990. "Morals and Moralism in the Debate Over Euthanasia and Assisted Suicide." *New England Journal of Medicine* 323:750–752.

Cerne, F. 1990. "Mercy or Murder? Physician's Role in Suicide Spurs Debate," *American Hospital Association News* 26 (July 2):1, 5.

Conwell, Y., M. Rotenberg, and E. D. Caine. 1990. "Completed Suicide at Age 50 and Over." *Journal of the American Geriatrics Society* 38(6) (June):640–644.

Fletcher, J. 1974. "Four Indicators of Humanhood: The Enquiry Matures." *Hastings Center Report* 4 (December):4–7.

Gillon, R. 1986. "The Principle of Double Effect and Medical Ethics," *British Medical Journal* 292, 193–194.

Jonsen, A., 1988. "What does Life Support Support?" In W. Winslade, ed., *Personal Choices and Public Commitments: Perspectives on the Humanities*, pp. 61–69. Galveston, Tex.: Institute for the Medical Humanities.

"Keine Negeraerzte in der amerikanischen Standesorganisation." 1939. *Archiv fuer Rassen- und Gesellschaftsbiologie* 33:276.

Kennedy, F. 1942. "The Problem of Social Control and the Congenitally Defective: Education, Sterilization, Euthanasia." *American Journal of Psychiatry* 99:13–16.

Kevorkian, J. 1991. *Prescription: Medicide—The Goodness of Planned Death*. New York: Prometheus Books.

"Kevorkian Cleared of Murder Charge." 1992. *Chicago Tribune* (July 22): Sec. 1, 3.

"Kevorkian Helps Another Woman Commit Suicide." 1992. *Chicago Tribune* (November 24): Sec. 1, 5.

Kimsma, G., and E. van Leeuwen. 1993. "Dutch Euthanasia: Background, Practice, and Present Justifications," *Cambridge Quarterly* 2(1):19–31.

Kushner, T. 1993. "*CQ* Interview: Derek Humphry Discusses Death With Dignity." *Cambridge Quarterly of Health Care Ethics* 2(1):57–61.

Lauter, H., and J. E. Meyer. 1984. "Active Euthanasia without Consent: Historical Comments on a Current Debate." *Death Education* 8:89–98.

Lifton, R. J. 1986. *Nazi Doctors.* New York: Basic Books.

Loewy E. 1987. "Treatment Decisions in the Mentally Impaired: Limiting But Not Abandoning Treatment." *New England Journal of Medicine* 317:1465–1469.

Miller, P. J. 1987. "Death With Dignity and the Right to Die—Sometimes Doctors Have a Duty to Hasten Death." *Journal of Medical Ethics* 13:81–85.

Mueller-Hill, B. 1988. *Murderous Science: Elimination by Scientific Selection of Jews, Gypsies, and Others, Germany 1933–1945.* New York: Oxford University Press.

Pellegrino, E. D., and D. C. Thomasma. 1989. *For the Patient's Good: Toward the Restoration of Beneficence in Health Care.* New York: Oxford University Press.

Proctor, R. N. 1988. *Racial Hygiene: Medicine under the Nazis.* Cambridge, Mass.: Harvard University Press.

Proctor, R. N. 1992. "Nazi Doctors, Racial Medicine, and Human Experimentation," In G. Annas and M. A. Grodin, eds., *The Nazi Doctors and the Nuremberg Code*, pp. 17–31. New York: Oxford University Press.

Quill, T. 1991. "Death With Dignity: A Case of Individualized Decisionmaking." *New England Journal of Medicine* 324(10):691–694.

Rachels, J. 1975. "Active and Passive Euthanasia," *New England Journal of Medicine* 292:78–80.

Ramm, R. 1942. *Aertzliche Rechts- und Standeskunde.* Berlin: Gruyter.

Remmelink Concludeert (Medical Decisions at the End of Life). 1992. Zwolle: W. E. J. Tjeenk Willink.

Rosenblum, V. G., and C. D. Forsythe. 1990. "The Right to Assisted Suicide: Protection of Autonomy or an Open Door to Social Killing?" *Issues in Law and Medicine* 6(1) (Summer):3–31.

Rosner, F., P. Rogatz, R. Lowenstein, H. M. Risemberg, A. J. Bennett, A. Buscaglia, E. J. Cassell, P. B. Farnsworth, A. L. Halpern, and J. B. Henry. 1992. "Physician-Assisted Suicide." *New York State Journal of Medicine* 92(9):388–391.

Roth, K. H., ed. 1984. *Erfassung zur Vernichtung, von der Socialhygiene zum "Gesetz ueber Sterbehilfe."* West Berlin: Verlagsgesellschaft Gesundheit.

Stanley, J. M., ed. 1989. "The Appleton Consensus: Suggested International Guidelines for Decisions to Forgo Medical Treatment." *Journal of Medical Ethics* 15:129–136.

Thomasma, D. 1988. "The Range of Euthanasia." *Bulletin of the American College of Surgeons* 73 (August):3–13.

Thomasma, D. 1990. "The Ethics of Caring for Vulnerable Individuals." In *Reflections on Ethics*, pp. 39–45. Washington, D.C.: American Speech-Language-Hearing Association.

Thomasma, D. 1992. "Mercy Killing of Elderly People with Dementia: A Counterproposal." In R. Binstock, S. Post, and P. Whitehouse, eds., *Dementia and Aging: Ethics, Values, and Policy Choices*, pp. 101–117. Baltimore, Md.: Johns Hopkins University Press.

Thomasma, D., and G. C. Graber. 1990. *Euthanasia: Toward an Ethical Social Policy.* New York: Continuum.

Tomlinson, T., and H. Brody. 1990. "Futility and the Ethics of Resuscitation." *Journal of the American Medical Association* 264:1276–1280.

Van der Wal, G. 1992. *Euthanasie en hulp bij zelfdoding door huisartsen.* Rotterdam: WYT Uitgeefgroep.

16

Managing the Unmanageable: The Case Against Euthanasia

Carlos F. Gomez

There has been, in the last three or four years, an important—yet almost imperceptible—shift in the debate over euthanasia and physician-assisted suicide. The question, which initially began as a proposition that the practice *ought* to be allowed, has now been turned into a negative query: why ought euthanasia *not* be allowed? In other words, the burden for argumentation now begins to fall more heavily on those, such as myself, who believe the practice to be inherently dangerous as a matter of public policy and, moreover, to be inimical to an ethic central to the practice of medicine. In other language, the *notion* of euthanasia seems to have achieved some sort of validation, though the *practice* of euthanasia remains problematic from a policy standpoint. Two recently defeated proposals that would have given legal sanction to euthanasia—Initiative 119 in Washington state in 1991, and Proposition 161 in California in 1992—failed, I think, less because people objected to the idea per se than because they worried about the regulatory safeguards for the practice.[1] To some extent, I would argue, the question before the public has become less *whether* euthanasia ought to be legalized, than *how* and *when*.

The extent to which this notion has become entrenched in the popular imagination finds expression, for example, in the popularity of Derek Humphry's how-to manual on suicide, *Final Exit*, which topped the *New York Times* best-seller list for most of the summer of 1991. Similarly, Betty Rollin's earlier book, *Last Wish*, an account of how she and her husband helped her terminally ill mother to commit suicide, found new life as a made-for-television movie. Of Dr. Kevorkian and his roving sideshow of death, all one can say is that his handiwork is the source of a seemingly endless stream of popular reportage, as well as a seemingly endless list of dead patients.

More important, the notion of euthanasia as a conceivable practice has entered the medical profession itself. Beginning, in recent times, with the "It's Over, Debbie" article in early 1988,[2] an old debate over the permissibility of physician-assisted suicide and euthanasia seems to be raging with new life.[3] And if "Debbie" provided a new literary push toward acceptance of euthanasia, subsequent articles have continued along the same narrative stream. Dr. Timothy Quill's article on his patient, referred to as "Diane," was a more thoughtful and eloquent expression of one physician's response to, yet again, a cancer patient's desperate situation.[4] Unlike the "Debbie" case—in which a weary-sounding resident pushes an apparently lethal dose into an agonal patient—Dr. Quill provides medicine that, given knowingly and in sufficient quantities, the patient self-administers, bringing about her own death. Dr. Quill's activity is perhaps more appropriately described as physician-assisted suicide, yet he forms part of a larger chorus of voices that is pleading that—under specific circumstances—physicians be allowed to administer or prescribe medicine with the specific and unambiguous intent of bringing about the patient's death.

These calls for euthanasia, moreover, cannot reasonably be dismissed as the odd ranting of isolated eccentrics. A panel of twelve distinguished physicians, in a landmark article in the *New England Journal of Medicine* that addressed the care of hopelessly ill patients, argued (with only two dissents) that under specific circumstances, they would help a terminally ill patient commit suicide.[5] Even more recently, a trio of physicians, including Dr. Quill, published a specific proposal that would have made the actions in the "Diane" case a matter of accepted public policy.[6] In this same issue of the *New England Journal of Medicine*, Howard Brody—again, another prominent and well-respected physician-ethicist—argued that physician-assisted suicide is a compassionate response to what he calls "a medical failure," i.e., a dying that is needlessly protracted and painful.

My point in detailing the evolution of this trend in end-of-life care is to point out that it cannot be dismissed as a movement at the margins of respectability. On the contrary, it is now a centerpiece of current public moral dialogue. It is now a debate that often centers around programmatic specifics, e.g., when will euthanasia be acceptable? who may ask for it? how will we control it? In other words, it is no longer a debate in the realm of the abstract; it is an urgent matter, its proponents argue, that needs quick embodiment in policy and law. The debate has, in a subtle yet very profound way, altered the way in which we view the needs and wants of patients, and how the medical profession views its appropriate response and responsibility.

While some have argued that this debate has been worthwhile,[7] I am going to sound a dissonant note here, and suggest that the debate over the permissibility of euthanasia has been, at best, misguided and confused. Moreover, I hope to demonstrate that current proposals for euthanasia and physician-assisted suicide are most emphatically *not* an appropriate response to cries of dying patients and the families for appropriate care. In fact, I am going to make the case that these proposals, both as they have been imagined and as they have been specified, are dangerous to patients.

I am going to make my case in three stages. First, I am going to argue that the evidence now available to us on the actual practice of euthanasia, evidence from the ongoing experiment in the Netherlands, suggests that the Dutch are not constructing a paradigm that we should emulate, but that they are spinning out, bit by bit, a cautionary tale. Second, I will suggest that the public face of euthanasia in the Netherlands is deceivingly benign, and that claims about the practice's safefuards have been uncritically accepted—and repeated—by advocates of the practice in the United States. Finally, I will argue that the profession of medicine has damaged itself in this debate. More important, we have damaged a significant segment of the public whom we claim to serve; that is, we have failed miserably in the care of dying patients. In doing so, we have unwittingly helped to spawn a movement that takes at least part of its origins in the public's very justified anger: anger over the treatment of the terminally ill; anger over the health care system's inaccessibility and byzantine ways; anger over the cost and burden inflicted on the families of the chronically debilitated and ill.

As I unravel this story, and as I make the case against proposals for legalizing euthanasia, I want to suggest, in parallel fashion, that the medical profession has failed in the things most important to its core ethic, and that rather than attend first to these failures, we are overreaching ourselves, almost out of a sense of guilt, if we believe we can tame and contain the practice of euthanasia. What I will argue, finally, is that the appropriate response of the medical profession should not be to accede to calls for the decriminalization of euthanasia, but to try to recapture and reconstruct a healthier sense of what it means to doctor—what, in the words of Albert Jonsen, should be the profession's "appropriate frame of reference"[8]—and what it means to care *for*, as opposed to managing the problems *of*, dying patients.

Euthanasia in the Netherlands: Taming the Whirlwind

The Dutch and their experiment with euthanasia, now almost twenty years old, became, almost unwillingly, central to the early arguments of proponents of the practice. Holland, with her generous social welfare programs and universal health care coverage, would provide, so it was said, a model of how a liberal, humane, and tolerant society could come together on so fractious an issue. More important, it would provide something sorely needed in the euthanasia debate: an empiric base. The model of physician-assisted suicide and euthanasia developed by the Dutch would provide a response to people (such as myself) who argue that this is an inherently dangerous practice. The Dutch would demonstrate to the rest of the world that this sort of thing does not necessarily degenerate into indiscriminate killing on the part of the medical profession; that physician-assisted suicide is both compassionate and merciful, and not just mercy-killing cloaked under the veil of compassion. The Dutch experience was, and is, an important piece of evidence in this debate.

What I want to illustrate with the Dutch model, however, is exactly the opposite: that what began, ostensibly, as an exercise in patient autonomy— perhaps the *ultimate* exercise in patient autonomy—has become something altogether different. Moreover, I want to suggest that the Dutch experiment with euthanasia argues that this practice cannot be regulated, and should therefore not be allowed. Finally, I want to suggest that the Dutch experiment has by now given us sufficient evidence to believe that were the practice transplanted to the United States, our own experience would be no better and, arguably, a good deal worse.

The Dutch experience with euthanasia is, I think, so illustrative and important that it merits developing at some length the legal and political context in which it is practiced. To begin with, euthanasia is still formally forbidden in the Netherlands. There are two statutes in the Dutch penal code that delineate specific punishment for a citizen who "robs another of life at his express and serious wish" and "incites another to suicide, assists him therein, or provides him with the means."[9] The statutes, though over a century old, seem to speak directly to the issue at hand: neither killing at a person's direct—and, the article adds—*serious* request, nor aiding a person in his or her suicide, is to be countenanced by the law.

Yet every commentator on the practice of euthanasia in the Netherlands agrees that it occurs with some frequency and regularity.[10] How, then, is this the case? That is, how do the Dutch reconcile their practice with the prohibitions of the law? At least one answer lies in the evolution of case law over the past twenty years, with which the Dutch have crafted an opening for the practice of euthanasia, without abandoning the general prohibition against killing framed by the penal code. There are several cases cited by jurists on this issue, a few of which merit brief review here, for they trace the evolution of public policy regarding euthanasia in the Netherlands.[11] In 1973 a physician admitted to giving her nursing home-bound mother a lethal dose of morphine. The district prosecutor charged the physician with murder, and brought the case to trial in Leeuwarden. In her defense, the physician pleaded that her mother had requested the injection, that she was suffering horribly, and that as her daughter, the physician was simply responding compassionately to a serious and reasoned request. The court found the physician guilty, yet adjudicated the case in what was then a novel manner. Though the court found the defendant guilty, the court refused to pass the sentence mandated by the law. Instead, in consideration of what the court called "the circumstances under which the [crime] was perpetrated . . . and the perfect purity of [the defendant's] motives beyond doubt,"[12] it held in abeyance (for one year) a prison sentence of one week. If, at the end of the year, the doctor was not found guilty of any other punishable act, the sentence would be completely suspended.

The Leeuwarden case was a landmark in the practice of euthanasia because, though the court found fault with the specifics of the case (there was no written documentation of the mother's request, for example), it found itself incapable of meting out punishment. What was at fault, the court seemed to suggest, was not the intent itself—which, one should recall, the court called "pure"—but the mechanics of the act. For the first time, the court suggested, however indirectly, that it might tolerate euthanasia if some mechanism were found to evaluate and regularize it. The act itself—the aiding of a suicide or the administration of a drug with intended lethality—was not, of itself, punishable. For obvious reasons, the court could not bring itself to give wholesale, unrestricted license to the practice. The question that remained was not whether the practice would be tolerated, but *how* and under what regulatory structure the courts would sanction such a practice.

Two subsequent cases brought more definition to this question. In 1977 a disciplinary medical court—a rough equivalent to our state licensing boards—acquitted a physician of charges that he acted inappropriately when he administered an intentional overdose of barbiturates to a terminally ill patient. According to the court, the physician's actions did not violate the canons of the profession; moreover, the disciplinary court refused to hand the matter over to the public prosecutor's office. This was a matter for the profession to solve within itself, it seemed to say, and the civil courts, by tacitly accepting the outcome of the disciplinary hearing, seemed to agree.

A second ruling, in 1982 by the district court in Rotterdam, further confirmed this impression. Here, the court found guilty of manslaughter a lay person who performed an act of euthanasia. The ruling here was instructive. First, the court set out a limit on what it would tolerate, i.e., it seemed to establish the outer boundary of what it would consider acceptable practice. Second, it confirmed what the disciplinary court in 1977 had only implied: that assisted suicide, in the hands of the medical profession, would become something *other* than the crime outlined in the penal code. An operative analogy here, I think, is to the wielding of a knife: in the hands of a lay person, it constitutes grounds for assault, or worse; in the hands of a physician, appropriately used as a scalpel, it becomes a therapeutic tool. In the particular case of euthanasia, what is murder in the hands of a lay person becomes, according to this court doctrine, therapy in the hands of a physician.

Having established that the practice was to be restricted to the medical profession, the court still left unanswered what latitude it would give the physicians in their practice of euthanasia. The following year, the district court at Alkmaar adjudicated a case that would eventually provide an answer. The case in question involved a physician, with clearly documented evidence of a terminal patient's wishes, who administered a lethal overdose to the patient. The public prosecutor brought charges against the physician, but the Alkmaar court held that, despite the clear prohibitions in the penal code, the physician could be acquitted on the grounds that he was protecting the patient's right to "self-determination." In an important shift in legal emphasis, the Alkmaar court suddenly created a new test for euthanasia, one that would eventually become decisive: when medical or legal principles collide with patients' wishes, the physician may find excuse from the prohibitions of statutory law, and accede to the patient's request for assistance with suicide. In other words, if no general harm can be proven, and if the patient's request is well-documented, physicians and their patients may mutually agree to an act of euthanasia.

The prosecutor in the case, unhappy over what seemed to be the court's making up law out of whole cloth, appealed the decision to a higher court in Amsterdam.[13] The appellate court, reviewing the findings of the case, agreed with the prosecutor that the law had been violated, and overturned the acquittal. However, it did not assign punishment and did not remand the case for retrial.

The matter might have stopped here, in a sort of legal limbo, with the penal code still formally intact, though bereft of sanctions on this matter, but the physician in question felt that his actions had been cast in doubt. Moreover, despite there being no penalty against him, he had, in fact, been found guilty of a crime. He thus appealed the ruling from the Amsterdam court, taking his case, finally, to the Supreme Court at the Hague. There, in what was to be the defining adjudication in the case, the Supreme Court struck down the lower court's ruling because it had decided the case, it said, in too narrow a fashion. In considering the case, argued the Supreme Court, the lower court in Amsterdam should have invoked the principle of *force majeure*, quite literally, a "greater force," a principle of law under which, for example, the penal code acquitted defendants of crimes committed under duress. According to the Supreme Court, a physician acting in response to the repeated pleas of a patient for release from life is analogous to someone forced to commit a crime against his or her will. The physician is, in a sense, bending to a greater or more insistent will; in this case, the will of a dying patient who wants death to come sooner rather than later. Coupled with the earlier ruling of the Alkmaar court—which established the principle of self-determination as a key defense—the Supreme Court recast the matter of euthanasia into an almost unrecognizable form.

The Supreme Court sent the case back to a different appellate court, and gave specific instructions that the matter be decided using these two principles—patient self-determination and *force majeure*—in addition to the prohibitions of statutory law. Given these constraints, the appellate court, not surprisingly, acquitted the physician. Perhaps most important, the court affirmed earlier guidelines stipulated by the Rotterdam court in 1982, giving them, in essence, the force of law. The guidelines listed below, in more or less unchanged fashion, still govern the practice in the Netherlands today:

- There must be great suffering on the part of the patient.
- The desire to die must emanate from a conscious person.
- The request for euthanasia must be voluntary.
- The person must have been given alternatives and must have had time to consider them.
- There must be no other reasonable solution to the patient's problem.
- The death must not inflict unnecessary suffering on others.
- More than one person must be involved in the decision.
- Only a physician may actually euthanize the patient.
- Great care must be exercised in making this decision.

In outlining these guidelines, the courts addressed the fears expressed by some that if this was to become a paradigm for patient care, some constraining force need be applied.

The court's guidelines attempt to speak, in one fashion or another, to those fears. First, the guidelines suggest that euthanasia is a practice of last resort; that the patient's suffering be "unbearable" and that there be no alternatives. In other language, euthanasia should not be pedestrian practice and should be done only when, in a memorable phrase of the K.N.M.G. (roughly, the Dutch equivalent of the American Medical Association) the physician's back is "up against the wall."[14] Moreover, the guidelines suggest, euthanasia is not a way of forcing the chronically debilitated and burdensome from our presence: it must be voluntary and uncoerced. It is, moreover, a practice subject to control: only physicians may practice it (thereby invoking the canons of the profession that promote beneficence and protect against malfeasance), and at least one other physician has to agree that the euthanasia is warranted. One last provision, not stipulated in the guidelines but part of the tacit agreement between the courts and the medical profession, insists that these acts be given at least some public, extra-professional airing, i.e., the public prosecutor needs to be notified.

The Dutch thus bow in both directions at once: the stipulations of the penal code remain in effect, yet public policy—at least as it has evolved through case law and accepted medical practice—satisfies an expressed desire for the practice by crafting an ad hoc opening for euthanasia. Yet if this all sounds a bit too unworkable and informal, it is precisely because that happens to be the case. The Dutch approach to this matter has been the triumph of optimism over prudence. When pressed about potential for abuses, for example, or the regulatory force of these guidelines, apologists for the practice from the Netherlands are almost uniformly reassuring; the thought that Dutch practitioners might abuse this practice is beyond the realm of possibility.[15] The early articles on this practice that were written by the Dutch in English-language journals were all uniformly favorable and sought to allay fears that were being expressed abroad.

A Public Accounting of a Private Matter

Yet the reality of the practice in the Netherlands, despite the almost unbridled enthusiasm expressed by both the Dutch and their admirers, suggests, at least to me, a grimmer picture. It betrays a dissonance between what I will call the public and the private face of euthanasia in the Netherlands. Publicly, the practice looks clean, well-regulated, tolerable, an aid to the dying; privately, the practice strikes me as troublesome, perplexing, a good deal more *dirty* than is claimed in public. Having developed the public, legal context for this practice in the Netherlands, I hope next to demonstrate that euthanasia—the *actuality* of giving over to physicians the license to kill, irrespective of good intentions—carries almost incalculable risks for patients. I hope to use the Dutch experience as a sort of lens in which advocates of the practice in the United States—along with the rest of us involved in this debate—might see more clearly what this new therapy entails.

One should note at the outset that publicly the Dutch suffer and die in ways similar to ourselves. That is to say, their dying population, like ours, is increasingly old, and we suffer the same common maladies of an advanced and sedentary society: we commonly die of coronary artery disease, cerebrovascular accidents, and malignancies. In that sense, the dying Dutch look much like our own, at least publicly.

What is becoming different in private—and here I draw on details from my own and other published studies of the *act* of euthanasia in the Netherlands—are the details of the practice. Dutch physicians who practice euthanasia typically proceed in one of two ways. When a patient is unable or unwilling to self-administer lethal amounts of a drug, a physician will narcotize them with a gram of pentobarbital intravenously, then after induction (if the patient is still alive) the physician injects curare or a curare-like drug, which induces complete neuromuscular blockade. The patient quickly dies of respiratory arrest. When patients are able or willing to administer the medicine themselves, Dutch physicians use a variety of medicines and combinations of medicines, but which typically induce central nervous system depression and, again, respiratory arrest, followed by death. In two cases documented in an earlier study, the patients were killed with a bolus of potassium chloride, inducing a lethal cardiac arrhythmia.[16] I raise the specifics of death by euthanasia for two reasons. One, there is something that is, on the face of it, brutalizing about the details of the practice, details that are too often subsumed in more general, and more euphemistic, talk about euthanasia. The intent of physicians giving a neuromuscular blocking agent without ventilatory support—the unalloyed, undiluted intent—is to kill, and the details of such a practice make this clear. Similarly, the use of inappropriately high doses of narcotics—a gram of morphine, for example, delivered intravenously in a few minutes—suggests an intent other than analgesia. Two, detailing the actual practice of euthanasia in the Netherlands helps to separate the practice of withholding or withdrawing treatment from patients, and killing them outright. That is to say, the Dutch have collapsed the distinction between the two and see no difference between the administration of a drug with intended lethality and turning off a ventilator, for example, at a patient's or designated proxy's request.

I emphasize this distinction because advocates of euthanasia and physician-assisted suicide have used this blurring of lines to their advantage. Patients and their families alike recoil in horror, appropriately, to an indeterminate and indefinite dying amidst a panoply of invasive technologies—ventilators, central venous lines, heart monitors and the like. But the reality of current medicolegal practice in the United States is that no one need die a death punctuated by the stops and starts of intrusive and unwanted medical technology. That much has been established by both case law and accepted medical practice. But the larger point here is that this is not, in fact, what lies at the heart of the euthanasia movement. The argument is not for better crafted or more easily applied "right-to-die" laws, it is for the very different practice of outright killing.

That this matters as more than just an academic distinction is borne out by the continuing evolution of the practice in the Netherlands. If the original *public* appeal of euthanasia legislation in the Netherlands was its sense of empowerment, its idea of enhancing patient autonomy, in *private* practice it has actually come to encompass a range of activities—and of patients— that its original proponents said would clearly be beyond accepted limits. In my own study, for example, a two-day-old child with Down's syndrome and duodenal atresia was euthanized with the tacit consent of the parents. A seventy-year-old man, suffering the devastation of a stroke, was euthanized without being able to consent (or dissent), because the physician in question was sure that "no one would want to live this way," though "this way" was, at that point, only five days into the patient's potential recovery. All told, there were four cases out of twenty-six in which it was clear that the patient could not have been able to consent to the practice, and two in which the notion of volition could have been called into question.

But these numbers I cite are small and, as critics have pointed out, are subject to distortion. The Dutch themselves, however, have not only confirmed what I only hinted at in my study—that the practice of euthanasia now extends to incompetent and unconsenting patients—but have gone much further. In a summary report of the Remmelink Commission, chaired by the attorney-general of the Netherlands, the authors detail what is, to date, the largest study of the practice ever conducted.[17] The study comprised interviews with 400 physicians on the practice of euthanasia and reviewed the causes of death of 8,500 patients. The authors conclude from this survey that euthanasia is a rare occurrence (accounting, they say, for only 1.8 percent of all deaths) and that it was "almost never" (to use the language of the authors) subject to abuse.[18] However, the data from the report have yet to receive the scrutiny that they deserve.

The authors of the report chose, for reasons that are not clear, not to count as acts of euthanasia instances in which physicians gave lethal doses of pain medication, not with the intent of alleviating pain per se, but to hasten or bring about death. In other words, the intent was not to palliate, but to kill. Adding these cases to the tally would bring the number of cases of euthanasia in the Netherlands to almost 8,100, or about 6 percent of all deaths. More to the point, the authors of the report chose to discount an additional 1,000 cases in which other, unspecified methods were used to bring about the death of patients who, the report notes, were incapable of giving consent. These were not acts of withdrawing or withholding life-sustaining treatments; they were injections of lethal substances given with the specific intent of killing the patient. The committee chose not to include these cases because the physicians were "providing assistance to the dying," and these acts were not, according to the authors, problematic. Adding these cases to the final tally brings the total count documented by the Remmelink Report to 9,100 cases of euthanasia out of an annual mortality rate of 130,000, or about 7 percent of all deaths in the Netherlands in a given year. If similar rates of euthanasia took hold in an America that has passed euthanasia legislation, there would be something on the order of 140,000 cases of euthanasia per year.

Some defenders of this practice in the United States continue to maintain, even in the face of the data now arriving from the Dutch, that it is not conclusive or decisive;[19] that even if one grants that the practice in the Netherlands looks different than what was originally intended, that in itself does not predict what will happen in the U.S. In one sense, I agree with them: there is no way of assuring ourselves that we will be as restrained as the Dutch have been. In a country where we routinely deny basic medical care to millions of people, there is nothing that suggests to me that we will behave more prudently than the more generous and equitable Dutch. In other words, my prediction is that as bad as I think the practice of euthanasia is in the Netherlands, I do not think, ironically, that we will be that good. Proponents of euthanasia legislation in the United States ought to face squarely not only what I hope to have shown to be the quagmire of medical killing into which the Dutch have gotten themselves, but also what I believe will be an inherently more dangerous and less controllable practice in the United States.

Conclusion: Death and Dying in a Land of Scarcity

My arguments against euthanasia have been, to this point, indirect. I have tried to demonstrate that what available data we have on the practice suggest that the public face of euthanasia differs from the private reality. In the protected space in which physicians and patients meet—away from the glare of regulatory lights, emboldened by a new ethic that accepts some forms of medical killing—this practice that purports to exalt patients' autonomy, and to respond with compassion, becomes, in substantial numbers of cases, an exercise in unilateral decision making on the part of physicians.[20] Moreover, the limits on what the practice may entail, the patients whom one can euthanize, seems to be rather elastic. Dutch physicians may refer to the guidelines—as they did, for example, when I interviewed them on their practice of euthanasia—but when pressed, seem willing to extend the practice beyond what is publicly said to be allowed, and certainly what the courts have said they will countenance. Even more worrisome, they seem to do so with impunity.

The larger point to be made here, finally, is not only that this demonstrable discrepancy between public statement and private reality is all taking place in a country of relative affluence, seemingly well-governed by democratic institutions, with a generally equitable social and medical welfare system. More important, it is being accepted with remarkable alacrity in this country, with its gross inequities and deranged medical system, now groaning under the fiscal burden of decades of unbridled and illogical growth. My point here is that the euthanasia movement is making its presence felt at a time when, as a common polity, the United States will clearly have to make some enormously painful and divisive choices. The costs of health care in this country, as a percentage of our gross national product, simply cannot be sustained at the current rate of growth, which now graphically resembles a hyperbolic curve, increasing at an exponential rate, never quite reaching its asymptote. Given the magnitude of our problem, and the difficulty that we will inevitably encounter in producing some sort of coherent health care system, why would we confound an already delicate situation—one that will inevitably involve rationing and triage—with the license to kill?

Said even less delicately, the people whom I most fear for are not those who read articles of this sort—not those of us who vote, and lobby, and write, and engage and manipulate the political system to our advantage—but the marginalized, the stigmatized, the discouraged, the disenfranchised. I worry about those who now overpopulate the public hospitals and clinics in this country, simply because private institutions will not take care of them. Patients with AIDS, women of color, the demented and those just this side of dementia; the patients whom I care for in my own clinic—the ones with whom I have trained, and who are teaching me to be a doctor; it is their vulnerability to abuse that worries me the most.

How will they fare were physician-assisted suicide and euthanasia legalized? I simply point to their plight now, and leave their potential future for us to ponder. If this is to be a new experiment in end-of-life therapy, how will we protect them from becoming the unwitting and unwilling subjects of this exercise. For my own part, I have seen enough of this practice, under more enlightened circumstances, to come away anxious and afraid. What physicians failed to do in the Netherlands—that is, to address the underlying fears of their dying patients—they now do in what I think I have shown to be a more simplistic, and more brutal, fashion.

Those who now advocate a change in the legal status of euthanasia should, I would submit, take a much closer, more critical look at the Netherlands. Moreover, those within the medical profession who are espousing such a change should accept that at least part of the public's enthusiasm for the practice derives from a failure to provide very basic care—especially adequate analgesia—on the part of physicians. Those of us in the profession wholly opposed to the euthanasia movement should also admit that there are some deaths, irrespective of our attempts to manipulate symptoms and medicine, that strike patients, families, and their physicians as unnecessarily painful and demoralizing. But what I ask, finally, is that before we seriously countenance allowing physicians to practice euthanasia, we should insist that they—that we—practice good medicine; that we doctor well; and that we reanimate a moribund ethic that places the patient's comfort, health, and well-being before our parochial obsession with the marvels of our technical wizardry.

Notes

1. See, for example, Rob Carson's argument in "Washington's I-119," *Hastings Center Report* 22(2):7–9, 1992, where he argues that it was an exaggerated fear of abuse that ultimately defeated Washington's euthanasia initiative.

2. "It's Over, Debbie," *Journal of the American Medical Association* 259:272, 1988.

3. Listen, for example, to an early voice in this debate in J. Rachels, "Active and Passive Euthanasia," *New England Journal of Medicine* 292:78–80, 1975.

4. T. E. Quill, "Death and Dignity: A Case of Individualized Decison-Making," *New England Journal of Medicine* 322:1881–1883, 1990.

5. S. H. Wanzer, D. D. Federman, S. J. Adelstein, et al. "The Physician's Responsibility toward Hopelessly Ill Patients: A Second Look," *New England Journal of Medicine* 320:844–849, 1989.

6. T. E. Quill, C. K. Cassel and D. Meier, "Care of the Hopelessly Ill; Criteria for Physician-Assisted Suicide," *New England Journal of Medicine* 329:1380–1384, 1992.

7. C. K. Cassel and D. Meier, "Morals and Moralism in the Debate over Euthanasia and Assisted Suicide," *New England Journal of Medicine* 232:750–752, 1990.

8. A. R. Jonsen, "Beyond the Physician's Reference: The Ethics of Active Euthanasia," *Western Journal of Medicine* 149:195–198, 1988.

9. H. J. Schmidt, *Geschiedenis van het Wetboek van Strafrecht* [*History of the Penal Code*], vol 2., p. 440; cited in C. F. Gomez, *Regulating Death: Euthanasia and the Case of the Netherlands* (New York: Free Press, 1991).

10. The actual numbers and the epidemiology of the practice, however, remain in some dispute. A landmark 1991 article in *Lancet*, which summarized the results of a survey on the practice, suggested that the numbers involved were relatively

small; subsequent commentators (including myself) on both the practice of euthanasia in the Netherlands and the way the results of the survey were reported, have been more critical. Compare, for example, P. J. van der Maas, J. J. van Delden, L. Pijnenborg, and C. W. N. Looman, "Euthanasia and Other Decisions Concerning the End of Life," *Lancet* 338:669–674, 1991, and a more critical reading of the numbers of cases of both voluntary and *involuntary* euthanasia in: H. A. M. J. ten Have and J. V. M. Welie, "Euthanasia? Normal Medical Practice?" *Hastings Center Report* 22:34–38, 1992.

11. See Gomez, *Regulating Death*; J. Keown, "The Law and Practice of Euthanasia in the Netherlands," *Law Quarterly Review* (January):453–463, 1992; and M. de Wachter, "Active Euthanasia in the Netherlands," *Journal of the American Medical Association* 262:3315–3319, 1989, for a more complete review of this issue.

12. Gomez, *Regulating Death*, p. 31.

13. Unlike Anglo-American common law, the Dutch legal system, which derives from Napoleonic law, permits double jeopardy.

14. K.N.M.G. "Standpunt Inzake Euthanasie," cited in "Final Report of the Netherlands State Commission on Euthanasia: An English Summary," *Bioethics* 1:168, 1987.

15. Ibid.; see also, for example, H. Rigter, "Euthanasia in the Netherlands: Distinguishing Facts from Fiction," Special Supplement, *Hastings Center Report* 19:31–32, 1989.

16. Gomez, *Regulating Death*.

17. van der Maas et al., "Euthanasia and Other Medical Decisions."

18. Ibid., p. 674.

19. See, for example, Margaret Battin's "Voluntary Euthanasia and the Risk of Abuse: Can We Learn Anything from the Netherlands?" *Law, Medicine, and Health Care* 2:133–143, 1992.

20. See, for example, the very critical review of the Remmelink Report data in ten Have and Welie, "Euthanasia? Normal Medical Practice?"

17

The Changing Role of the Physician in the Care of the Dying

Robert J. Miller

The two trends or social-political movements that will have the most impact on the care of the dying over the next decade will be the medical cost-containment efforts and the increasing individual autonomy, or patient's rights, movement. These forces will have both positive and negative influences on terminal care.

Efforts to control cost will force physicians to consider alternatives to the most high-tech aggressive approaches and consider other options, e.g., supportive, home-based, hospice-type care for patients with incurable conditions. Reimbursement pressures, however, may limit available funding and encourage rationing approaches that could discriminate against patients in need of terminal care.

The movement toward increasing autonomy may benefit patients by encouraging open and better communication between health care providers and patients and their families to include their values and priorities in treatment decisions. The extension of the right-to-die movement to include euthanasia poses potential dangers for the terminally ill.

What will be the end result of these forces and how will this change the role of the physician? If the preponderance of these forces is detrimental, how best can we protect and promote competent and compassionate terminal care?

Economic Forces and the High Cost of Caring for the Dying

Demographic and economic projections predict increasing growth and costs among both the elderly and the dying. Political forces and increasingly vocal special interest groups will probably be enough to ensure the quality of care for the elderly and maintain their "disproportionate" share of the health care dollar. But what of the dying? Who speaks for them? And how will they be served?

There is little doubt that an aging America will increase the costs of health care (Schneider and Guralnik 1990).Some argue that the money being spent on the elderly is already excessive and probably should be reduced (Chakravarty and Weisman 1988; Smith 1989). Others argue that providing a lower quality of care for the elderly is unethical (Kennedy 1988) and economically misguided (Levinsky 1990). There is clearly a need for more research on the appropriate and ethical care of this group (Wennberg 1990; Lonergan and Krevans 1991). While there has been considerable discussion of the economic impact of the elderly, there has also been discussion concerning the escalating costs of caring for the dying.

Medical costs at the end of life are very high. This is not a recent development; in 1961, before the advent of Medicare, the health care costs of those who died was almost three times greater than those who survived (Scitovsky 1984). Studies suggest that the intensity of the treatment for terminal cancer patients continues to increase up to the very time of death (Holli and Hakama 1989). It seems reasonable to expect that the sickest patients would cost the most to care for and those who go on to die, even more. But as society begins restricting health care, we can expect that efforts will be made to identify those patients who are not likely to survive so that the health care dollars can be spent on someone else.

Health Care Financing Administration (HCFA) data report that each year 19–22 percent of Medicare money is spent on the 5 percent who die (Bayer et al. 1983.) HCFA personnel recently completed a study to determine if the fraction of money spent on the dying was increasing or decreasing. They compared data from 1976 with 1985 and found that the percent of money spent on the 5.2 percent who died each year had actually fallen from 28.2 percent (1976) to 26.7 percent (1985) (*American Medical News* 1991 [January 7]:23). There was evidence to suggest that efforts to maintain the life of the most elderly was being cut back. The money to care for an older survivor is 66 percent higher than younger Medicare recipients but the amount spent on those who die is 56 percent lower (*American Medical News* 1990 [November 9]:18). Does this show good judgment in the terminal care of the elderly or is their care less aggressive because of age discrimination?

We still are spending almost four times as much ($8,061 vs. $2,041) caring for a dying octogenarian as for those who are surviving.

There is an assumption that excessive money is being spent and that it can be reduced without compromising care, and there is considerable evidence that much medical care is inappropriate. Studies show excessive overutilization of diagnostic tests and treatments (Brook 1989). There is a natural bias for physicians to recommend the treatments that they perform themselves (Belanger, Moore, and Tannock 1991) or benefit from economically (Hillman et al. 1990). There is evidence that physicians will recommend aggressive palliative treatment that they would not accept themselves (Mackillop, O'Sullivan, and Ward 1987). There is also clear evidence that economic forces are having an impact on how dying patients are treated, but whether outcome suffers is unclear from available data (Mayer and Patterson 1988).

Efforts to cut hospital costs shift sicker patients to nursing homes or outpatient settings. The implementation of Medicare's prospective payment system shifted the dying from hospital to nursing home so that from 1981 to 1985 the number of patients dying in nursing homes increased 18–26 percent (Sager et al. 1989). How did this affect the quality of their terminal care?

A major problem in evaluating terminal care and applying cost-effective approaches is the lack of reliable instruments to measure outcome in terminal care. Studies suggest overall that health care quality has not suffered from the changes associated with the prospective payment system (Kahn et al. 1990; Rubenstein et al. 1990). But measuring quality or cost-effectiveness in the care of terminal patients is difficult if not impossible with current tools (Detsky 1989; Goodwin et al. 1988). Some type of instrument is needed that will measure quality of care over the remaining survival time in these patients. New tools such as quality-adjusted life years could potentially discriminate against the terminally ill (La Puma and Lawlor 1990). The system proposed in Oregon to develop a priority list for Medicaid expenditures uses a system that divides the cost of a treatment by the number of years of benefit (*American Medical News* 1990 [May 18]:2). What sort of score would terminal care earn in such a system?

Rationing Health Care

Since there is a growing recognition that health care is already being rationed, the Oregon legislature decided to rank medical interventions with the goal of providing basic health care benefits to more people by limiting the number of services covered. If the system had won federal approval it would have expanded the number of people covered under Medicaid in Oregon from 130,000 to 207,000. A panel developed a priority list or ranking of medical interventions by dividing the cost of the treatment by the number of years a person receiving such treatment would benefit. They also made use of the quality of well-being (QWB) scale, which blends individual attitudes, community values, expected health outcomes, and comparative benefits for different treatments (*American Medical News* 1990 [May 18]:2). They eventually ended up with a list of 709 services. Among the 587 considered "essential" they did include comfort care for the terminally ill (Steinbrook and Lo 1992).

Despite the fact that the system is probably an ethical way to resolve the limits on health care dollars, some complained that it did not give enough weight to the quality of life of the disabled and, after an eleven-month review, Health and Human Services Secretary Louis Sullivan rejected the program, saying it violated the Americans with Disabilities Act (*American Medical News* 1992 [August 17]:1, 11). Such programs will eventually be utilized so that society can set priorities at a public level. The challenge for palliative care medicine will be to make the case for appropriate palliative care within whatever type of system is developed.

Since most systems require both a quality factor and time factor it is likely that physicians will be expected to make accurate predictions of expected survival and estimate the quality-of-life benefit associated with different palliative interventions before they will be authorized. There is no evidence that physicians can accurately predict survival of terminal patients (Bruera et al. 1992; Pearlman 1988; Forster and Lynn 1988; Evans and McCarthy 1985). Similarly, tools to measure quality of life are still being developed in terminal patients (Goodwin et al. 1988; Levine et al. 1988; Goldhirsch et al. 1989; Schipper and Levitt 1985).

With little objective evidence to go on, advocates for the care of the dying will need to make the case that the dying period is an important time that can be very meaningful in a person's life and that prolonging this period while making it comfortable is worthwhile. In a medical world controlled by outcome measurements, accurate quality-of-life instruments and tools are urgently needed in palliative care and palliative care specialists must develop the research tools needed to collect the necessary data.

Autonomy and the Right-to-Die Movement

At the same time that a highly sophisticated technology is offering the medical profession an increasing array of interventions that can be utilized to slow the dying process, the individual has been taking an increasing role in the deliberation of what treatments to accept. Calls for increasing rights of self-determination (described as consumer rights), a patients' bill of rights, and informed consent have increased. After the Supreme Court decision in the Nancy Cruzan case, many more states enacted living will and durable power of attorney laws. At the federal level the Patient Self-Determination Act was passed in an effort to ensure patients' rights to make decisions about their care. Have these laws improved the care of the dying and are they responding to a real or perceived need?

The increasing clamor over right-to-die court cases, living will laws, and durable powers of attorney finally led to the passage in 1990 of the Patient Self-Determination Act. This legislation requires that Medicare/Medicaid health care providers, including hospices, have written policies and procedures concerning advance directives. The intent of the law is to offer patients the opportunity to participate in decisions concerning life-prolonging treatment, such as whether they desire attempts at cardiopulmonary resuscitation (CPR) or rather a do-not-resuscitate (DNR) order.

Generally in the past, DNR orders were written without the clear involvement of the patient (Stolman et al. 1989). In their study of DNR orders at a chronic care facility, Johnson, McNamee, and Campion (1988) found only 14 percent of the cases where it was clear that the patient was consulted in the decision. A study of the impact of a new law in New York that standardized the use of DNR orders revealed that although documentation of DNR had increased from 22 percent to 93 percent after passage of the legislation, involvement of the patient in the decision had only increased from 13 percent to 16 percent (Kamer et al. 1990). It is apparent that medical professionals make these decisions on their own, but even if patients are properly consulted in these options, what type of choices do they make? Are they better served by having a voice in these decisions?

The choices patients make concerning life-prolonging procedures often appear to be "inappropriate" to the health care team. Danis et al. (1991) presented a series of scenarios to 126 competent nursing home patients and found that 20 percent indicated they would want CPR even if they had terminal cancer and 19 percent would desire it even if they were in a permanent coma. In a similar study, Emanuel et al. (1991) found that 16 percent of patients stated they would want to be resuscitated even if they had dementia, 10 percent if in a persistent vegetative state, and 8 percent even if demented and terminally ill. Similar studies of other elderly patients also show comparable numbers of respondents who would make these "inappropriate" choices (Uhlmann, Pearlman, and Cain 1988; Zweibel and Cassel 1989; Frankl, Oye, and Bellamy 1989).

It is generally known that when confronted with such "incorrect" choices, the medical staff endeavors to "assist" the patient in realizing that the correct choice is a DNR order. Since the futility of resuscitation in terminal cancer patients has been well documented (Podrid 1989; Taffet, Teasdale, and Luchi 1988; Vitelli et al. 1991), we might ask if it is necessary to present an option to patients that is not medically realistic. It has been argued that input from the patient and/or family is appropriate only if there are clinically legitimate alternatives (Ewer 1991). Despite the considerable debate about the ethical necessity of always involving patients and their families in every decision (Murphy 1988; Schiedermayer 1988; Youngner 1990; Hackler and Hiller 1990), the consensus clearly favors involving them whenever possible and at least informing them when a decision has been made by the medical staff (Council on Ethical and Judicial Affairs 1991). Ultimately, the measure of benefit from patient involvement will require some consideration of the quality of decisions that are made.

What, if anything, has been accomplished by the new legislation remains unclear (La Puma, Orentlicher, and Moss 1990; White and Fletcher 1991). Obviously, having confused elderly patients fill out forms they don't understand that are then ignored by medical staff who disagree with their choices will accomplish nothing. Advance directives, no matter how thoughtfully conceived, do not take into account how frequently patients change their minds as their disease state progresses. In the Netherlands, two-thirds of those patients initially requesting euthanasia changed their minds as the disease progressed, and two-thirds of those remaining also changed their minds when alternative therapy was made available (Battin 1992). Legal documents on their own will do nothing to prove the care of the dying. Ideally, DNR orders and discussions of living wills and surrogates should trigger a complete discussion of the patient's values. By training the medical staff in ethics, communication, and compassion, the new emphasis on patient autonomy can result in clarifying what is desired by the patient (Sulmasy et al. 1992).

Euthanasia: The Ultimate Solution

A natural evolution as patients express their autonomy over their health care and the right to refuse or discontinue life-prolonging therapy is the request for assisted suicide or euthanasia. As pain control and palliative care have improved and as hospice care has become increasingly available it was somewhat startling to observe the rush toward legalized euthanasia. As noted by Roy (1991) many of those who considered themselves "right to die liberals" and were comfortable with allowing people the right to refuse therapy, somehow believed they would be content to let God pick the actual time and place of death. Despite the fact that organized medicine still opposes physician-assisted suicide (Orentlicher 1989), many reasonable people now see a place for assisted suicide in the care of the dying (Quill 1991; Wanzer et al. 1989; Weir 1992).

Despite the increasing public support for removing physician-assisted suicide from the criminal statutes, the majority of those working in the hospice movement remain strongly opposed. Whereas some ethicists have trouble defining the distinctions between withdrawing life support (sometimes called passive euthanasia) and active euthanasia, the hospice staff clearly draws a sharp line between the two (Miller 1992). Those who work directly at the bedside with the dying are aware of the potential for abuse and manipulation of these patients. They believe the risk of degeneration into involuntary euthanasia (the slippery slope argument) is too strong to support decriminalization at the present time.

The strongest argument against euthanasia is that it does not meet the real needs of the dying: the need for communication and understanding, competent and compassionate palliative care, and the possibility for the patient and family to find meaning and beauty at the end of one's life. Euthanasia does nothing to help society come to grips with our mortality and would serve as one more mechanism to sanitize and avoid confronting death. Legalized euthanasia may also interfere with the task of developing and improving palliative care (Miller 1992). As society carefully reviews medical expenditures, looking for areas of excess, euthanasia would be an obvious cost-effective solution to the "overutilization" of health care by the dying. How much harder will it be to develop quality-of-life instruments documenting the importance and value of the terminal stages of life once society has implicitly said these final days should simply be eliminated?

Medical Care after Euthanasia is Legalized

The recent effort to legalize physician-assisted suicide in Washington (Initiative 119) failed to pass, as did a similar effort in California (Proposition 161, Death with Dignity Act). Similar legislation is pending in other states, and at some point it will be passed. Eventually a national health plan will be in place and physicians will be replaced by "health care providers" working nine to five and dispensing health care to consumers according to rigid patient care guidelines while being scrutinized by peer review committees and computers that update their cost-control profiles. Who then looks out for the dying? In the past, before the Hippocratic oath, doctors were feared. When the doctors of the future are killers as well as curers will we as a society trust them to protect us when we are most vulnerable?

Preliminary analysis of the Netherlands experience demonstrates that there will be abuses. Despite strict guidelines requiring repeated requests for euthanasia and careful documentation, in 0.8 percent of all deaths the guidelines were not followed (Battin 1992). The challenge of physicians will be to learn from their experience and work to avoid abuses.

Defining the Role of the Physician in the Future

The hospice movement in this country started at a grassroots level with very little physician input. Many of the earliest hospice programs were heavy on volunteer support and emphasized social, emotional, and spiritual support. Some of the earliest programs were actually hostile to physicians. They felt that physicians viewed the hospice movement as a counterculture movement that developed out of a rejection of a medical system that seemed obsessed with technology and treatment for treatment's sake. As hospice programs began to provide more complete medical care and assume a role in the health care system, there was a need for more physician involvement to ensure that the medical care was of the highest possible quality. In 1988 the Academy of Hospice Physicians was formed as an organization of physicians interested in and committed to hospice and palliative care. From 124 founding members it has grown in four years to over 1,100 members from seventeen countries. I served as its first president, and as we endeavored to develop a philosophy and mission statement for the new organization, it became clear that the hospice had a lot more to give to physicians than we had to give in return. The hospice emphasis on treating the whole patient, involving family, sharing the burden of care among an equal interdisciplinary team, and finally meeting not just physical needs, but attending to the social, emotional, and spiritual were all important concepts that were missing from most physicians' training. The agenda that has been developed for the Academy of Hospice Physicians should be applied to all physicians in the future. We are emphasizing the need for physician education in total patient care, medical ethics in clinical practice, research into optimal patient care techniques, and participation in social and political issues that have an impact on the care of the dying. The physician of the future needs to be an educator, a scientist, a politician, and philosopher.

The changing model of the doctor-patient relationship has left many physicians with the notion that the only alternative to an old-fashioned paternalistic approach to patients is one of simply providing patients with the treatment alternatives and accepting whatever decision they make. Many physicians feel it is inappropriate to directly order a patient to do something. For instance, since the dangers of cigarette smoking or excessive alcohol consumption are so well known, they assume it would be inappropriate to order a patient to stop smoking or drinking. A recent study found that problem drinkers did in fact do better if they were specifically warned by their doctor to stop drinking, but ironically only 22 percent recall their physician telling them to do so (Walsh et al. 1992). Emanuel and Emanuel (1992) have emphasized that there are doctor-patient models that include helping interpret information and counseling patients, and that the ideal physician is a caring physician who integrates the information and relevant patient values to make a recommendation and, through discussion, attempts to persuade the patient to accept it. Even in situations where the information and outcome are uncertain (e.g., a diagnosis of Alzheimer's disease), the physician needs to involve the patient and family in the process (Drickamer and Lachs 1992), and should do so while still maintaining hope.

At the scientific level the physician needs to become involved in clinical research and develop outcome measures so that the most appropriate interventions can be utilized. There is a need to determine if certain high-cost interventions are really necessary for comfort care.

At the political level, the physician needs to fight for patient rights, particularly as they have an impact on the doctor-patient relationship (Annas, Glantz, and Manner 1990). They need to work toward public and social education efforts that will increase awareness of palliative care and bureaucratic obstacles. Such efforts as the Wisconsin Pain Initiative, which was started in 1985 to increase public awareness of the need for pain control and appropriate access to narcotics as needed, have now spread to other states (Foley 1989). Other obstacles such as triplicate narcotic forms may be ill advised and need to be opposed through public education and political activism (Blum, Simpson, and Blum 1990.) Political conservatism may continue to interfere with efforts to develop optimal palliative care (Cotton 1992) and needs to be resisted.

At a philosophical level, the new physician needs to do more than manage symptoms. In the Netherlands, the most common reason cited by patients requesting euthanasia was loss of dignity (mentioned by 57 percent) and only 5 percent stated pain as the only reason (Battin 1992). It seems clear that training physicians to become merely pain control experts will not prevent requests for euthanasia. In fact, controlling the signs and symptoms of the dying may be detrimental if it allows society to continue avoiding dealing with the reality of death.

If palliative care physicians just manage the pain and symptoms of the terminally ill, society can continue to avoid dealing with the issues of death and dying. While acknowledging spiritual needs, we have by and large avoided addressing issues that many feel are better left to theologians and philosophers. Could or should physicians do more to help society and individuals make sense of their mortality? The traditional medical approach has been to relieve physical and emotional hindrances so that the patient can make his or her own best death. By striving to be nondenominational, neutral, and not to take a position on the meaning of life, suffering, or death, it is difficult to argue effectively against euthanasia as a simple cost-effective solution to relieving suffering. It may be necessary for those involved in all aspects of palliative care to more actively investigate spiritual suffering and, rather than manage the symptoms of the dying, to work to help society legitimate and make meaningful the reality of dying. The goal of optimal terminal care should be to provide a death with dignity that means more than a calm, controlled acceptance of death, but one that helps our patients die in a way that transforms the dying process into a final opportunity for self-enhancement, growth, and a search for meaning. We need to help society recognize that dying is a part of life and should be an occasion for families to come together to express their love (Misbin 1991).

The 1990s will be a decade of increasing change with both challenges and opportunities. The direction of health care for the future will likely be decided, and how we treat the dying will reveal much about how we care about the living. The opportunity for dedicated physicians to use the force for change to improve the care of the dying is obvious and should not be squandered.

References

Annas, G. J., L. H. Glantz, and W. K. Manner. 1990. "The Right of Privacy Protects the Doctor-Patient Relationship." *Journal of the American Medical Association* 263:858–861.

Battin, M. 1992. "Voluntary Euthanasia and the Risks of Abuse: Can We Learn Anything from the Netherlands?" *Law, Medicine and Health Care* 1–2:133–143.

Bayer, R., D. Callahan, J. Fletcher, T. Hodgson, B. Jennings, D. Monsees, S. Sieverts, and R. Veatch. 1983. "The Care of the Terminally Ill: Morality and Economics." *New England Journal of Medicine* 309:1490–1494.

Belanger, D., M. Moore, and I. Tannock. 1991. "How American Oncologists Treat Breast Cancer: An Assessment of the Influence of Clinical Trials." *Journal of Clinical Oncology* 9:7–16.

Blum, R. H., P. K. Simpson, and D. S. Blum. 1990. "Factors Limiting the Use of Indicated Opioid Analgesics for Cancer Pain." *American Journal of Hospice and Palliative Care* 7(5):31–35.

Brook, R. H. 1989. "Practice Guidelines and Practicing Medicine. Are They Compatible?" *Journal of the American Medical Association* 262:3027–3030.

Bruera, E., M. J. Miller, N. Kuehn, T. MacEachern, and J. Hanson. 1992. "Estimate of Survival of Patients Admitted to a Palliative Care Unit: A Prospective Study." *Journal of Pain and Symptom Management* 7:82–86.

Chakravarty, S. N., and K. Weisman. 1988. "Consuming our Children?" *Forbes* (November 14):222–232.

Cotton, P. 1992. "Government Extinguishes Marijuana Access, Advocates Smell Politics." *Journal of the American Medical Association* 268:2573–2574.

Council on Ethical and Judicial Affairs, American Medical Association. 1991. "Guidelines for the Appropriate Use of Do-Not-Resuscitate Orders." *Journal of the American Medical Association* 265:1868–1871.

Danis, M., L. Southerland, J. M. Garrett et al. 1991. "A Prospective Study of Advance Directives for Life-Sustaining Care." *New England Journal of Medicine* 324:882–888.

Detsky, A. S. 1989. "Are Clinical Trials a Cost-Effective Investment?" *Journal of the American Medical Association* 262:1795–1800.

Drickamer, M. A., and M. S. Lachs. 1992. "Should Patients with Alzheimer's Disease Be Told Their Diagnosis?" *New England Journal of Medicine* 326:947–951.

Emanuel, E. J., and L. L. Emanuel. 1992. "Four Models of the Physician-Patient Relationship." *Journal of the American Medical Association* 267:2221–2226.

Emanuel, L. L., M. J. Barry, J. D. Stoekle et al. 1991. "Advance Directives for Medical Care—A Case for Greater Use." *New England Journal of Medicine* 324:889–895.

Evans, C., and M. McCarthy. 1985. "Prognostic Uncertainty in Terminal Care: Can the Karnofsky Index Help? *Lancet* 1:1204–1206.

Ewer, M. S. 1991. "Decision Making in Critical Illness: Who Knows Best?" *M.D. Anderson Oncolog* 36(1):1–5.

Foley, K. M. 1989. "Controversies in Cancer Pain. Medical Perspectives." *Cancer* 63:2257–2265.

Forster, L. E., and J. Lynn. 1988. "Predicting Life Span for Applicants to Inpatient Hospices." *Archives of Internal Medicine* 148:2540–2543.

Frankl, D., R. K. Oye, and P. Bellamy. 1989. "Attitudes of Hospitalized Patients toward Life Support: A Survey of 200 Medical Inpatients." *American Journal of Medicine* 86:645–648.

Goldhirsch, A., R. D. Gelber, R. J. Simes et al. 1989. "Costs and Benefits of Adjuvant Therapy in Breast Cancer: A Quality-Adjusted Survival Analysis." *Journal of Clinical Oncology* 7:36–44.

Goodwin, P. J., R. Feld, W. K. Evans, and J. Pater. 1988. "Cost-Effectiveness of Cancer Chemotherapy: An Economic Evaluation of a Randomized Trial in Small-Cell Lung Cancer." *Journal of Clinical Oncology* 6:1537–1547.

Hackler, J. C., and F. C. Hiller. 1990. "Family Consent to Orders Not to Resuscitate." *Journal of the American Medical Association* 264:1281–1283.

Hillman, B. J., C. A. Joseph, M. R. Mabry, J. H. Sunshine, S. D. Kennedy, and M. Noether. 1990. "Frequency and Costs of Diagnostic Imaging in Office Practice—A Comparison of Self-Referring and Radiologist-Referring Physicians." *New England Journal of Medicine* 323:1604–1608.

Holli, K., and M. Hakama. 1989. "Treatment of the Terminal Stages of Breast Cancer." *British Medical Journal* 298:13–14.

Johnson, P. V., M. McNammee, and E. W. Campion. 1988. "The 'Do Not Resuscitate' Order: A Profile of Its Changing Use." *Archives of Internal Medicine* 148:2373–2375.

Kahn, K. L., E. B. Keeler, M. J. Sherwood, W. H. Rogers, D. Draper, S. S. Bentow, E. J. Reinisch, L. V. Rubenstein, J. Kosecoff, and R. H. Brook. 1990. "Comparing Outcomes of Care Before and After Implementation of the DRG-Based Prospective Payment System." *Journal of the American Medical Association* 264:1984–1988.

Kamer, R. S., E. M. Dieck, J. McClung et al. 1990. "Effect of New York State's Do-Not-Resuscitate Legislation on In-Hospital Cardiopulmonary Resuscitation Practice." *American Journal of Medicine* 88:108–111.

Kennedy, B. J. 1988. "Aging and Cancer." *Journal of Clinical Oncology* 6:1903–1911.

La Puma, J., and E. F. Lawlor. 1990. "Quality-Adjusted Life-Years. Ethical Implications for Physicians and Policy Makers." *Journal of the American Medical Association* 263:2917–2921.

La Puma, J., D. Orentlicher, R. J. Moss. 1991. "Advance Directives on Admission. Clinical Implications and Analysis of the Patient Self-Determination Act of 1990." *Journal of the American Medical Association* 266:402–405.

Levine, M. N., G. H. Guyatt, M. Gent et al. 1988. "Quality of Life in Stage II Breast Cancer: An Instrument for Clinical Trials." *Journal of Clinical Oncology* 6:1798–1810.

Levinsky, N. G. 1990. "Age as a Criterion for Rationing Health Care." *New England Journal of Medicine* 322:1813–1815.

Lonergan, E. T., and J. R. Krevans. 1991. "National Agenda for Research on Aging." *New England Journal of Medicine* 324:1825–1828.

Mackillop, W. J., B. O'Sullivan, and G. K. Ward. 1987. "Non-Small Cell Lung Cancer: How Oncologists Want to Be Treated." *International Journal of Radiation Oncology, Biology, Physics* 13:929–934.

Mayer, R. J., and W. B. Patterson. 1988. "How is Cancer Treatment Chosen?" *New England Journal of Medicine* 318:636–638.

Miller, R. J. 1992. "Hospice Care as an Alternative to Euthanasia." *Law, Medicine and Health Care* 20:127–132.

Misbin, R. I. 1991. "Physicians' Aid in Dying." *New England Journal of Medicine* 325:1307–1311.

Murphy, D. 1988. "Do-Not-Resuscitate Orders. Time for Reappraisal in Long-Term-Care Institutions." *Journal of the American Medical Association* 260:2098–2101.

Orentlicher, D. 1989. "Ethics and Health Policy Counsel. Physician Participation in Assisted Suicide. From the Office of the General Counsel." *Journal of the American Medical Association* 262:1844–1845.

Pearlman, R. A. 1988. "Inaccurate Predictions of Life Expectancy. Dilemmas and Opportunities." *Archives of Internal Medicine* 148:2537–2538.

Podrid, P. J. 1989. "Resuscitation in the Elderly: A Blessing or a Curse?" *Annals of Internal Medicine* 111:193–195.

Quill, T. E. 1991. "Death and Dignity, A Case of Individualized Decision Making." *New England Journal of Medicine* 324:691–694.

Roy, D. J. 1991. "Is There Only One Right Way to Die?" *Journal of Palliative Care* 7:3–4.

Rubenstein, L. V., K. L. Kahn, E. J. Reinisch, M. J. Sherwood, W. H. Rogers, C. Kamberg, D. Draper, and R. H. Brook. 1990. "Changes in Quality of Care for Five Diseases Measured by Implicit Review, 1981 to 1986." *Journal of the American Medical Association* 264:1974–1979.

Sager, M. A., D. V. Easterling, D. A. Kindig, and O. W. Anderson. 1989. "Changes in the Location of Death after Passage of Medicare's Prospective Payment System. A National Study." *New England Journal of Medicine* 320:433–439.

Schiedermayer, D. L. 1988. "The Decision to Forgo CPR in the Elderly Patient." *Journal of the American Medical Association* 260:2096–2097.

Schipper, H., and M. Levitt. 1985. "Measuring Quality of Life: Risks and Benefits." *Cancer Treatment Reports* 69:1115–1123.

Schneider, E. L., and J. M. Guralnik. 1990. "The Aging of America. Impact on Health Care Costs." *Journal of the American Medical Association* 263:2335–2340.

Scitovsky, A. A. 1984. " 'The High Cost of Dying': What Do the Data Show?" *Milbank Memorial Fund Quarterly* 62:591–608.

Smith, L. 1989. "What Do We Owe to the Elderly?" *Fortune* (March 27):54–62.

Steinbrook, R., and B. Lo. 1992. "The Oregon Medicaid Demonstration Project—Will it Provide Adequate Medical Care?" *New England Journal of Medicine* 326:340–344.

Stolman, C. J., J. T. Gregory, D. Dunn, and B. Ripley. 1989. "Evaluation of the Do-Not-Resuscitate Orders at a Community Hospital." *Archives of Internal Medicine* 149:1851–1856.

Sulmasy, D. P., G. Geller, R. Faden, and D. M. Levine. 1992. "The Quality of Mercy. Caring for Patients with 'Do Not Resuscitate' Orders." *Journal of the American Medical Association* 267:682–686.

Taffet, G. E., T. A. Teasdale, and R. J. Luchi. 1988. "In-Hospital Cardiopulmonary Resuscitation. *Journal of the American Medical Association* 260:2069–2072.

Uhlmann, R. F., R. Pearlman, and K. C. Cain. 1988. "Physicians' and Spouses' Predictions of Elderly Patients' Resuscitation Preferences." *Journal of Gerontology: Medical Sciences* 43:M115–M121.

Vitelli, C. E., K. Cooper, A. Rogatko, and M. F. Brennan. 1991. "Cardiopulmonary Resuscitation and the Patient with Cancer." *Journal of Clinical Oncology* 9:111–115.

Walsh, D. C., R. W. Hingson, D. M. Marrigan, S. M. Levenson, G. A. Coffman, T. Heeren, and L. A. Cupples. 1992. "The Impact of a Physician's Warning on Recovery after Alcoholism Treatment." *Journal of the American Medical Association* 267:663–667.

Wanzer, S. H., S. J. Federman, S. J. Edelstein et al. 1989. "The Physician's Responsibility Toward Hopelessly Ill Patients. A Second Look." *New England Journal of Medicine* 320:844–849.

Weir, R. F. 1992. "The Morality of Physician-Assisted Suicide." *Law, Medicine and Health Care* 20:116–126.

Wennberg, J. E. 1990. "Outcomes Research, Cost Containment, and the Fear of Health Care Rationing." *New England Journal of Medicine* 323:1202–1204.

White, M. L., and J. C. Fletcher. 1991. "The Patient Self-Determination Act. On Balance, More Help than Hindrance." *Journal of the American Medical Association* 266:410–412.

Youngner, S. J. 1990. "Futility in Context." *Journal of the American Medical Association* 264:1295–1296.

Zweibel, N. R., and C. K. Cassel. 1989. "Treatment Choices at the End of Life: A Comparison of Decisions by Older Patients and Their Physician-Selected Proxies." *The Gerontologist* 29(5):615–621.

18

Physician-Assisted Dying: The Conflict with Fundamental Principles of American Law

David Orentlicher

On the issue of physician-assisted dying (i.e., physician-assisted suicide and euthanasia), people express considerable ambivalence. For example, on the November 1991 Washington state ballot, Initiative 119 proposed that physician-assisted dying be permitted for terminally ill patients who voluntarily requested physician-assisted dying in writing and who were certified by two physicians as having no more than six months to live (Misbin 1991). When the initiative was debated, preference polls indicated that approximately two-thirds of the public favored the concept (Carson 1992). Nevertheless, the initiative was defeated when 54 percent of the voters rejected it (Carson 1992). Similarly, in November 1992, a California ballot proposal to permit physician-assisted dying was defeated by a 54–46 percent margin (Weber 1993) after preference polls had suggested that the public supported the proposal (Reinhold 1992). Members of the medical profession are also divided. While there is growing support among doctors for physician-assisted dying (Brody 1992; Quill, Cassel, and Meier 1992; Wanzer et al. 1989), most doctors appear to view physician-assisted dying as inconsistent with their professional role (Overmyer 1991).

The ambivalence toward physician-assisted dying reflects the complexity of the issue and the strength of the arguments both in favor and against its use (Brock 1992; Callahan 1992; Kass 1989; Orentlicher 1989; Pellegrino 1993; Weir 1992; Wolf 1989). In addition, the ambivalence may reflect an irreconcilable tension between two of the important philosophies that animate American law: the inalienability of certain rights and egalitarianism. Inalienable rights are rights that are so fundamental that they cannot be bought, sold, or otherwise transferred voluntarily from one person to another (Black, Nolan, and Nolan-Haley 1990). Egalitarianism refers to the equal status of each person under the law.

Physician-assisted dying is resisted in large part, both ethically and legally, because it violates the sense that the right to life is an inalienable right. Proposals for physician-assisted dying include safeguards that respond to concerns about inalienability, but these safeguards create a conflict with the principle that we have an egalitarian system of government. Efforts to reconcile physician-assisted dying with egalitarianism, in turn, exacerbate the conflict with inalienability. The more we deal with one concern, the greater the problems with the other. As I will explain, prohibiting physician-assisted dying may be necessary to avoid problems with either inalienability or egalitarianism.

To better understand the tension between inalienability and egalitarianism, it is useful to consider these two principles in some depth. As a prelude, it is interesting to note that the two principles were enunciated in the same passage of the American Declaration of Independence: "We hold these truths to be self-evident, that all men are created equal, they are endowed by their creator with certain unalienable rights, that among these are life, liberty and the pursuit of happiness."

Defining Inalienable Rights

Although there are different understandings of the concept of inalienable rights ("Rumpelstiltskin Revisited" 1986), it is not critical for the purposes of this essay to resolve those differences. Since my purpose is to demonstrate the tension between inalienability and egalitarianism, it is sufficient simply to define inalienable rights in a reasonable and consistent way. There are two central aspects to the definition of inalienable rights. In this section, I will discuss what inalienability actually entails, what it means to characterize a right as inalienable. In the next section, I will discuss how it is decided whether a particular right should be considered inalienable.

I will identify four important characteristics of inalienable rights. First, a person cannot waive or give up an inalienable right, even if there is fully voluntary consent to do so (Kuflik 1986; McConnell 1984). For example, if I were to ask a friend to kill me, and he did so, he would still be subject to prosecution for homicide. My consent would not be a defense to the murder. The right to vote is another example of an inalienable right; I cannot sell my right to vote nor can I have someone else appear at the polling precinct in my place. I also cannot agree to become an indentured servant or go into slavery, nor can I agree to be battered by a family member (Kuflik 1986).

The second feature of an inalienable right is that it defines a person's relationships with others. An inalienable right cannot be transferred or waived with respect to someone else (McConnell 1984). This characteristic of inalienability may explain why the states that make assisted suicide a crime nevertheless do not make suicide a crime. Although most states prohibit assisted suicide (Quill, Cassel, and Meier 1992), suicide is no longer a crime in any state ("Physician-Assisted Suicide" 1992). Voting provides another example of how inalienability exists with respect to others. In the United States, unlike some other countries, I do not have to vote in public elections; I can decline to exercise my right. However, if I sell my vote to someone else, I will be violating the law.

As a corollary to the inability to waive or give up the right with respect to someone else, an agreement to give up the right is unenforceable. If I promise to sell my vote to a friend and I renege, the friend cannot obtain a court order to enforce my promise. In addition to being unenforceable, an agreement to give up the right may even result in legal liability. For example, it is against federal law to sell or buy a vote (18 U.S.C. 597). It is also against federal law to have an indentured servant (18 U.S.C. 1584).

A third important point about inalienable rights is that they are not necessarily absolute rights. For example, while I may not be able to voluntarily give up my right to life, I may still lose the right involuntarily by forfeiture (McConnell 1984). People who commit murders are subject to capital punishment; people who attack another may be killed by the other person in self-defense.

The fourth feature of inalienability is that it can be a broad or a narrow concept (McConnell 1984). If inalienability is conceived broadly, then a person can never waive an inalienable right through consent. The right might be lost for other reasons, as by forfeiture, but consent is never a basis for losing the right. Historically, the United States has treated euthanasia that way; euthanasia is not made acceptable because the patient agrees to its performance. If inalienability is conceived narrowly, then consent alone is not sufficient to give up the right, but consent plus other factors may make waiver of the right acceptable. Advocates of assisted suicide have implicitly defined the inalienability of the right to life narrowly. In their view, consent by the patient alone is not sufficient to justify assisted suicide; rather, there must be consent, *and* there must be terminal or incurable illness, suffering without prospect of relief, and other qualifying conditions (Quill, Cassel, and Meier 1992; Wanzer et al. 1989). Similarly, consent to indentured servitude is not sufficient to waive the right to be free of indentured servitude. Yet if there is consent plus national security concerns, then the right may be waived. Accordingly, people who volunteered to serve in the military were not free to withhold their services during the Persian Gulf War.

In order to discuss the concept of inalienable rights with respect to the right to life, it is necessary to give a definition of the right to life. Here, too, there are different understandings; for example, people disagree whether the right to life includes the right to medical treatment, irrespective of income (Annas et al. 1990). For the purposes of this discussion, it will be sufficient to conclude that, at the very least, the right to life includes the right of one person not to have his/her life taken by another. Accordingly, while euthanasia or physician-assisted suicide might violate this aspect of the right to life, a refusal of life-sustaining treatment would not. In addition, because another person participates more deeply in an individual's decision to die by euthanasia than by assisted suicide, euthanasia is more problematic than assisted suicide from the perspective of inalienability. This distinction may in part explain why euthanasia is prohibited by law in all states, but assisted suicide is not prohibited in every state.

Categorizing Rights as Inalienable

To understand how proposals for legalizing physician-assisted dying respond to the inalienability of the right to life, it is useful to examine the reasons certain rights are considered inalienable. While there is some disagreement on where to draw the line between alienable and inalienable rights (Tribe 1985), it is nevertheless possible to identify the concerns that lead us to characterize a right as inalienable.

Perhaps the most important concern is the ideal of preserving the moral worth of society. Permitting physician-assisted dying may undermine the high value that society places on life. If people can be killed simply because they consent, there is a serious risk that society will have less respect for human life and will become less troubled when there are actual violations of a person's right to life (McConnell 1984). That is, people may become less troubled when killing occurs without consent. Prohibiting physician-assisted dying prevents us from beginning the process of weakening the moral fibers of society. For many people, the concern about moral worth has religious aspects—people hold their bodies in a stewardship for some greater being or purpose. Because individuals do not own their bodies, they therefore have an obligation not to shorten their lifespan. The ban on slavery also reflects the need to preserve the moral worth of society. The dignity and essential moral worth of the individual is undermined if people are allowed to become slaves, even with their consent.

Second, inalienable rights preserve freedom of choice in areas of profound consequence to happiness (Kuflik 1986). The irreversibility of death explains why many people object to physician-assisted dying. Indentured servitude also illustrates this point. A person might agree to become a slave yet, after a few months, conclude that servitude was not a desirable choice. If the agreement were enforceable, then the person's preferences would be frustrated in an area critical to the person's sense of personhood and well-being. Divorce is another example of the need to preserve freedom of choice in areas of profound consequence. A married person cannot be bound by a promise never to file for divorce. Because the right to decide with whom to live and share a family is so fundamental, the civil law does not allow a person to give up that right (Kuflik 1986).

Inalienable rights serve the third purpose of avoiding the creation or perpetuation of hierarchies (Kuflik 1986). Inalienability helps prevent the domination of one group by another. Slavery is an obvious example. The right to vote is another. We do not want the wealthy buying up all the votes and then controlling elections at the expense of the poor. Concern about domination is particularly relevant to the right to life. One of the important arguments against physician-assisted dying is the fear that the handicapped and other vulnerable groups will be victimized if assisted suicide or euthanasia is permitted.

Authenticity is a fourth concern underlying inalienable rights (Kuflik 1986; McConnell 1984). If I report that I assisted someone's suicide, there may be no way to determine whether I am telling the truth; the other person can no longer serve as a witness. One of Dr. Jack Kevorkian's cases of assisted suicide, in October 1991, illustrates just this concern. The prosecutor charged that Marjorie Wantz died by euthanasia, rather than by assisted suicide, but there was no reliable way to distinguish between the two, and the charges were dismissed by the court (*State v. Kevorkian*, No. CR–92–115190–FC, slip op. at 17–19 [Mich. Cir. Ct. July 21, 1992]). In other cases, there may be legitimate doubt whether the dead person had a truly competent intent to end his/her life. The person's competence may have been compromised by a treatable depression or by the effects of the underlying disease or its treatment (Conwell and Caine 1991; Wanzer et al. 1989). Concerns about authenticity are also important to the inalienability of the right to be free from battering. Often women who are abused by their spouses are unable to object or resist, either out of fear of retribution or for economic or other reasons (Strube 1988). Men charged with battering might falsely claim that there was consent to the battering. If consent to battering made assault permissible, then many women would have less legal protection from abuse by their spouses.

Limiting Physician-Assisted Dying to Avoid Problems with Inalienability

Supporters of physician-assisted dying have generally advanced proposals that respond to the concerns of inalienability. In the Netherlands, strict criteria have to be satisfied before a person can undergo euthanasia. The patient must be experiencing intolerable and irreversible suffering, the patient must make repeated, competent, and consistent requests for euthanasia, and two physicians must determine that euthanasia is appropriate (de Wachter 1992). Similarly, when a group of distinguished physicians endorsed physician-assisted suicide, it was in the context of terminally ill, competent patients whose suffering is intolerable and unresponsive to therapeutic intervention (Wanzer et al. 1989). In both cases, the criteria are designed to respond to the concerns that have made the right to life inalienable.

The protective measures used in the Netherlands, and included in many domestic proposals for physician-assisted dying, can be characterized as either substantive or procedural protections. Substantive criteria set limits on who can seek physician-assisted dying; procedural criteria regulate the manner in which physician-assisted dying is carried out. As examples of procedural criteria, there are the requirements that a) the patient must make repeated, competent requests over a reasonable period of time; b) the request must be well documented in the record; and c) a second physician must agree that the physician-assisted dying is appropriate (Quill, Cassel, and Meier 1992). These procedural criteria respond to the concern about authenticity. We can minimize the possibility that the person's death was involuntary if all of these procedural hurdles are satisfied.

The substantive criteria respond to the other concerns underlying inalienability. Examples of substantive restrictions include the requirements that a) the patient must be terminally ill; and b) the patient must be suffering intolerably with no prospect of relief. These restrictions limit physician-assisted dying to the people who are truly suffering and whose prognosis is hopeless, people who therefore are truly in need of assistance in dying. For these patients, assisted suicide or euthanasia may be the most compassionate response possible. Proponents of physician-assisted dying contend that, by permitting the most compassionate response, we can enhance, rather than compromise, the moral worth of society.

The substantive criteria also respond to the concern that the powerless will be victimized. By restricting physician-assisted dying to the very narrow group of people who are terminally ill and suffering intolerably with no prospect of relief, we ensure that people's lives are not ended simply because of age and infirmity.

Finally, the substantive criteria respond to the concern about limiting freedom of choice in important areas. When a patient becomes terminally ill with intolerable suffering, there is already very little freedom to make choices about the way life will be lived (Rubenfeld 1989).

Problems with Egalitarianism

Although the substantive criteria for physician-assisted dying respond to concerns about inalienability, they may create serious problems with egalitarianism, the principle that people are entitled to equal treatment under the law. In an egalitarian society, each person is entitled to be treated with equality and evenhandedness by the government (Tribe 1988). However, if the state permits physician-assisted dying only for patients who meet a specific level of terminal illness and suffering, then it will be granting a right to certain persons that it denies to other persons. In terms of physician-assisted dying, there would not be equal treatment of all individuals under the law.

Of course, egalitarianism does not require that people always be treated in the same way. Because there are important differences among individuals, they may need to be treated differently in order to be treated as equals. As the U.S. Supreme Court has observed, "Sometimes the greatest discrimination can lie in treating things that are different as though they were exactly alike" (*Jenness v. Fortson*, 403 U.S. 431, 442 [1971]). If all citizens were required to appear at the polls in order to vote, greater hardship would be imposed on disabled individuals or people who are temporarily living overseas (Tribe 1988). Similarly, if all citizens were required to pay the same percentage of their income in taxes, greater hardship would be imposed on citizens with low incomes. In short, equal treatment does not necessarily mean equivalent treatment.

The difficult question for an egalitarian society is deciding when variations among individuals are relevant for purposes of drawing legal distinctions (Beauchamp and Childress 1989). A considerable body of law has developed to interpret the Fourteenth Amendment's guarantee of equal protection under the law. It is not critical for the purposes of this paper to define precisely the limits of egalitarianism. The important point is to highlight the egalitarian concerns that would arise from laws permitting physician-assisted dying.

As the development of equal-protection law has recognized, certain kinds of distinctions among individuals are less acceptable than others. For example, when the government draws distinctions on the basis of race, courts subject the distinctions to the most exacting scrutiny and, almost without fail, conclude that the distinctions are unconstitutional (Tribe 1988). On the other hand, governments have considerable freedom to draw distinctions between individuals on the basis of their occupation (*Williamson v. Lee Optical*, 348 U.S. 483 [1955]). If the state permits physician-assisted dying only for patients who meet a specific level of terminal illness and suffering, then it will be responding to concerns about inalienability but it will be making the kinds of distinctions among its citizens that are particularly troublesome on egalitarian grounds: distinctions that are based on judgments about the value of people's lives.

The reluctance to make such judgments has influenced the development of legal doctrine or public policy in other contexts. The evolution of the law in withdrawal-of-life-support cases illustrates this influence. When the right to refuse life-sustaining treatment was first recognized, it was often viewed as a right of terminally ill patients to refuse particularly burdensome, or "extraordinary," care. Living-will statutes typically restricted their coverage to terminally ill patients (many still do) (Orentlicher 1990a), and the early court cases focused on the patient's impending death and the invasiveness of the medical treatment. For example, in *In re Quinlan* (355 A.2d 647 [1976]), the New Jersey Supreme Court concluded that the right to refuse treatment depends upon the seriousness of the patient's prognosis and the degree of bodily invasion from medical treatment. Thus, at one time, the state drew an important distinction among its citizens: while there was a right to refuse life-sustaining treatment, the right belonged only to patients who were sufficiently sick and who were dependent upon burdensome treatment.

Recent cases have made it clear that the right to refuse life-sustaining treatment is not limited by the patient's prognosis or the medical treatment being provided. For example, the right may be exercised by patients who still can live for decades in a fully conscious state. In *Georgia v. McAfee* (385 S.E.2d 651 [Ga. 1989]), and *McKay v. Bergstedt* (801 P.2d 617 [Nev. 1990]), the right was recognized for two young men who had become quadraplegic and ventilator-dependent as a result of severe spinal cord injuries, but who had not suffered any loss of mental competence. The right to refuse life-sustaining treatment has also been expanded to include any medical treatment, including artificial nutrition and hydration (*Cruzan v. Director, Missouri Department of Health*, 110 S. Ct. 2481 [1990]). In short, over time, courts have gradually eliminated their reliance on substantive criteria when making decisions about the right to refuse treatment. The right is no longer denied to patients because they do not have a severe enough prognosis or because the medical treatment upon which they depend is not unduly burdensome. If the government were to require treatment based upon substantive criteria, it would be saying that some lives still had sufficient value that they must be maintained. It would also be taking the position that other lives were so devoid of value that they did not have to be maintained. As the court in *Bouvia v. Superior Court* (225 Cal. Rptr. 297, 305 [Cal. Ct. App. 1986]) observed, however:

> Who shall say what the minimum amount of available life must be? Does it matter if it be 15 to 20 years, 15 to 20 months, or 15 to 20 days, if such life has been physically destroyed and its quality, dignity, and purpose gone? As in all matters lines must be drawn at some point, somewhere, but that decision must ultimately belong to the one whose life is in issue.

This abandonment of substantive criteria in withdrawal-of-treatment cases ensures that the government will not be making the worst kind of value judgments for a government to make—judgments about the value of a person's life (Tribe 1988).

To be sure, procedural criteria continue to play an important role in cases about the withdrawal of life-sustaining treatment. States may require clear and convincing evidence of an incompetent patient's wishes before treatment is withdrawn or, when such evidence is absent, states may permit family members to decide whether treatment should be discontinued (Orentlicher 1990b). Similarly, living-will statutes may require that two witnesses co-sign a living-will document and that the patient's diagnosis be confirmed by two physicians before the living will is carried out. As already noted, procedural criteria are designed to ensure authenticity; in the context of withdrawal-of-treatment cases, they are designed to ensure that treatment is withdrawn only if the patient would have wanted treatment withdrawn. By ensuring authenticity, the procedural criteria protect the ability of patients to make their own decisions about the value of their lives, thereby serving the goals of both egalitarianism and inalienability.

The reluctance to make judgments about the value of life has also influenced public policy in several other areas. The history of hemodialysis for chronic renal failure is an important example. At one time, hemodialysis was rationed and the rationing criteria were based on a number of considerations, including social class and social worth (Evans, Blagg, and Bryan 1981). Discomfort with that approach resulted in 1972 legislation that made Medicare funds available for kidney dialysis for virtually all patients with chronic renal failure (Evans, Blagg, and Bryan 1981). The same kind of discomfort has resulted in controversy over a recent decision by a bone-marrow-transplant program to deny treatment to a patient because her IQ was less than 75 (Gianelli 1992).

Oregon's health care reform program to provide coverage for the uninsured has also encountered resistance, in part because of judgments being made on value-of-life grounds (Pear 1992). Under the Oregon plan, coverage will become available to all of the state's uninsured population, but only to the extent of a standard benefits package (Oregon Health Services Commission 1993). That is, by requiring coverage for fewer medical treatments than provided in typical private health insurance plans, the state can ensure that more people have health insurance. The proposed limitations on coverage were developed by ranking medical treatments from 1 to 696 and establishing a cutoff for coverage at treatment 565 and above (Orentlicher 1994). Concerns about value-of-life judgments arose in the construction of the ranking. Originally, the ranking was created by considering primarily the ability of a treatment to prevent death, the ability of treatment to relieve symptoms, the impact of symptoms on the patient's quality of life, and the cost of treatment (Oregon Health Services Commission 1993). After objections from the Bush (Sullivan 1992) and Clinton (Shalala 1993) administrations, Oregon reranked the various treatments without considering judgments about the impact of treatment on quality of life. As a result, only a treatment's ability to prevent death and a treatment's cost were the primary criteria for creating the ranking (Oregon Health Services Commission 1993).

Resolving the Conflict Between Egalitarianism and Inalienability

Concerns about egalitarianism in physician-assisted dying can be resolved by eliminating a role for substantive criteria. If the government does not limit the option of physician-assisted dying to only certain people, concerns about value-of-life judgments would not arise. In other words, from an egalitarian perspective, it may make sense to permit physician-assisted dying for everyone or no one, thereby removing from the government the task of deciding when life becomes intolerable. Indeed, some states, such as Michigan, do not have criminal prohibitions against assisted suicide at all (*State v. Kevorkian*, No. CR–92–115190–FC, slip op. at 5–16 [Mich. Cir. Ct. July 21, 1992]), and in the states that prohibit assisted suicide, the laws apply to all people (e.g., Ariz. Rev. Stat. Ann. 13–1103 [1989]); Fla. Stat. Ann. 782.08 [West 1992]; N.Y. Penal Law 125.15 [McKinney 1987]). As discussed previously, however, the principle of inalienability indicates that physician-assisted dying should be permitted for only certain people or no one. Accordingly, to satisfy both inalienability and egalitarianism, it may be necessary to prohibit physician-assisted dying altogether.

The tension between egalitarianism and inalienability is already being played out in the debate about physician-assisted suicide. Many advocates of assisted suicide believe that it should be restricted to patients who are terminally ill (Wanzer et al. 1989), reflecting concerns about inalienability. Other advocates, however, observe that many nonterminal patients may be suffering intolerably and therefore should not be denied assisted suicide. These commentators argue that it would be unfair to treat the nonterminal patients differently than the terminally ill patients (Quill, Cassel, and Meier 1992).

It may be argued that physician-assisted dying need not violate egalitarianism. Egalitarianism requires equal, not equivalent, treatment. In the context of dying, the substantive criteria draw meaningful distinctions between people. If the concern is avoiding undue suffering, then to treat people equally may require permitting physician-assisted dying for those who are suffering intolerably. However, this line of argument brings us back to the same question: Is it the proper role of government to decide when suffering becomes so intolerable that a person's life need not be maintained? In withdrawing or withholding life-sustaining treatment, this society has decided that it is not an appropriate decision for government.

The defeat of the Washington state initiative to permit phyisican-assisted dying resulted in part from concerns that there were insufficient safeguards to prevent abuse (Carson 1992). In other words, the principle of inalienable rights played an important role in the defeat of the initiative. The California ballot proposal included stricter safeguards to overcome the concerns demonstrated in Washington (Crigger 1992), but its defeat also reflected concerns about the potential for abuse (Reinhold 1992). Despite the outcomes in Washington and California, legislative proposals in other states are likely to be put to a vote. Indeed, referenda will be on the ballots in Oregon and Washington in 1994 (Price 1992).

The motivations behind proposals to permit physician-assisted dying are powerful, as are the motivations behind objections to the proposals. It is therefore difficult to predict whether physician-assisted dying will be permitted for those who are terminally ill and suffering intolerably. If permission is granted, it is unlikely that a limited permissiveness will take us down the slippery slope to an expansive right to physician-assisted dying. Concerns about inalienability provide a strong bulwark against that possibility.

The author gratefully acknowledges the helpful comments of Teri Randall.

References

Annas, George J., Sylvia A. Law, Rand E. Rosenblatt, and Kenneth R. Wing. 1990. *American Health Law*. Boston: Little, Brown.

Beauchamp, Tom L., and James F. Childress. 1989. *Principles of Biomedical Ethics*. 3d ed. New York: Oxford University Press.

Black, Henry C., Joseph R. Nolan, and Jacqueline M. Nolan-Haley. 1990. *West's Law Dictionary*. 6th ed. St. Paul, Minn.: West.

Brock, Dan W. 1992. "Voluntary Active Euthanasia." *Hastings Center Report* 22(2):10–22.

Brody, Howard. 1992. "Assisted Death—A Compassionate Response to a Medical Failure." *New England Journal of Medicine* 327(19):1384–1388.

Callahan, Daniel. 1992. "When Self-Determination Runs Amok." *Hastings Center Report* 22(2):52–55.

Carson, Rob. 1992. "Washington's I-119." *Hastings Center Report* 22(2):7–9.

Conwell, Yeates, and Eric D. Caine. 1991. "Rational Suicide and the Right to Die: Reality and Myth." *New England Journal of Medicine* 325(15):1100–1103.

Crigger, Bette-Jane. 1992. "New California Initiative." *Hastings Center Report* 22(2):8.

de Wachter, Maurice A. M. 1992. "Euthanasia in the Netherlands." *Hastings Center Report* 22(2):23–30.

Evans, Roger W., Christopher R. Blagg, and Fred A. Bryan, Jr. 1981. "Implications for Health Care Policy: A Social and Demographic Profile of Hemodialysis Patients in the United States." *Journal of the American Medical Association* 245(5):487–491.

Gianelli, Diane M. 1992. "Transplant Program Scrutinized, Researcher's Criteria Challenged." *American Medical News* (September 7):2, 16.

Kass, Leon R. 1989. "Neither for Love nor Money: Why Doctors Must Not Kill." *Public Interest* 94 (Winter):25–46.

Kuflik, Arthur. 1986. "The Utilitarian Logic of Inalienable Rights." *Ethics* 97 (October):75–87.

McConnell, Terrance. 1984. "The Nature and Basis of Inalienable Rights." *Law and Philosophy* 3(1):25–59.

Misbin, Robert I. 1991. "Physicians' Aid in Dying." *New England Journal of Medicine* 325(18):1307–1311.

Oregon Health Services Commission. 1993. *Prioritization of Health Services: Report to the Governor and Legislature*. Portland: State of Oregon.

Orentlicher, David. 1989. "Physician Participation in Assisted Suicide." *Journal of the American Medical Association* 262(13):1844–1845.

Orentlicher, David. 1990a. "Advance Medical Directives." *Journal of the American Medical Association* 263(17):2365–2367.

Orentlicher, David. 1990b. "The Right to Die after *Cruzan*." *Journal of the American Medical Association* 264(18):2444–2446.

Orentlicher, David. 1994. "Rationing and the Americans with Disabilities Act." *Journal of the American Medical Association* 271(4):308–314.

Overmyer, Mac. 1991. "National Survey: Physicians' Views on the Right to Die." *Physician's Management* 31(7):40–76.

Pear, Robert. 1992. "Plan to Ration Health Care is Rejected by Government." *New York Times* (August 4):A6.

Pellegrino, Edmund D. 1993. "Compassion Needs Reason Too." *Journal of the American Medical Association* 270(7):874–875.

"Physician-Assisted Suicide and the Right to Die with Assistance." 1992. *Harvard Law Review* 105(8):2021–2040.

Price, Joyce. 1992. "Michigan Committee Approves Assisted-Suicide Bill." *Washington Times* (October 8):A5.

Quill, Timothy E., Christine K. Cassel, and Diane E. Meier. 1992. "Care of the Hopelessly Ill: Proposed Clinical Criteria for Physician-Assisted Suicide." *New England Journal of Medicine* 327(19):1380–1384.

Reinhold, Robert. 1992. "California to Decide if Doctors Can Aid in Suicide." *New York Times* (October 9):A1.

Rubenfeld, Jed. 1989. "The Right to Privacy." *Harvard Law Review* 102(4):737–807.

"Rumpelstiltskin Revisited: The Inalienable Rights of Surrogate Mothers." 1986. *Harvard Law Review* 99(8):1936–1955.

Shalala, Donna. 1993. Letter Barbara Roberts, Governor of Oregon. March 19.

Strube, Michael J. 1988. "The Decision to Leave an Abusive Relationship: Empirical Evidence and Theoretical Issues." *Psychological Bulletin* 104(2):236–250.

Sullivan, Louis W. 1992. Letter to Barbar Roberts, Governor of Oregon. August 3.

Tribe, Laurence H. 1985. "The Abortion Funding Conundrum: Inalienable Rights, Affirmative Duties, and the Dilemma of Dependence." *Harvard Law Review* 99(1):330–343.

Tribe, Laurence H. 1988. *American Constitutional Law*. 2d ed. Mineola, N.Y.: Foundation Press.

Wanzer, Sidney H., Daniel D. Federman, S. James Adelstein, Christine K. Cassel et al. 1989. "The Physician's Responsibility Toward Hopelessly Ill Patients: A Second Look." *New England Journal of Medicine* 320(13):844–849.

Weber, Doron. 1993. "A Way Around Kevorkian." *USA Today* (August 9):13A.

Weir, Robert F. 1992. "The Morality of Physician-Assisted Suicide." *Law, Medicine, and Health Care* 20(1–2):116–126.

Wolf, Susan M. 1989. "Holding the Line on Euthanasia." *Hastings Center Report* 19 (1) (Supp.):13–15.

19

AIDS and Empowerment: The Ethical Issues

James Serafini

> Over the whole earth, wherever there are men, is found the conception of the invisible dead. It is tempting to call it humanity's oldest conception. There is certainly no horde, no tribe, no people which does not have abundant ideas about its dead. Man has been obsessed by them; they have been of enormous importance to him; the action of the dead upon the living has been an essential part of life itself. —Canetti, *Crowds and Power*

The topic of this part of this volume, death and empowerment, would have utterly humbled me even five years ago. Now I feel confident that I have something useful to say about this phenomenon due to my startling experience first with AIDS and then with AIDS Coalition to Unleash Power (ACT UP). This essay presents my own experiences as a context for observations on death and empowerment. It also outlines the historical, sociological, and religious aspects of American culture, with particular emphasis on the gay white male subculture, that I believe have led to the success of AIDS activism.

There are critical junctures in the course of human events: the time comes when one's back is up against the wall and survival involves something more than ingenuity and care. Something extraordinary is called for, a degree of concern and action that might seem groundless to those not engaged by the experience. Such an extraordinary human event is the AIDS epidemic.

AIDS has captured not only our bodies but the imagination and soul of many of us. AIDS pushes the terrible polarity of sex and death right into our faces. Creation and destruction, the primitive, essential qualities of life, now define our everyday existence. And in a powerful transference of energy, I gained strength from that polarity. At the midpoint of a successful, upper-middle-class life, I am enthralled and horrified by the forces with which I am dealing. I am captivated by the continuity of my emotional commitment to be effective in my struggle with this beast. Yet the dimensions of the moral space I struggle in are so great that I find myself to be a hero and a coward, full of faith and despairing, vindictive, and compassionate.

As a member of ACT UP and as a Catholic, I believe in an activist faith. In 1973 that meant being one of the cofounders, along with John McNeil, of Dignity New York. In 1983 it meant being a volunteer at the Gay Men's Health Center (GMHC). In 1987 it meant joining ACT UP. In 1989 it meant going inside St. Patrick's Cathedral to bear witness to both my activism and my faith.

When I joined ACT UP in August 1987, I had not yet been tested. In fact, I knew nothing about my own blood. However, in October 1987, influenced by my experiences in ACT UP, I got tested and had my T-cells done. I had over 800, a relatively high number. But that result nonetheless changed my perception and my attitudes. I began to pay more attention to the Treatment + Data announcements at the general meetings. In March 1989 I had my T-cells done again and, much to my surprise, as well as my doctors', they had fallen to 467, even though I was perfectly healthy. My focus and perception of the AIDS crisis changed again. Later the next year, they fell to 197, and then below 100. All the scientific statistics indicated that I was heading for disaster. My attitude toward my whole life, from the guys I dated to whether to paint my apartment, was affected. If you are not positive, you will find it really difficult to have any notion of what that experience of watching your T-cells fall is like.

The best example I can offer comes from the German submarine movie *Das Boot*. In a scene near the end of the movie the German sub has been hit and is sinking. The captain and his men are gathered together around the depth gauge and they watch it fall. It falls past the first safety limit and then passes the real danger limit. The sub is entering a depth that imposes a pressure that is greater than its construction can withstand. The men wait in eerie silence for the ship's skin to implode on them. Monitoring my T-cells is exactly like watching that depth gauge, and I watched both terrified and fascinated, waiting for my immune system to implode and take me to a depth I wan't built to survive. This experience is shared by all too many members of ACT UP, and it gives us an intense focus and fills us with a burning urgency to act in this crisis. It also gives us a profoundly authentic voice, an authenticity that is based on a direct experience of our mortality and that goes beyond any derived from an ideology that is merely "politically correct."

This experience can also make one impatient and arrogant, sometimes as a defense against the desperate feelings of vulnerability. Yet it is precisely because of that vulnerability that most of us in ACT UP realize that this struggle is a profound test of our humanity; we are in the foxholes of mortality. Consequently, our commitment to medical reform and political confrontation springs spontaneously out of anger and a deep sense of compassion for our men, women, and children.

On December 17, 1982, I recorded in my diary,

> A very good week—I made a serious decision not to have casual sex after a terrible dream Tuesday night about AIDS. I must be careful; this AIDS thing is very serious, and I've had these problems with swollen glands now on and off for a year.

There are aspects of the present situation that make me apprehensive about ACT UP's continuing growth and effectiveness. The AIDS crisis has now lasted twice as long as the Second World War. The accumulation of vulnerabilities is enormous. The desire to hide, to retreat, and to protect the self is natural, even healthy. Yet for ACT UP to continue its work and to grow, people have to select themselves, as patients and as activists. With a disease that may be asymptomatic for as much as ten years, there is very little pressure for individuals to accept a new identity as "patient"; there is no obvious external necessity, such as a broken arm or kidney failure, to force the issue on an individual. One's T-cells can fall, even like my precipitous plunge, and yet one may not suffer any obvious physical change. It is hard for most people to take care of themselves when they feel fine, let alone take complicated regimens of medication. It is understandable, even natural, for HIV-positive individuals to continue to refuse to accept a stigmatized, fatal destiny. This dynamic force of a natural psychological resistance to know or act on the implications of being HIV-positive has to be taken into account when one considers the future possibilities for ACT UP. When ACT UP began there were absolutely no viable treatments. The fact there are now three drugs available, AZT, ddI, and ddC, relieves some of the pressure on many HIV-positive individuals to act. Thus, it is ironic that the very drugs that in some ways are available only as a result of ACT UP's insistence also reduce the potential pool of recruits for the activist movement by creating in the minds of many a reassuring, but false, sense that the HIV crisis is being effectively managed.

This reduction in the number of potential recruits for activism is further affected by the epidemiological shift in the affected population. The percentage of gay white males constituting new HIV-positive cases has been falling for the last six years. That is good news for gay white males, but for continued AIDS activism, it is a mixed blessing as gay white males still comprise the vast majority of people involved in the three main branches of AIDS activism: political, research/pharmaceutical, and treatment access. For any number of complicated reasons, the other affected groups have not yet assumed the activist role that their numbers would warrant. Too often, in fact, intravenous drug users, women, and various minorities are represented by well-intentioned people who are themselves HIV-negative. This shift is dangerous and it undermines the empowerment from these affected groups.

The false optimism often engendered by many of the so-called advances in the fight against AIDS is an insidious form of propaganda that seeks merely to pacify HIV-positive individuals. This is potentially destructive to the activist movement. To be fair, however, in terms of the treatment of opportunistic infections, the last five years has seen genuine and significant advances. But the situation with antivirals remains essentially the same as it was in 1987.

The past five years of the AIDS crisis form a striking contrast with the first five. The first five years were characterized by the silence of the medical establishment. It was not until HIV was discovered and the HIV antibody assay was established that doctors began suggesting something could be done. AIDS came along at the peak of American medicine's technological triumph and utterly humiliated its armies. I remember my lover, Matthew, who died in 1983, slipping away over a period of a year, and doctors simply had nothing to say. No testament to their sense of powerlessness and frustration could be greater than the general silence of mainstream medicine and its institutional cohorts: the Centers for Disease Control, the National Institutes of Health, the pharmaceutical companies. However, once a virus and an antibody assay enabled doctors to diagnose who is infected, they began to talk and to feel more in control. The medical system needs control to operate coherently. During the previous forty years, American medicine and researchers had grown to think of themselves as not only infallible but invincible.

AIDS crushed that conviction of invulnerability, leaving a hole in the armor of American medicine that became the nursery of ACT UP. The forty years of imperial progress in medicine left most doctors shaken before the profound mysteries of sex and death that AIDS revealed to them. They and their patients were thrust into a tragic romance whose dimensions caused even those who had witnessed the depths of twentieth-century brutality to recoil.

When the silence ended, however, it was replaced not with an interesting and useful dialogue about AIDS but with a terrible political dialectic. For five years the combination of silence and death had created enormous anxiety that would encourage America's neurosis over AIDS information. Silence was replaced, in fact, by moral outrage and the pseudo-medical struggle over testing. This information neurosis led to a hysteria involving not only political and religious conservatives versus homosexuals but well-intentioned liberals who thought gay men would be best served by mandatory testing and reporting, if not outright quarantining. Yet there was no cure, no treatment, and only a bare bones understanding of the syndrome. Therefore, testing and the knowledge of one's HIV status became the key to reestablishing some sense of control for established medical authority.

Even among organizations like GMHC and Body Positive, an education and support organization for people who are HIV-positive, an unwitting collusion takes place that supports imperial American medicine's image of being effective and on top of the AIDS epidemic. Body Positive, on whose board I sit, publishes a monthly magazine. Its introductory essay, called "You Are Not Alone," states:

> Testing positive for HIV does not mean you have AIDS, but HIV is probably the greatest threat to your life you have ever faced. This virus may remain inactive in your body for a long time, but it may not. *If you are healthy now, you may still go on to develop some sort of health problems* related to HIV. You may develop AIDS. There remain many uncertainties surrounding HIV, and though there is currently no "cure" for HIV infection, there are treatments. You need to learn what information is available and work to make informed choices about your health.
>
> Many HIV+ people now live fulfilling and happy lives. *Many are healthy and show no symptoms of disease.* Many have chosen to take certain treatments and drugs that show promise to preserve and lengthen their lives. So as serious as this is, there is hope! You do not have to look at testing HIV positive as though you've just been given a death sentence. (emphasis added)

But AIDS activism was built on the conviction and the reality that it *was* a death sentence. These paragraphs are too reassuringly pat. They involve a serious distortion of the medical and social reality of AIDS.

This is just one of the most glaring examples of the false sense of control and effectiveness American medicine has created around AIDS, similar to what it has succesfully created around cancer. This has the insidious effect of undermining patient empowerment. By reducing the sense of urgency it allows gay men to pass the period in which they are asymptomatic in a reassuring medical delusion that everything is, and will continue to be, fine. It took six years for ACT UP to get started. There had to be an enormous pile of bodies before people were pushed into an angry, empowered realization of what was happening to them, of which the palpable experience of death was an absolutely essential ingredient. People were essentially radicalized by their familiarity with death. It took a great conscious act of the will to break the silence, and perhaps only an intimacy with death and dying could mobilize the will sufficiently to engage the enormous tasks presented by AIDS in America.

In 1987, with the introduction of AZT, the medical establishment solidified its control. This was done with the unwitting help of AIDS activists, who helped push for the premature closure on placebo-controlled clinical trials of AZT. (I helped push for the early release of AZT, and I have no regrets about that decision. However, I realize that as a consequence of that activism we have operated in confusion concerning the therapeutic usefulness of AZT. To a real extent, ddI and ddC, AZT's sister drugs, have also been affected by a similarly confused clinical picture concerning efficacy and dosage.)

Thus, it is fair to suggest that ACT UP is a new kind of sexual/political community aligned with some aspects of the left and even some aspects of the right. Borrowing from the right, ACT UP favors deregulation of the drug industry and open access to drugs, that individuals have the right in treatment to assume considerable risks if they are informed and they so choose. We engage the old left on its narrow economic and class focus, and we are seeking to change even the left's attitude, which holds class and economic issues often over the new parameters of sexual liberation. ACT UP finds itself in a unique power position. Issues that even the most liberal left had not previously regarded as properly political at all, such as sexual identity, treatment access, and drug research, are now viewed as deeply political.

One of the more interesting questions of historical analysis has been why some movements take hold while others fade. At the heart of the coverage of ACT UP lie the questions, "How did ACT UP get so big, so effective, so fast? How has it maintained its position of power despite lackluster years and strong internal dissension?" The answer on one level is that *ACT UP works*: it produces results, not just ideological schemes. This was especially true in the first three years of its work when the results were the most pronounced. ACT UP works because its members had the critical realization early on that AIDS patients were only the latest individuals to have been colonized by an imperial American medicine and held captive within its technological empire. As HIV-positive individuals, as a captive people, our role was simple: listen, pay, obey, three words that describe perfectly the ideal patient in the imperial medical system. I am convinced that our previous historical experience as an oppressed minority helped us have the intuition that a new colonial reality now existed in the medical context of HIV. Not that this insight was articulated consciously, but the intuition that as an oppressed people we had little or no worth, especially when ill, fueled our audacity and imagination. It led ACT UP members to a deep conviction that the individuals "handling" the AIDS crisis had no idea what they were doing and cared even less. This is a strong reason so many HIV-positive individuals refuse to accept the message of ACT UP. ACT UP demands an identification with one's mortality and most people would understandably prefer to distance themselves from such an imminent reality, which also, unfortunately, separates them from a great deal of power. The identification with one's mortality and the realization of institutional incompetence can only be usefully assimilated into consciousness when accompanied by an insistent expression of willfulness, the conviction that one must act. Thus, ACT UP becomes a gymnasium of the will: it strengthens and trains weak and atrophied abilities to choose and act. If this process of strengthening does not take place, this kind of realization about the incompetence of established institutions and their lack of compassion can easily become a source of debilitating depression and despair.

ACT UP has succeeded in effecting essential and deep changes in the Food and Drug Administration's drug-approval process; funding for AIDS care and research; and making minorities, women, and children an issue years before anyone else noticed, precisely because it took the oppositional position of a colonized people throwing off its incompetent authority. That is, ACT UP has a serious respect for the power of the institutions as well as a deep cynicism and distrust of it.

As the death rates climbed in New York through the early 1980s, a small group of gay men became fed up with living as gay "colonists" of the dominant social and medical culture and with passing for straight at work and being compliant with the federal CDC. After 1984, anxiety over HIV testing became an added burden; HIV testing was a double-edged sword, allowing for diagnosis and discovery. Many feared that their sexual identity could be determined by a blood test. In fact, their sexual history and practices might reasonably have been deduced and used against them. Many in the gay community had lost their nerve and their will under the burden of oppression and AIDS. ACT UP stimulated the consciousness of gay men, especially through such actions as the famous confrontation at New York's St. Patrick's Cathedral. The values of imperial American medicine were similar to those that had always dominated and oppressed the psyche of gay men. Thus, gay men, especially those who were HIV-positive and who were to join ACT UP, accepted and acknowledged their status openly and on a deeper level even embraced the stigma of HIV for which the dominant culture had shunned them. This set up a powerful dynamic so that ACT UP did not come to form an organization as much as a community.

Aspects of recent gay male psychosocial history uniquely served the emergence of powerful and effective grassroots groups such as ACT UP,

GMHC, and Body Positive. In fact, if any group of individuals was disposed by their history to organize resistance to a new fatal infectious disease, it was gay men in the early 1980s. I conclude this for several reasons. First, in the ten years following Stonewall, gay men had made a journey from being a criminal class to an openly tolerated subculture. This was especially true in the gay urban centers such as New York, Los Angeles, and San Francisco. To effect this change, gay men had to develop effective means of communication independent of the media and established mainstream institutions. Gay men were therefore uniquely adapted to a life in which person-to-person discourse was dominant, where information about gay life was passed literally from man to man. Such information ran the gamut from where to buy a good shirt, to where the good bars were, to who was a good doctor. Thus, from the beginning of the AIDS crisis gay men had established a network of doctors who were familiar with their lifestyle and who were dedicated to their treatment.

An activist breast cancer movement has recently developed, similar in many ways to ACT UP. In fact, some women came to Treatment + Data meetings for advice and support. Yet women have been dying of breast cancer in increasing numbers for two generations. Imagine if all those cases of breast cancer were concentrated in twenty large cities. Within a year or two, most women would know at least another woman personally who had had breast cancer, if they themselves were not affected. Death has its most startling effect on people's consciousness when it is a palpable experience, and this is what the few hundred AIDS deaths in New York, San Francisco, and Los Angeles provided. The intensely closed sexual/social interaction among gay men provided thousands of men with a personal involvement in a very short time with someone who had the new "gay disease." Consequently, a relatively small number of deaths had an impact that would not have been felt had they been more evenly distributed. But these deaths occurred within a community where news traveled fast and reliably, which was essential because AIDS was initially ignored by the government and the mass media.

Many HIV-positive gay men now found themselves further marginalized. It did not even occur to most to expect significant help from the larger society since they had learned as early as their teenage years that they would have to make it on their own. So most gay men had early training in accepting a fuller responsibility for shaping their own destiny, which they did with energy, acuity, and imagination. Few grassroots movements have been so concerned with the aesthetics of their image and the continuous successful control of that image. Most men, like myself, were young (under thirty-five) and entering the height of our professional and financial power. We had access, and we also had a cynical attitude toward medical and political authority that was a result of our experience with a homophobic society. This cynicism proved to be an asset in the struggle against death.

While these sociological and psychological conditions fostered the development of skills and attitudes that drove ACT UP initially, something more was needed to transform ACT UP from just another grassroots organization into a committed, crusade-like movement.

> In order to have members, or even adherents, an organization must have some way of representing itself, and it carves out a distinct identity through both mythic and ritual means. Organizations propagate myths regarding their origin and purpose, while members engage in symbolic practices that serve to mark them off from nonmembers. These myths often assert the group's superiority. It is, according to Arnold, a "unifying force . . . as mysterious as the law of gravitation." (Kertzer 1989:17–18)

It is an irony of this tragedy that in the struggle for an effective organization with a continuous source of energy, ACT UP borrowed from an idiosyncratic form for its general meetings. Meetings soon began resembling the religious revival meeting, a form that provided a ritualized, almost sacred context for our work.

The AIDS crisis has even appropriated the terminology of the religious experience. There may not be two words that describe this complex confluence better than *convert* and *positive*. When one seroconverts, one becomes HIV-positive. The most important event in fundamentalist religious life is the experience of conversion. Likewise, when one seroconverts one "becomes" the AIDS crisis; the crisis is no longer taking place "out there" but in one's bloodstream. For many of us the conversion is not only physical but profoundly psychological that binds one to others who have converted. We form a new community.

Many people who were and are involved in ACT UP experience it as a community of the faithful. This conviction places making a commitment to ACT UP on an emotional level similar to a religious experience. It is ironic that many of the same emotional underpinnings of ACT UP should be found in the American fundamentalist experience, but many activists, after they seroconvert, undergo an astounding ontological transformation that has as its parallel religious conversion. At Stonewall the sexual entered the civil space. It was an expression of freedom through the open assertion of the sexual, and it became a movement, gay liberation, that linked the ideology of independence and self-expression to biology. With AIDS the dynamic process was essentially reversed. Our biology links us to a new ideology. This fusion of identity and biology lay the groundwork for gay men's struggle with AIDS.

The intense experience of conversion, combined with the dynamic of gays being outside the mainstream has transformed the marginalized status of many who are HIV-positive feel into a chosen status that empowers. What externally may make one shunned can also make one unique, set apart, chosen, stronger. In keeping with ACT UP's empowerment goals, membership is through self-selection; one simply chooses to join. There are no officers and all members have an equal authority to speak. ACT UP encourages its members to be empowered by an unmediated experience of the crisis in their own bloodstream, so that there is a powerful identification between "being" and the epidemic.

I argue in this essay that since the end of World War II, medical practice and research in the West have developed into an empire of technique driven by an ideology of conquest and dominance that holds the conquest of disease is best accomplished through the submission of the body and the patient's choice to the authority of medicine. One of the founders of modern scientific methodology, Sir Francis Bacon, warned against abuses of science. He said that a time would come when scientists would put Nature to the rack in order to compel her to answer their questions. Bacon warned us that however we might twist and force her, we still have to be *free* to listen to the answers that Nature gives us back.

The reality, however, is that most of us—researchers, patients, physicians—are *not* free and in fact are abused and/or neglected by a system that, like its twin the military-industrial complex, is run by an elaborate old-boy network that ensures financial and ideological control through an interactive system of consultantships and grants. In addition, powerful lobbies such as the American Medical Association have long obstructed health-care reform. Like the military-industrial complex, the research-pharmaceutical complex is long on waste and bureaucracy and short on results.

Time and experience have shown that it is not enough to push the medical/pharmaceutical/governmental establishment from behind, hoping it will somehow catch up with the epidemic. If we have learned anything over the past few years, it is that there must be basic changes in the rules of the game. ACT UP recognizes that the very structure of research has to be called into question. Yet today, unfortunately, even among activists, not enough of us are aware of the fact that challenging a scientific or methodological paradigm is a serious and a necessary step for AIDS activists. Starting in earnest with our treatment agenda for the Montreal conference in 1989, and continuing with our agendas for San Francisco in 1990, Florence in 1991, and Amsterdam in 1992, we offer not only criticism but alternatives to the present model and focus of research and treatment.

ACT UP's proposal for parallel-track research (first proposed at our Montreal meeting in 1989) has already effected significant changes in the drug development process. The parallel-track proposal was first adopted to expand access to the drugs ddI and ddC. Speedy, simple drug trials and more extensive testing of drugs against specific opportunistic infections are a direct challenge to the research status quo. Part of ACT UP's tactics has been to disrupt "science as usual," yet the disruptions were targeted to change areas of research that we had decided were most likely to achieve important results.

In fact, the most effective aspect of AIDS activism has been the extensive reform of the FDA and the AIDS Clinical Trial Group (ACTG), a huge medical enterprise that employs thousands and is responsible for most of the HIV drug research in America. These reforms were initiated at a meeting of Treatment + Data in April 1989, right after the quarterly meeting of the ACTG. ACT UP was represented at the ACTG meeting in an unofficial capacity. It was soon apparent that researchers were moving slowly with their research protocols. By most estimates it would take five or six years for any new drug to get to patients. Placebo-controlled trials, we felt, were unethical in the context of this particular disease. Members of Treatment + Data were sought for their expertise. Political pressure was placed on the ACTG by large ACT UP demonstrations, which had begun to get thorough media coverage. Given these circumstances, I suggested at our small committee meetings that we take a new course with the FDA that would take advantage of problems in the ACTG and the political and social pressure that we could bring to bear. Six of us got together and wrote what turned out to be the Montreal Treatment Agenda.

Choice has always been a central issue for ACT UP. Our individual choice to act against socially and medically imposed constraints. Once individuals make that choice, we join with others to form a community of choice and within that community we act and gain our strength. We have, in effect, developed an empowering community mechanism whereby the quality of research and medical care is evaluated and the information is disseminated. This has been accomplished in a culture where patient choice over medical procedure was historically restricted. When patients complied with little thought, they were less able to believe in their own moral and medical freedom. This, in turn, constricted the development of the strengths of character necessary to enable patients to make important decisions in cooperation with established medical authority.

By the 1980s we had arrived at a situation in the practice of medicine where the exercise of conscious decision making, the expression of the individual's authority to know and choose, was struggling. Those who wanted to make a choice about their own medical care and give feedback to the medical system were considered revolutionaries, such as the women's collective who wrote *Our Bodies, Ourselves* and the gay men and women who pressured the American Psychiatric Association to change its designation of homosexuality as a pathology.

American medicine had become stuck in a "SWAMP"; the individuals who thrive in it are straight, white, academic, medical professionals. Yet what do we do in the face of this monolithic bureaucracy? Try to destroy or coopt it somehow? No, I believe that there is a need for authority, including medical authority. The majority of medical people are good men and women acting in a system driven by a narrow, conservative ideology from which they do not have the means or the will to liberate themselves. The responsibility falls to the activist community to liberate American medicine and research.

ACT UP believes it is never ethical for medical authority to supersede the individual's right to knowledge and choice. A necessary role for medical research expertise is to inform and assist the patient in making a well-developed medical choice. ACT UP aims to see a system where the accessibility to complete information and care and the exercise of choice through knowledge is commonplace.

In 1987, when I was told that I was HIV-positive, I had to develop an ability to discriminate among my medical options very quickly. I had relatively high T-cells. Should I begin treatment? Should I wait? What would be lost by not getting treatment? What might be gained? Since my T-cells were at 800, there was not much need to begin treatment. A year and a half later, when they fell below 600, the issue became more pressing, and a year later, when they fell below 300, I had to make a treatment decision. The decision to prophylax against PCP was not difficult to make; deciding on antiviral therapy was not as easy because the benefits were not as clear-cut. It is often the case that prophylaxis for opportunistic infections is a relatively simple choice, but other decisions pose more problematic choices.

There were serious differences among all four prominent AIDS clinicians with whom I consulted, and the final medical decision fell to me. Many people do not realize that in a medical situation where there is a great deal of uncertainty, pathogenesis, treatment and also prognosis create a space for choice. This space can and should be filled by the patient's decision about his or her treatment options.

Two areas complicate the predicament for the HIV-positive individual. First, both doctors and patients often find the uncertainty over early intervention and care of HIV-positive individuals to be very anxiety-provoking. In addition, the remarkable effectiveness of antibiotics over the last forty years has weakened the patient's ability to discriminate and for doctors to deal with the idiosyncratic nature of the treatment and progression of HIV. To put it bluntly, antibiotic therapies have made doctors and patients lazy and somewhat cavalier.

Second, too few doctors are well trained in dealing with HIV disease. Many of the experienced doctors have gained their experience over the past ten years of clinical care, which has been stressful, and many have closed their practices. I have spoken to many of these doctors in New York City and San Francisco. One of their concerns is that HIV-positive individuals require an enormous amount of information about new treatments and research, and that this often takes up more than 75 percent of the time spent in office visits and phone calls. In the coming years, it is questionable whether people who seroconvert are not going to have these kinds of physicians available to them. In addition, medical students have already begun to avoid some of the great urban teaching hospitals because of the prospect of having to treat HIV-positive individuals.

I use these two points to conclude that the government's involvement in early care should be to promote the education of HIV-positive individuals as advocates for their own health. Patients will need to be educated to understand the complexities of a long-term chronic illness. We simply will not have enough physicians with the skills to educate and treat the growing HIV-positive population.

Those of us who are HIV-positive can handle this aspect of the health crisis posed by HIV since patients can often, with the right information and emotional support, make sensible medical decisions for themselves, especially in the early stages of the disease. They need information, among other things, on T-cell tests, beta-2, and plasma viremia assays, which must be made available and affordable through government support at public health clinics. The crisis in American medicine can be partially avoided through an extensive and accessible education program for HIV-positive individuals and their doctors.

My experience with ACT UP and Body Positive has shown me that a wide range of individuals, men and women of very different educational backgrounds, can assume a significant decision-making responsibility for their own care. The nature of HIV disease is such that one needs much fine tuning to receive good care. For example, there is an enormous variation in the clinical status of individuals with the same number of T-cells. This is significant since T-cell levels are the principal diagnostic markers used today. An interesting medical lesson of AIDS is that immune systems and their markers are idiosyncratic. (This tends not to be true, of course, at the extremes of T-cell counts, above 600 or below 50. At those extremes, the clinical pictures are much more predictable in the short run.)

One of the reasons I am persuaded that gay men have dealt so well with this disease, both physically and psychologically, is that they have made sure that they had the information they needed to act. Body Positive has trained thousands of HIV-positive individuals to be serious partners in their own care. The government must see to it that patient education and empowerment become a central goal of early intervention, for without this educational empowerment there will not be good medical care for most individuals who will seroconvert in the coming years. Outside of a clearly effective treatment or cure, patient education will carry an increasing burden of responsibility for improving and extending the life of HIV-positive individuals. Perhaps this model could even be extended to other chronic or life-threatening diseases.

An axiom in Catholic moral theology has, I believe, powerful implications for our approach to the issue of trials and treatment: *Ubi dubium ibi libertas*, "where there is doubt, there is freedom." Within this principle is a sound basis for pushing for patients to make an independent choice to assume risks with an experimental drug or treatment, since treatment of HIV infection still takes place in the context of uncertainty. Yet until ACT UP pressured the government for its own agenda, the FDA and the ACTGs reflected an opposing view, "where there is doubt, there is no freedom." In this crisis, it is an unnecessarily restrictive and authoritarian stand to maintain. The principle "where there is doubt, there is freedom" supports the right of patients to take well-informed risks with treatments and drugs.

It seems clear that the doubt surrounding the natural history of HIV infection gives HIV-positive communities a right to demand that established models for nonpredictive research trials be changed radically. Kuhn supports our claims for patient-community parity with the scientific establishment: "As in political revolutions, so in paradigm choice there is no standard higher than the assent of the relevant community" (Kuhn 1970:93).

Having generated a community we now have a profound responsibility to fight for better HIV education, care, and research; we have a right to parity with the medical/governmental establishment in all aspects of this huge endeavor. We demand the free access to information, through accessible education programs, so we are free to learn and to take risks intelligently: this is the kind of empowerment that ACT UP works toward.

References

Canetti, Elias. 1984. *Crowds and Power*. Translated by Carol Stewart. New York: Farrar, Straus, and Giroux.

Kertzer, David I. 1989. *Ritual Politics and Power*. New Haven, Conn.: Yale University Press.

Kuhn, Thomas S. 1970. *The Structure of Scientific Revolutions*. Chicago: University of Chicago Press.

About the Contributors

George J. Annas, J.D., M.P.H., is the Edward Utley Professor of Health Law, Chair of the Health Law Department, and Director, Law, Medicine, and Ethics Program, Boston University Schools of Medicine and Public Health. He writes a regular column on "Legal Aspects of Medicine" for the *New England Journal of Medicine*. His most recent book is *Standard of Care: The Law of American Bioethics* (Oxford University Press, 1993).

Robert H. Blank, Ph.D., is a Professor in the Political Science Department at the University of Canterbury, Christchurch, New Zealand. Among his recent books in biomedical policy are *Rationing Medicine*, *Regulating Reproduction*, *Fetal Protection in the Workplace* (all from Columbia University Press), *Life, Death, and Public Policy*, *Mother and Fetus*, and *Fertility Control*. He is also coeditor of *Compelled Compassion* and *Health Insurance and Public Policy*.

Andrea L. Bonnicksen, Ph.D., is Professor of Political Science at Northern Illinois University. She is the author of two books, including *In Vitro Fertilization: Building Policy from Laboratories to Legislatures* (Columbia University Press, 1989), and she is book review editor for public policy for the journal *Politics and the Life Sciences*. She was a 1990–91 Rockefeller Foundation Fellow at the Institute for the Medical Humanities, University of Texas Medical Branch, Galveston, Texas, and she is currently studying policy issues relating to the preimplantation diagnosis of human embryos.

Lynton K. Caldwell, Ph.D., is Arthur F. Bentley Professor of Political Science Emeritus and Professor of Public and Environmental Affairs at Indiana University. He has written over two hundred refereed articles and ten books, including *Biocracy: Public Policy and the Life Sciences* (1987) and *Between Two Worlds: Science, the Environmental Movement and Policy Choice* (1990). He is a Fellow of the American Association for the Advancement of Science, the Royal Society of Arts, and he has served on science advisory boards at the National Research Council, the Sea Grant Program, and the U.S. Army Corps of Engineers, the Army Environmental Policy Institute, the National Institutes of Health, and the International Joint Commission. He is noted as principal architect of the National Environmental Policy Act of 1969 and "inventor" of the environmental impact statement.

Daniel Callahan, Ph.D., is the cofounder and president of the Hastings Center. He received his doctorate in philosophy from Harvard. He is the author or editor of thirty books, including *The Troubled Dream of Life: Living with Mortality* (1993); *What Kind of Life: The Limits of Medical Progress* (1990); and *Setting Limits: Medical Goals in an Aging Society* (1987). He is an elected member of the Institute of Medicine, National Academy of Sciences, and has received numerous awards and honorary degrees.

Christine K. Cassel, M.D., F.A.C.P., is Chief of the Section of General Internal Medicine; Director of the Center on Aging, Health, and Society; and Professor of Medicine and Public Policy at the University of Chicago. Among her numerous publications are three textbooks and more than one hundred articles published in medical, policy, and scientific journals. Dr. Cassel is past president of Physicians for Social Responsibility and of the Society for Health and Human Values. She was appointed to the U.S. Congress Biomedical Advisory Committee in 1988, and she has served as a consultant to the Veterans Administration, the Institute of Medicine, the Health Care Financing Administration, the National Institute on Aging, and the Agency for Health Care Policy and Research.

Cynthia R. Daniels is a faculty member in the Political Science Department at Rutgers University where she teaches in the Women and Politics Ph.D. program. She is the author of *At Women's Expense: State Power and the Politics of Fetal Rights* (Harvard University Press, 1993), which analyzes the rise of "fetal protectionism" in law and popular culture in the United States and assesses the meaning of gender difference for women's standing as liberal citizens. She has previously taught at Harvard University and has been the recipient of fellowships from the Bunting Institute (1989–1990) and the Woodrow Wilson Foundation.

H. Tristram Engelhardt, Jr., holds an M.D. with honors from Tulane University School of Medicine and a Ph.D. from the University of Texas at Austin. Currently, he is Professor in the Department of Medicine, as well as in the Departments of Community Medicine, and Obstetrics and Gynecology, Baylor College of Medicine. In addition, he is Professor in the Department of Philosophy, Rice University, Adjunct Research Fellow, Institute of Religion, Houston, Texas, and Member of the Center for Ethics, Medicine, and Public Issues. Dr Engelhardt is editor of the *Journal of Medicine and Philosophy* and coeditor of the *Philosophy and Medicine* book series with over forty volumes in print. He has written over 190 articles and chapters of books and coedited more than twenty-five volumes. His most recent book is *Bioethics and Secular Humanism: The Search for a Common Morality* (Trinity Press International/SCM Press, 1991).

Carlos F. Gomez, M.D., Ph.D., is a physician at the University of Virginia School of Medicine. He is the author of numerous works, including *Regulating Death: Euthanasia and the Case of the Netherlands* (Free Press, 1991).

Clifford Grobstein, Ph.D., is Professor of Biological Science and Public Policy Emeritus at the University of California, San Diego, where he was previously Dean of the Medical School. Among his many publications are *From Chance to Purpose: An Appraisal of External Human Fertilization* (1981) and *Science and the Unborn: Choosing Human Features* (1988).

Elizabeth McCloskey, M.A., served as Legislative Assistant to Senator John C. Danforth (R-Mo.) from 1989 to 1992 during which time she advised the senator on medical ethics, health care, education, and welfare issues. Prior to joining Senator Danforth's staff, Ms. McCloskey worked in the Sex Crimes Unit of the Manhattan District Attorney's office. Ms. McCloskey holds a master's degree in social ethics from Yale Divinity School. She has published numerous articles on the subject of the Patient Self-Determination Act and on other topics. Currently, she is a columnist for *Commonweal* and a Research Associate for the National Advisory Board on Ethics in Reproduction.

Andrew H. Malcolm, M.S., is the author of *Someday* (Harper Perennial), an autobiography examining the personal and professional impact of medical technology on his family's life. He was an editor, foreign and national correspondent, and columnist for the *New York Times*, and he is now Executive Assistant for Policy and Communications for the Governor of Montana. His other books include *This Far and No More*, the true story of a mercy killing; *The Canadians*, a profile of that people and country and its complex relationship with the United States; *Final Harvest*, a true murder mystery set in the Midwest; and *Huddle: Fathers, Sons, and Football*, an autobiographical examination of how fathers teach sons the rules of life through a game.

Diane E. Meier, M.D., is an Associate Professor of Geriatrics and Internal Medicine at the Mount Sinai School of Medicine in New York City. She was educated at Oberlin College and Northwestern University Medical School, and completed residency and fellowship training at Oregon Health Sciences University. Her current research interests include ethical aspects of decision making at the end of life, and metabolic bone diseases. She is Chief of the Geriatric Clinic and Co-Director of the Osteoporosis and Metabolic Bone Diseases Program at Mount Sinai.

Robert J. Miller, M.D., is the Medical Director of the Cancer Care Center at St. Anthony's Hospital in St. Petersburg, Florida and Assistant Clinical Professor at University of South Florida Medical School. He is a founding member and has served as the first president of the Academy of Hospice Physicians, is on the board of directors of the International Hospice Institute and the Hospice of the Suncoast, the largest home-based program in the United States. He has done research and published in the field of palliative care, terminal care, medical ethics, and hospice medicine. He is currently researching various aspects of terminal care with emphasis on developing outcome measures and quality of life instruments suitable for the dying patient.

Albert S. Moraczewski, O.P., Ph.D., S.T. Mag., is *Editor of Ethics and Medics* from the Pope John Center. Dr. Moraczewski is Adjunct Professor, Department of Psychiatry and Behavioral Sciences, Baylor College of Medicine, Houston, Texas.

David Orentlicher, M.D., J.D., is Ethics and Health Policy Counsel for the American Medical Association. He is a Lecturer in Law at the University of Chicago School of Law and Adjunct Assistant Professor of Medicine at Northwestern University Medical School.

Timothy E. Quill, M.D., is Associate Chief of Medicine at the Genesee Hospital, Associate Professor of Medicine and Psychiatry at the University of Rochester School of Medicine and Dentistry, and a primary care internist in Rochester, New York. He also directs a fellowship program at the University of Rochester in Advanced Biopsychosocial Studies.

James A. Serafini has a Ph.D. in psychology and has had a private psychotherapeutic practice in New York City for twenty years. He has been a member of ACT UP/New York's Treatment + Data Committee for three and a half years. He is on the board of directors of Body Positive, a support and education organization for HIV-positive individuals. He is past president of Dignity/New York, a group for gay and lesbian Catholics. In addition, he has recently done research work at Sloan-Kettering Cancer Center and Columbia University in New York and will soon publish an article on homophobia and Catholicism.

Robert L. Sinsheimer holds a Ph.D. in biophysics from MIT and served as Chancellor of the University of California at Santa Cruz from 1977 to 1987. His research has been concerned with the physicochemical characterization of nucleic acids and viruses, viral genetics, DNA replication, and the biological effects of ultraviolet radiation. Currently, he is engaged in research at the University of California at Santa Barbara attempting to use the atomic-force microscope to study DNA structure.

Carson Strong, Ph.D., is Professor in the Department of Human Values and Ethics at the College of Medicine of the University of Tennessee, Memphis. He holds a doctorate in philosophy from the University of Pennsylvania. His publications cover a variety of topics in medical ethics, but areas of special interest include ethics in reproductive and perinatal medicine, as well as clinical ethics teaching. He is coauthor of *A Casebook of Medical Ethics* (Oxford University Press).

David C. Thomasma, Ph.D., is the Michael I. English Professor of Medical Ethics and Director of the Medical Humanities Program at Loyola University Chicago

Medical Center, and also Chief of the Ethics Consult Service and a member of the Hospital Ethics Committee. He has published 210 articles and 15 books. His most recent books are (with John Monagle) *Medical Ethics: Politics, Protocols, Guidelines and Programs* (Aspen Publications, 1992) and *Medical Ethics: A Guide for Health Professionals* (Aspen Publications, 1988) and *Medical Ethics: Policies Procedures, Guidelines* (Aspen Publications, 1992); (with Glenn Graber) *Theory and Practice in Medical Ethics* and *Euthanasia: Toward an Ethical Social Policy* (both with Continuum Press, 1989, 1990 respectively), and *Human Life in the Balance* (Westminster Press, 1990); (with Edmund Pellegrino) *The Virtues in Medical Practice* (Oxford University Press, 1993).

Robert F. Weir, Ph.D., is the Director of the Program in Biomedical Ethics in the College of Medicine, and Professor of Pediatrics and Religious Studies at the University of Iowa. He is the author of *Selective Nontreatment of Handicapped Newborns*, *Abating Treatment with Critically Ill Patients*, and numerous articles on biomedical ethics in professional journals.

Kevin Wm. Wildes, S.J., Ph.D., is Assistant Professor of Philosophy, Senior Research Scholar of the Kennedy Institute of Ethics, and member of the Center for Clinical Bioethics in the School of Medicine at Georgetown University, as well as affiliated with Georgetown's Department of Philosophy.

.